Redefining transatlantic security relations

Published in our
centenary year
～ **2004** ～
MANCHESTER
UNIVERSITY
PRESS

Redefining transatlantic security relations

The challenge of change

Dieter Mahncke,
Wyn Rees
and
Wayne C. Thompson

Manchester University Press
Manchester and New York

distributed exclusively in the USA by Palgrave

Published by Manchester University Press
Oxford Road, Manchester M13 9NR, UK
and Room 400, 175 Fifth Avenue, New York, NY 10010, USA
www.manchesteruniversitypress.co.uk

Distributed exclusively in the USA by
Palgrave, 175 Fifth Avenue, New York,
NY 10010, USA

Distributed exclusively in Canada by
UBC Press, University of British Columbia, 2029 West Mall,
Vancouver, BC, Canada V6T 1Z2

British Library Cataloguing-in-Publication Data
A catalogue record for this book is available from the British Library

Library of Congress Cataloging-in-Publication Data applied for

ISBN 0 7190 6210 1 *hardback*
        0 7190 6211 X *paperback*

First published 2004

13 12 11 10 09 08 07 06 05 04   10 9 8 7 6 5 4 3 2 1

Typeset in Photina
by Servis Filmsetting Ltd, Manchester
Printed in Great Britain
by Bell & Bain Ltd, Glasgow

Contents

Contents

Acknowledgements

The authors would like to thank those officials in national governments and in international organisations who gave interviews for the research in this book. Dieter Mahncke would like to thank Alicia Ambos for her able research assistance and both her and Christopher Reynolds for their comments and suggestions. Wyn Rees would like to thank the British Academy and the University of Leicester for funds they provided to support his research.

Introduction

Wyn Rees and Dieter Mahncke

This book focuses on the recent experience and the future of the transatlantic security relationship. Although security is only one facet of a multi-issue relationship, arguably it has been and will continue to be the most important. In order to understand the interaction of the United States and Europe over security, one has to differentiate between the 'transatlantic Alliance' (NATO) and the 'transatlantic relationship'. The terms tend to be used interchangeably, but they represent different things. NATO is a military organisation, established under the Washington Treaty of 1949. It is a collective defence structure in which states of varying size and strength have come together to accord precision and predictability to their security relations. During the Cold War the Alliance embodied the interests of all sides in resisting external aggression and provided the 'glue' between the allies in the face of the perceived threat from the Soviet Union and its Warsaw Pact allies.

The idea of a defence organisation exclusive to the continent, the European Defence Community (EDC), foundered in 1954. For the rest of the Cold War, NATO was the bedrock of Western security. The majority of West European states did not attempt to counterbalance the superior power of the United States because they regarded it as their security guarantor against the Soviet Union and because they did not believe that the United States threatened their interests. American power allowed European states to concentrate their attention and resources on economic recovery. Moreover, except for France, the Western European partners did not believe that they could manage their security affairs alone.

At the same time as NATO helped to resolve the tensions among European states, it also provided a vehicle for the exercise of US leadership. The United States was clearly the most influential country within an organisation that operated on the principle of unanimity. Its nuclear forces were integral to the Alliance's military strategy and a four-star American general was the Supreme Allied Commander Europe (SACEUR), while the top civilian post, that of NATO

Secretary General, was occupied by a European. This is not to deny periodic tensions in Alliance relations: in fact, it appeared as if NATO was frequently in 'crisis' after its formation. Tensions varied and included issues of military doctrine and nuclear retaliation, the importance and manner of conducting *détente* towards the Soviet Union and the American belief, particularly among some members of Congress, that the Europeans were not bearing their fair share of the defence burden. Yet despite internal tensions the Alliance retained its cohesion and grew from its original membership of twelve to sixteen states by the late 1980s.

In addition to the transatlantic relationship within NATO, there was a broader US–European relationship that was built upon the shared principles of the two sides. It encapsulated a range of other values such as a commitment to democratic pluralism, free-market economics, human rights and to shared areas of culture. This wider community of values was evident in the approach of the United States, France and the United Kingdom towards the occupation of West Germany in cultivating democracy and an open market. It was apparent in the assistance the United States gave towards the economic reconstruction of Europe through the provision of Marshall Aid after 1947. It was also a vital ingredient in America's positive encouragement of the process of European integration.[1]

A pattern of complex interdependence was generated between the United States and Europe which enabled the two sides to move beyond the limits of a traditional military alliance. In the view of Deutsch, the transatlantic relationship evolved into a 'pluralistic security community'. This denotes a situation in which traditional concepts of competing power relationships and the threat of violence between the members have been transcended.[2] It contrasts with the classical understanding of an alliance where states align in order to balance the threat of a hegemonic power. According to the latter perspective, states are likely to break away from the alliance once the external threat has disappeared. Holsti argues that the cohesion of an alliance 'is largely dependent upon the intensity and duration of that threat'.[3]

It is testament to the enduring community of values and interests within the transatlantic relationship that the two sides did not break apart when the Cold War was over. As the Warsaw Pact disbanded and the Soviet Union fragmented, the external military threat to Western Europe was removed. Neo-realist commentators at the time[4] predicted that the absence of an external threat would remove the internal strength from Western international institutions. These commentators foresaw that organisations such as NATO and the European Community/Union would unravel because the motivations that had brought them together had been removed. Neo-realists predicted the re-emergence of traditional, self-interested policies among the major Western powers that would result in competition and conflict.

Despite a period of uncertainty in the transatlantic relationship in the early 1990s, as the principal actors took stock of the new environment, the structures that were established during the Cold War did not collapse. NATO proved that it was not a narrowly focused organisation in the way that it did not become redundant once the Soviet Union disappeared. The shared transatlantic fund of values and interests ensured that the Alliance not only survived but restructured itself and adapted to new tasks. Along with the European Union, the Alliance began the process of enlarging its membership to include former adversaries from Central and Eastern Europe and to develop a new relationship with Russia and the successor states of the Soviet Union.[5] The Western security community took upon itself the task of extending stability to the eastern half of the continent to those states that were willing to adopt the established criteria of market economies, democratic government and the rule of law.

The post-Cold War period

This study concentrates on two principal security challenges that confront the transatlantic allies in a time of considerable change. The first is the widening of the security agenda. In the post-Cold War environment, freed from the threat of major warfare against the Soviet Union, it has become possible for the Americans and the Europeans to conceive of security as encapsulating more than just the absence of inter-state war. Security concerns have enlarged from the traditional preoccupation with military threats to a range of more diffuse issues. (Note: this broader agenda can be stretched to include a variety of issues, such as migration, but this book cannot hope to cover all issues.)

This is not to suggest that military security is no longer important in transatlantic relations. For example, Russia's military capabilities have continued to be a matter of residual concern on both sides of the Atlantic and the risk of military conflicts on the rim of Western Europe remains a major worry. It is striking that, since the Cold War ended, the Americans and the Europeans have been active in a wide variety of operations in which military force has been employed. On these occasions, Western involvement has frequently demanded innovative forms of intervention in complex, ethno-national conflicts. Governments have been called upon to consider how their forces can contribute to tasks such as peace enforcement and peacekeeping, in places where their immediate national interests have not been engaged. Interventions in Bosnia and Kosovo have highlighted the way in which the contemporary application of military power can result in prolonged commitments in which forces must strive to keep hostile communities apart and contribute to national reconstruction.

Among the security issues that figured during the Cold War, but subsequently gained greater salience, is the threat from the proliferation of Weapons of Mass Destruction (WMD). The superpower condominium during the Cold War helped to suppress this problem, but it has increased in significance as the patronage offered by the two major powers has declined. The Americans and the Europeans regard the threat from hostile or unstable countries acquiring nuclear, chemical or biological weapon technology, or the means of their delivery by ballistic missiles, as one of the foremost threats to security. A relatively weak state can develop the means to put both its neighbours and the wider international community at risk through obtaining such lethal weapons.

The broader security agenda now extends to non-traditional threats such as transnational terrorism and international organised crime. They are not new threats, but they have been accorded a much higher priority now that the threat of large-scale, inter-state conflict involving the West has diminished. They present particular difficulties because they transcend the boundary between internal and external security. Furthermore, terrorism and organised crime present difficult challenges because they require new instruments to combat them and because the transatlantic allies have little prior experience of co-operating together against these problems.

The United States has tended to express greater concern about these emerging security threats than its European allies.[6] In a January 1994 speech in Brussels, President Bill Clinton argued that

> the immediate threat to our East is not of advancing armies, but of creeping instability. Countering that threat requires not only military security, but also the promotion of democratic and economic renewal. Combined, these forces are the strongest bulwark against Europe's current dangers: against ethnic conflict, the abuse of human rights, destabilizing refugee flows, the rise of aggressive regimes and the spread of weapons of mass destruction.

Linked with the challenge posed by an expanding security agenda is the question of whether the transatlantic allies will share common perceptions about the nature of these threats. During the Cold War the threat was unmistakable and the margin of disagreement was limited. This broader array of contemporary threats offers much greater opportunity for the United States and Europe to differ about the extent of the danger and its relevance to their own security. The United States has taken the lead in thinking more broadly about the sorts of security threats that the transatlantic allies are likely to face in the years ahead.[7]

The second principal security challenge for the transatlantic relationship is to determine a new balance between issues relating to continental Europe and global concerns. Henry Kissinger asserted in 1973 that 'the United States is a global power, while Europe is a regional power'. This dichotomy between 'global America' and 'regional Europe' was, and remains, striking. It is mitigated to some extent by the global economic involvement of the European Union and by the long-held extra-European interests of countries such as the United Kingdom, France, Italy and Germany. Yet at the outset of the twenty-first century there remains a kernel of truth in this idea. Among the European states, only Britain and France can lay claim to be capable of projecting military power beyond the continent and thereby possessing the means to contribute to high-intensity operations outside Europe.

The Cold War premise in transatlantic relations was that America's own interests would ensure that the security of Europe remained its foremost concern.[8] In the post-Cold War environment this assumption no longer holds. Whilst the United States demonstrated by its actions in the 1990s, such as in Kosovo and in relation to NATO enlargement, that it remains committed to the security of Europe, policy makers in Washington have come to the view that the continent has achieved a reliable degree of stability. Hence America's focus of attention has been shifting elsewhere. US security interests have long been defined within a global context because of the worldwide involvement of the United States in economic, ideological and military terms. America stands as the strongest and most technologically advanced power in the world. The events of 11 September 2001 provided a huge stimulus to America's perception of itself as a global security actor. The willingness of the United States to use its coercive power in international affairs, if necessary in a pre-emptive manner against imminent threats, has increased markedly.

This shift in America's attention has reflected its appreciation that the new security threats are increasingly global in nature. The proliferation of weapons of mass destruction and their attendant means of delivery are not just problems on the borders of Europe but stretch into Central and South East Asia. The nuclear stand-off between India and Pakistan has shown how America can be faced with confrontations between its allies, while North Korea has demonstrated the danger of how a covert weapons programme can potentially place nuclear weapons in the hands of unstable countries. In addition, the post-11 September 'War against Terrorism' has exposed al-Qaida's global network of operations and its willingness to strike at targets all over the world.

America has called upon its European allies to assume a wider array of global security responsibilities. The United States has wanted its allies to help to address this broader security agenda outside the European continent in a similar way to its Cold War request for them to bear a larger share of the defence burden. In a speech in Stuttgart in 1996 Secretary of State Warren Christopher stated, 'Europe and America will be taking joint action against global threats that we can only overcome by working together.'[9] For its part, Europe has found it difficult to respond to this American urging. The ability of European states to act collectively on the global stage, in areas other than economic policy, has been limited. With NATO focused on the defence of the continent, it was only in the early 1990s that the European Union began to develop the capacity to act in a cohesive fashion through its nascent Common Foreign and Security Policy (CFSP). It was not until 1999 that the Union decided to develop a capability for military crisis reaction. Hence the European Union's ability to act alongside the United States in global security matters is at a very early stage.

The United States has not been satisfied with the response Europe has made to its calls for global security challenges to be taken seriously. American policy makers have accused their transatlantic allies of being content to leave it to the United States to address extra-European security problems and even hiding

behind the United States on awkward international issues.[10] This has contributed to a deep sense of injustice in Washington over European 'free riding' on
the back of American efforts. The United States perceives itself to be the producer of the global 'public good' of security and regards its European allies as
behaving as little more than consumers. The eagerness of European governments to decrease their defence spending in the aftermath of the end of the Cold
War, and their subsequent unwillingness to reverse that decline as new threats
have been identified, has earned the contempt of many among the US elite and
contributed to a debate over the issue of America reassessing the balance
between its foreign security commitments. For example, prior to the inaugura-
tion of George W. Bush as President, the prospect of a division of labour
between Europe and America was mooted by National Security Adviser
Condoleeza Rice in which the United States would withdraw from its peacekeeping duties in the Balkans in order to concentrate on global security concerns. The new administration appeared to be signalling that it was willing to
reappraise the traditional transatlantic relationship.

The counter-argument made by the Europeans has been that the significance
of their efforts in peacekeeping and peace building have gone largely unac-
knowledged by Washington. Whilst the United States has undoubtedly been the
dominant actor when force has been employed in recent international crises,
European states have often provided the lion's share of the resources for policing the subsequent peace agreements and for undertaking the massive reconstruction efforts in the states involved. The Europeans have felt aggrieved that
they have not received appropriate credit for undertaking these long-term commitments and have been critical of what they have regarded as the failure of the
United States to treat them as equals in conflict situations. The perception has
arisen in European capitals that in matters of international security affairs the
United States wants subordinates rather than partners.

If the question of a rebalancing of global security efforts between Europe
and America is not agreed in the future, then transatlantic tensions may
increase. One result of this may be that the United States will be increasingly
attracted to acting unilaterally in military crises. Although its European allies
impress upon Washington the need to act through multilateral forums in order
to ensure legitimacy, the United States has less need to do so. The realities of
American military power, and the inability of European allies to contribute in
meaningful ways, mean that it may be simpler for the United States to conduct
operations alone. Acting unilaterally removes the need for the United States to
build a consensus among its allies and accords the US military the maximum
degree of flexibility in offensive operations.

Issues and questions

Considering the intensity and importance of the transatlantic relationship,
both its current status and, more important, the perspectives for its develop-

ment warrant attention on the part of practitioners and analysts alike. In fact, the relationship is characterised by its importance for those involved, by its complexity and by the new challenges with which it is confronted at the beginning of the twenty-first century.

This volume sets out to look at these issues in three main parts: the first focuses on transatlantic relations and European security; the second investigates the significance of newly arising global challenges for US–European relations, and the third concentrates on the combating of terrorism and international crime.

The first part is entitled 'Transatlantic security: joint venture at risk?' and is concerned with the 'traditional' arena of transatlantic relations, namely the maintenance of security in Europe. This area of interest, involving the security dialogue between North America and Western Europe and focused around NATO, has been the subject of countless books and articles. However, this dialogue has become considerably more complex since 1989. It has extended geographically to include all of Europe, it has to deal with new challenges, and it has had to take on new tasks.

These issue areas are analysed in Part I in four chapters. Chapter 1, 'Maintaining European security: issues, interests and attitudes', starts out by looking at the role of the Atlantic Alliance in maintaining security in Europe and determining what are American and what are European interests and attitudes. While it may be assumed that a large measure of agreement exists with regard to the issues, and even with regard to the interests, there is likely to be at least some disagreement in the assessment of the challenges and even more on the evaluation of the response to the challenges. Two main areas stand out here: the development of European political and military capabilities and the development of NATO. Consequently, these issues are dealt with in detail, and they are analysed under various headings and viewpoints in Chapters 2–3. The aim is not to provide a comprehensive description of developments. Rather, it is to discuss the interests and assessments of the actors and the implications for the actions undertaken or not undertaken. Emphasis is placed on American assessments on the one hand and European views on the other. However, differences among the Europeans themselves play a major role and are taken into consideration. In every case, an attempt is made not only to reveal agreement or disagreement but also to evaluate implications for action and for the problem at hand.

The main instabilities and threats to security and stability that may arise in Europe or on its perimeter are discussed in Chapter 2, 'Instability and crises: risks and challenges for European security'. It examines how the Europeans have reacted to these challenges, looking specifically at the improvement of crisis reaction capabilities of the European Union, including the decision to establish a rapid reaction force in the framework of the European Security and Defence Policy (ESDP). But the need to meet new challenges is not the only motivating force. Another is the perennial debate on burden sharing between the Americans and the Europeans, more recently under the heading of the so-called 'capabilities gap'. ESDP is one effort to overcome it, although closely related are the moves towards improving EU–NATO co-operation. The chapter concludes with an overall assessment of the issue of burden sharing in the transatlantic relationship, arguing that while the Americans bear a larger share on the military side the Europeans make a significant contribution to peacekeeping and peace building.

Chapter 3 concentrates on 'The changing role of NATO' to determine whether and in what way the Alliance can perform crucial functions in maintaining European security by ensuring transatlantic co-operation, a division of labour and a fair sharing of the burden. It picks up new challenges and tasks that the Alliance is confronted with: by bringing Russia 'into the system', extending security to Central and Eastern Europe through enlargement and by reforming the Alliance to make it more relevant for taking on new tasks, the most important of which are combating international terrorism and the proliferation of WMD.

Chapter 4, 'Perspectives: European security and the future of transatlantic relations', attempts to draw some conclusions from the preceding analysis for the future of the relationship. It comes to the rather critical conclusion that because closer European union, and consequently a more effective European Union as an international actor, are not to be expected in the foreseeable future, bilateral relations are likely to become more important. Yet, at the same time, the transatlantic relationship will continue to be the crucial element for the maintenance of security and stability in Europe. Americans may continue to be dissatisfied with the European contribution, but in return they are enjoying a position of privileged leadership. On the other side, Europeans may continue to be dissatisfied with American leadership and their subordinate role, but under the circumstances they have no alternative nor need they be particularly uncomfortable with the situation.

Obviously, these developments in the transatlantic relationship stemming from the security of Europe cannot be separated from broader global security concerns. Part II, 'Transatlantic responses to global challenges', looks at how the transatlantic relationship has addressed new security challenges outside Europe. Chapter 5, 'European–American co-operation through NATO and the European Union', and Chapter 6, 'American–European global co-operation', investigate how Europeans and North Americans are reacting to the new challenges and requirements, and what consequences for transatlantic relations can be discerned.

Chapters 5–6 focus upon the following main areas: global challenges affecting both Americans and Europeans, different foreign policy attitudes and approaches prevalent among the two sides, and institutional provisions in which American and European policies are discussed and co-ordinated. Global security issues or matters beyond the traditional concern of the North Atlantic Alliance include the Mediterranean and the Middle East as well as the Far East

(Korea, Taiwan and the South China Sea). They also include the cultivation of bilateral relations with Russia and the pursuit of American and European interests in Eastern Europe and Central Asia. In addition, arms control and the problem of the proliferation of weapons of mass destruction are analysed.

Chapters 5–6 discuss at some length the subject of unilateralism in American foreign policy compared with a belief more widespread among Europeans that in today's highly interdependent world security threats are best dealt with through a greater emphasis on dialogue and engagement. Reasons are considered that explain why the United States, with its different history and its superpower status, is more prone to emphasise sovereignty, the capacity for unilateral action and the use of military force. Europeans, on the other hand, are in the throes of European integration and are more firmly convinced that multilateralism and institutionalism are the most effective ways of fostering interdependence and ensuring stability.

Such different transatlantic approaches lead to disagreement and frequently to tension. One of the purposes of this study is to investigate the implications for American–European relations and what means may be used to ameliorate differences and co-ordinate actions in the common interest. A characteristic of transatlantic relations is that there is a dense network of interactions. In addition to numerous bilateral contacts, there are a host of institutions such as NATO, the Group of Seven (G-7) and the Organisation for Security and Co-operation in Europe (OSCE). But, despite the numerous bilateral and multilateral contacts, both Europeans and Americans believed in the 1990s that there was a need for an additional, explicitly European–American forum. The result of this desire was the creation of the 1995 New Transatlantic Agenda (NTA) and the Joint Action Plan (JAP).

The third part of the book, 'Emerging security challenges', investigates transatlantic co-operation in two areas that have hitherto received relatively little attention. Chapter 7, 'Combating terrorism in transatlantic relations', looks at the way in which the United States and Europe have worked together to fight international terrorism. Although neglected in the 1990s, since 2001 this subject has been accorded a special degree of priority. Chapter 8, 'Transatlantic co-operation against organised crime and drug trafficking', analyses US and European co-operation against a range of threats which are imprecise and difficult to measure yet are widely acknowledged to be of growing concern.

Chapter 7 begins with a definition of the phenomenon of terrorism and a description of its changing nature since the end of the Cold War. It analyses the evolution of diverse American and European approaches towards international terrorism based on different historical experiences. It is argued that these different experiences and perceptions have rendered co-operation difficult to achieve. Co-operation has been pursued through a variety of bilateral and multilateral channels, such as the European Union, NATO and the G-7/G-8, thereby exemplifying the complexity of the issue. The chapter goes on to consider transatlantic disagreements in relation to so-called 'states of concern'. It investigates the reasons why the United States chooses to confront states suspected of harbouring terrorists with a range of coercive instruments up to, and including, the use of military force, whilst European countries hesitate in this respect. Focusing on the aftermath of the terrorist attacks on New York and Washington in September 2001, the chapter questions to what extent these events have created a new momentum toward a more successful US–European counter-terrorist strategy. It looks specifically at the four main areas of transatlantic co-operation: police and judicial co-operation, terrorist financing, border controls and sharing of intelligence. The chapter concludes with an inquiry concerning the 'life span' of European support for America's way of dealing with the War on Terrorism.

Chapter 8 concentrates on the difficulties of finding transatlantic common ground in combating international crime and drug trafficking. It starts by tracing the differing European and American historical patterns in dealing with organised crime, pointing out, for example, why drugs are defined as a security threat in the United States while Europeans have tended to follow a 'softer' approach, at least towards certain drugs. This leads to discussion of the arguments and frustration within the transatlantic partnership concerning different perceptions of the extent of the challenges posed by transnational organised crime.

With special reference to Europol, the chapter refers to the difficulties of the United States in dealing with EU inconsistency and complexity in relation to the 'Justice and Home Affairs' pillar. New European–American initiatives in identifying and combating organised crime and drug trafficking are discussed particularly in view of the New Transatlantic Agenda. They refer to such issues as the trafficking in women, combating 'cyber-crime', regional drug trafficking and the difficulty of reaching a transatlantic agreement on money laundering. Finally, the chapter investigates transatlantic attitudes and activities towards enhanced global co-operation, such as in the framework of UN conventions or the G-7/G-8. It concludes with recommendations on how US–European co-operation might be improved.

The book closes by presenting some general conclusions for the development of transatlantic relations at the beginning of the twenty-first century. It once more raises the basic questions that have guided the investigation by the authors and discusses the main issues that will be relevant for the transatlantic relationship in the coming years.

Notes

1 P. Winand, *Eisenhower, Kennedy and the United States of Europe* (New York: St Martin's Press, 1996).
2 K. Deutsch *et al.*, *Political Community and the North Atlantic Area: International Organisation in the Light of Historical Experience* (Princeton NJ: Princeton University Press, 1957), p. 7.

3 K. Holsti, *International Politics: A Framework for Analysis* (4th edn, Englewood Cliffs NJ: Prentice Hall, 1983), p. 89.

4 See, for example, J. Mearsheimer, 'Back to the future: instability in Europe after the Cold War', *International Security*, 41: 1 (1990), pp. 5–57.

5 S. Croft, J. Redmond, W. Rees and M. Webber, *The Enlargement of Europe* (Manchester: Manchester University Press, 1999), and J. Sperling (ed.), *Two Tiers or Two Speeds? The European Security Order and the Enlargement of the European Union and NATO* (Manchester: Manchester University Press, 1999).

6 M. Chalmers, 'The Atlantic burden-sharing debate: widening or fragmenting?' *International Affairs*, 77: 3 (2001), p. 569. See chapters 14 and 16 of D. Calleo, *Rethinking Europe's Future* (Princeton NJ: Princeton University Press, 2001).

7 T. Frellesen, 'Processes and procedures in EU–US foreign policy co-operation: from the transatlantic declaration to the New Transatlantic Agenda', in E. Philippart and P. Winand (eds), *Ever Closer Partnership: Policy Making in US–EU Relations* (Brussels: Lang, 2001), p. 317. See J. Holmes, *The United States and Europe after the Cold War: A New Alliance?* (Columbia SC: University of South Carolina Press, 1997).

8 See, for example, P. Gebhard, *The United States and European Security* (Adelphi Paper 286, London: Brassey's, 1994), and W. Rees, 'US–European security relations: surfing or sinking?' in J. Monar (ed.), *The New Transatlantic Agenda and the Future of EU–US Relations* (The Hague: Kluwer, 1998), p. 30.

9 Secretary of State Warren Christopher, 'A New Atlantic Community for the Twenty-first Century', speech in Stuttgart, 6 September 1996, Washington File, pp. 3 and 6.

10 R. Morningstar, speech at the College of Europe, Bruges, 17 April 2001. Interviews with P. Mulrean by Alicia Ambos and Wayne Thompson, 6 March and 21 June 2001.

Part I

Transatlantic security: joint venture at risk?

Dieter Mahncke

1

Maintaining European security: issues, interests and attitudes

The ensuing four chapters deal with transatlantic security under three main headings. The first chapter gives a general introduction to the issues that are to be dealt with and addresses interests and attitudes on the two sides of the Atlantic.[1] Chapter 2 analyses the challenges and risks, looking at instabilities both within Europe and on Europe's perimeter as well as at risks and threats emanating from outside. It continues with a discussion of European efforts to respond to new demands by developing crisis management capabilities both in the civilian and the military field. Chapter 3 examines the development and role of NATO in meeting the new risks and challenges. In this context the issue of terrorism cannot be ignored. While it is dealt with extensively in Part III of this study, it also requires attention in the framework of the transatlantic discussion of the functions and role of the Alliance. The same applies to the relationship with Russia, which is dealt with more extensively – though from a different perspective – in Part II. Finally, Chapter 4 concludes with an outlook on the future of European security and its interconnection with transatlantic relations.[2]

The uncertainties of alliance

When the North Atlantic Treaty was originally signed in April 1949 the purpose was to form a military alliance that would pool resources, but equally – or more important – to assure the European allies and warn the Russians of American military assistance in case of aggression. In the course of the years the Alliance was buttressed with a sizeable organisation, first in Fontainebleau, then in Brussels and Mons.[3] Throughout the years the main purpose of the Alliance was to affirm American support against potential Soviet aggression, in terms of both conventional forces and the extension of the US nuclear umbrella over Europe.[4]

The Alliance was successful and achieved its purposes. The Cold War ended peacefully with the fall of the Berlin Wall in 1989, the dissolution of the

Warsaw Pact in March 1991 and the collapse of the Soviet Union in December 1991. The use of military force had never been necessary.

Already before 1989 two developments had taken place that few would have expected when the Alliance was founded. First, it had not only developed a major military organisation during peacetime but had also become a major instrument of transatlantic political co-operation. Second, it had become the main instrument of American military and political involvement in Europe. Western positions and policies were regularly and intensely discussed, developed and formulated in the NATO framework.

There are two further striking developments that nobody would have expected – either in 1949 or in 1989. One is that the Alliance would for the first time use force and indeed wage war after the Cold War had ended, and this would occur not in defence of any of its members but outside the Alliance area in the Balkans. The other is perhaps even more remarkable, namely that for the first time Article 5 of the Atlantic Treaty, which stipulates that an attack against one member would be considered an attack against all, was invoked – however symbolically – not in defence of a European ally but because of an attack against the United States.

Has all of this changed the nature of the transatlantic security relationship? In what ways has NATO changed, what new tasks has it been attributed, and what will such new demands and obligations (and expectations) do to the Alliance? Is the Alliance a suitable instrument for meeting the new challenges? What effects have the events in New York and Washington of 11 September 2001 had? Have they moved the allies closer together in confronting new challenges to their security? Have these events stopped the 'drifting apart' which many analysts detected in transatlantic relations after the Cold War?[5] Or have they actually led to an opposite development: growing disagreement over new challenges and what to do about them, disappointment, dissatisfaction and frustration on both sides and consequently a declining emphasis on the Alliance by both the United States and the European allies?[6] Indeed, what future do transatlantic relations and the Alliance have, specifically with regard to the maintenance of security?

The events of 11 September 2001 have shown that while in the past the Alliance was formally responsible for the security of all of its members but in fact exclusively concerned with European security, it is now an Alliance that is confronted by similar security risks for all its members. The member perhaps most in danger is ironically the United States, hitherto the country that appeared to be an almost unassailable distant fortress. America's perceived invulnerability had previously been put in question by the advent of Sputnik and mutual assured destruction capabilities. But as the nuclear threat declined after the end of the Cold War, the United States had once again gained such a position, perhaps even more so than before. That is now definitely past. On the one hand, the issue of European security in its Cold War sense seems basically settled but, on the other, it has also become more complex and more difficult to define, and its relationship to transatlantic security has seemingly become less clear. In any case, other issues, primarily international terrorism and the proliferation of weapons of mass destruction, appear more important, certainly from the perspective of the United States. Many Americans find the expected support of European allies in meeting these new challenges and risks likely to be insufficient and hence of little importance and certainly of little weight. On the other hand, many Europeans feel significantly less dependent on the United States – ignoring the fact that in any major crisis they would still not be able to act effectively without its help – and are hence willing to let disagreements and a sense of frustration with an overbearing ally gain the upper hand. This has always been true to some extent of France; what is new is that it has also become visible in Germany, previously the *Musterschüler*, the most faithful follower of the Alliance line.

The European reaction on 11 September 2001 was swift and firm in expressing sympathy and commitment. There was no European government amongst the allies that hesitated to tell the United States and the world that they considered it an assault against all, and none that demurred from the invocation of Article 5. Two reasons were probably decisive for this reaction. First, the spontaneous feeling that the Europeans owe to the Americans who had stood by them when they were threatened and had not retreated even when the risks were high (as, for example, during the Berlin crises in 1948–49 and 1958–61). Second, there was the realisation that it might also happen to the Europeans. Hence, if this was the new threat, it was better to stand together from the beginning. But one may well ask to what extent this was a 'spur of the moment' and strongly emotional reaction. The months after 11 September soon revealed that there was sympathy in the particular instance but abiding disagreement on many fundamental issues just below the surface. For not a few Europeans sympathy had been of a 'yes, but . . .' nature: Yes, this is terrible and unacceptable, but is not the United States itself to blame for it?

When analysing transatlantic security relations, we are thus confronted by a range of questions, and it is difficult to answer them at a time when the relationship is in a state of flux. What can be said with certainty is that the relationship is changing: with regard to interests and attitudes on both sides, with regard to new risks and challenges and with regard to the possible answers. Analysing the questions and potential answers may, however, shed some light on where we might be heading, what alternatives there are, and what the implications of making various choices may be.

European and American interests and attitudes

It is relatively easy, even banal, to list the American interests in the transatlantic security relationship. In the course of the Second World War the United States' leadership became convinced that a continuing American involvement would be necessary after the war. In 1917 as in 1941 the United States had come to the aid of the European democracies not (primarily) for altruistic reasons but because American governments were convinced, under the leadership of Woodrow Wilson and Franklin Roosevelt, that a stable, prosperous and friendly Europe was in the interest of the United States.[7] Certainly, it would not be in the American interest if Europe were to fall under the control of a hegemonic power, particularly if that power was unfriendly to the United States. The function of preventing a hegemonic power from developing in Europe had for several centuries been a task undertaken by Britain. In 1917 as in 1941 it had become obvious that Britain was no longer capable of meeting this challenge, but it was only with Britain turning to the United States for help during the Greek civil war and the subsequent declaration of the Truman Doctrine in 1947[8] that the staff formally passed into American hands – at the very moment when once again there was danger of Europe falling prey to a hegemonic power.

The United States had turned its back on Europe in 1920 when it refused to ratify the Versailles Treaty in a fit of isolationism,[9] leaving the European states once again – as many Americans now see it – to bungle up their affairs. After 1945 they were determined not to make the same mistake again, and even though American involvement and military presence grew slowly and step by step, the United States had decided to stay in place and have a voice in European affairs.[10] Of course, this was decisively encouraged by the growing confrontation with the Soviet Union. Thus American commitment was evidently motivated by self-interest: the confrontation with the Soviet Union, the belief that control of the European continent would give the Soviet Union a decisive advantage in what was a conflict of both power and ideology, but also the conviction that a stable and prosperous Western Europe would be in both the political and the economic interest of the United States. This does not, however, mean that there were no altruistic motives. The United States was also in Europe to ensure freedom and help build democracy. As is the case in most democracies, American foreign policy was motivated by self-interest as well as ideals.[11]

Throughout the Cold War various US administrations and at least some members of Congress and the general public had a differing understanding of the American commitment in Europe. The administrations were usually firm and reliable in their commitment, even while emphasising the need for a balanced 'burden sharing' of European defence.[12] This was not always the case amongst the members of the US Congress. Only a small number in the US Senate or the House of Representatives called for a complete withdrawal. However, during the 1960s under the leadership of Senator Mike Mansfield from Montana and to a lesser extent again in the 1980s under prodding from Representative Patricia Schroeder from Colorado there were quite a few who felt that the US military commitment was larger than necessary. Some of these believed that American forces should be reduced regardless of what the Europeans did while others thought that the United States should at least threaten to reduce its forces unless the Europeans made a greater effort to increase and improve their own contributions.[13]

As to the general public, there was a widespread impression that the United States was 'defending Europe' while the Europeans were allowed to concentrate on their economic development and were contributing little or at least not enough to their own defence.[14] The European contribution was never, then or now, put into perspective.[15] Remarkably, this does not seem to have changed since 11 September 2001. One might have expected that the attacks and the subsequent reactions by the European NATO members would have made more Americans aware not only of the usefulness of having allies (as, for example, during the Gulf War) but of the American need of them. On the European side, the American feeling that the confrontation with terrorism would not be concluded by success in Afghanistan alone but would have to be continued and carried into other regions as well met with some scepticism,[16] a scepticism that grew even stronger and changed into outright opposition when the US administration made it clear that it was not only willing to use force on an extensive scale but also to do so unilaterally (without a UN mandate) and preventively.[17] No doubt, for many Americans this covered up the favourable European reaction after 11 September and fuelled the feeling that the Europeans were in fact leaving them alone. The climax was reached during the German election campaign in September 2002 when the Social Democratic candidate, Chancellor Gerhard Schröder, played on both the fear of war (against Iraq) and underlying anti-American feeling (particularly in East Germany where it had, of course, been nurtured during Communist rule).[18] While this seriously impaired the German–American relationship, it is not quite clear whether it also had an effect on the overall American attitude towards the Europeans. But attitudes are shaped by a combination of factors, and this is likely to be one of them, at least for some time to come.

In sum, then, there is a continuing American interest in a stable and prosperous Europe. However, for several reasons that interest has gone down the list of priorities: primarily because it seems assured but at the same time because other issues seem more pressing. Threats to US security are no longer seen in Europe, despite continuing instabilities, but now emanate from international terrorism and the proliferation of weapons of mass destruction. Moreover, the United States has developed a favourable relationship with Russia and evidently needs neither the Europeans nor NATO to do this.

On the other side of the Atlantic, European interest in maintaining the American commitment has always been intertwined with European dependence on that commitment. In the early years of the Cold War the European democracies were dependent on the United States for defence as well as economic assistance. Initially, there was at least as much concern – perhaps even more – about Germany as about the Soviet Union, certainly on the part of France. However, in the time between the Treaty of Dunkirk in 1947[19] and the Washington Treaty in 1949 the emphasis clearly shifted to the perception of a Soviet threat.

With regard to defence, the European allies were dependent on the American contribution to European conventional defence and on the American nuclear deterrent. Beyond that they were dependent on American armaments, which they paid for, to be sure, but which they were at least initially not producing themselves (and which the United States was more than happy to sell). But for most of the time the Europeans were also dependent on American leadership, which they needed, waited for and often criticised when it came.

On the whole, the European public understood this well. Of course, there were exceptions, such as the Vietnam demonstrations in the 1960s or opposition to NATO's dual track decision in 1979 and the consequent decision to deploy American Pershing II and land-based cruise missiles in Europe in 1983, when the so-called peace movement organised a series of mass demonstrations in a number of European countries. But, generally, US involvement was supported. Tensions in transatlantic relations usually arose more as a result of concerns or dissatisfaction within European governments. These were either of a substantive nature, for example with regard to the NATO strategy of 'flexible response' in the early 1960s or missile defence in the 1980s and 1990s, or they were motivated by some diffuse discontent with American leadership.

While substantive differences normally get a lot of media attention, they are generally not fundamental to the relationship. The more serious difficulties involve underlying feelings and motives. They included uncertainty with regard to the reliability of the American commitment, about which Europeans – particularly the Germans – tended to be highly sensitive in view of their exposed position and high dependence on the United States; a feeling of not being treated according to (self-perceived) 'rank' or of not being given a commensurate role – often a concern of France – or simply a general dissatisfaction with having to accept leadership rather than leading. Prodded by France, an increasing number of Europeans have come to feel that 'Europe' needs a stronger voice in transatlantic relations, needs more independence, or at least autonomy.[20] These feelings have grown in the post-Cold War period as the dependence of the European allies on immediate American protection has declined. Moreover, those in Europe critical of the United States now obtain support from the extreme right, where resistance to American 'pop culture' and materialism is strong, or from the extreme left, where there is the image of the United States as arrogant, a ruthless promoter of selfish economic interests, and militaristic.

There is an underlying strain of anti-Americanism in Europe, although to any significant extent it can probably be found only in France and Germany. It remains uncertain how politically effective it might become, but it is safe to say that it is likely to have some effect and that transatlantic relations in future will be more heavily burdened by differences on both perceptions and policies. Alliances are held together most effectively by a common threat. Next to that, though much less forcefully, common suffering and common needs tie nations together. Interests, a third factor, range behind either of these two. Common values we find trailing far behind any of these, as a lonely fourth.[21] Interestingly enough, political statements today tend to emphasise the latter: after the Soviet threat has disappeared and interests frequently tend to be more divisive than unifying, this is hardly surprising. But it may not be enough to ensure a relationship that ensures common solutions are found for common problems.

Notes

1 Canada will not be dealt with specifically; the focus will be the United States. The geographical proximity of Canada to the United States inevitably affects Canadian policies, but quite frequently Canada will lean toward European positions.

2 A general comment on terminology needs to be made here. Throughout the following chapters the term 'European Union' or 'EU' will be used when reference is specifically made to the European Union. Otherwise the more general expressions 'Europe' and 'Europeans' will be used, sometimes referring to the European Union, but often referring to 'the Europeans' in a broader sense. This is done for several reasons: because the European Union does not encompass all Europeans, because European views are not found only in the European Union and because Europeans act sometimes in the framework of the European Union, sometimes as a group smaller and sometimes as a group larger than the European Union.

3 For a history of the beginnings of the Alliance see Robert E. Osgood, *NATO: The Entangling Alliance* (Chicago: University of Chicago Press, 1962), and Henry A. Kissinger, *Nuclear Weapons and Foreign Policy* (Boulder CO: Westview Press, 1962); an overall history is presented by Peter Duignan, *NATO: Its Past, Present and Future* (Stanford CA: Hoover Institution Press, 2000).

4 For a discussion on extended deterrence see, for example, Robert M. Soofer, *Missile Defenses and Western European Security: NATO Strategy, Arms Control and Deterrence* (New York and London: Greenwood Press, 1988); also Dieter Mahncke, *Nukleare Mitwirkung. Die Bundesrepublik Deutschland in der atlantischen Allianz 1954–1970* (Berlin and New York: de Gruyter, 1972).

5 See on this Joseph S. Nye, 'The US and Europe: continental drift?', *International Affairs*, 76: 1 (2000), pp. 51–9; Peter W. Rodman, *Drifting Apart? Trends in US–European Relations* (Washington DC: Nixon Center, 1999), www.nixoncenter. org/publications/monographs/ drifting.pdf); Werner Weidenfeld, *America and Europe: Is the Break Inevitable?* (Gütersloh: Bertelsmann Foundation, 1996). An entirely different conclusion can be drawn from the detailed analysis of growing co-operation in transatlantic relations by Eric Philippart and Pascaline Winand (eds), *Ever Closer Partnership: Policy Making in US–EU Relations* (Brussels: Lang, 2001): 'EU–US relations, in spite of trade disputes and occasional manifestations of self-centeredness or unilateralism, are on a relatively stable course' (p. 426).

6 An article that seems to pull all these doubts together is Robert Kagan, 'Power and weakness', *Policy Review*, 113 (June–July 2002), www.policyreview.org/JUN02 /kagan.html; see also Peter van Ham, 'Security and culture, or, Why NATO won't last', *Security Dialogue*, 32: 4 (2001), pp. 393–406.

7 For a broad discussion of 'Identity and power in American foreign policy' see the perceptive study by Henry R. Nau, *At Home Abroad* (Ithaca NY and London: Cornell University Press, 2002).

8 See, for example, Simon Serfaty, *Stay the Course: European Unity and Atlantic*

Solidarity (Washington Paper 171, Center for Strategic and International Studies, Westport CT: Praeger, 1997), pp. 76 ff. Digital versions of the 'Truman Doctrine Study Collection' are held at the Truman Presidential Library in Missouri (www.whistlestop.org/study_collections/doctrine/ large/doctrine.htm).

9 The idea of a particularly strong strain of isolationism in American politics is based almost exclusively on this period, although isolationism is only one strain, and not the strongest; see on this the excellent study by Günter Moltmann, *Atlantische Blockpolitik im 19. Jahrhundert. Die Vereinigten Staaten und der deutsche Liberalismus während der Revolution von 1848–1849* (Düsseldorf: Droste, 1973).

10 See also the introduction to this study. An interesting observation one might make here is that most of those persons responsible for US policy in 1945 had experienced the First World War and its aftermath as politically conscious adults who were now determined to avoid previous mistakes. If personal experience is prerequisite to sensible policy, this does not bode well for the future of transatlantic relations.

11 See on this the classic study by Robert E. Osgood, *Ideals and Self-interest in American Foreign Relations* (Chicago: University of Chicago Press, 1953); also Nau, *At Home Abroad*.

12 At times an administration would work together with the Europeans to make clear to the Congress that the Europeans were in fact bearing a fair share of the burden. The issue of burden sharing took up some part of the transatlantic relationship, particularly during the 1960s and to an extent again in the 1980s. See Elke Thiel, *Dollar-Dominanz. Lastenteilung und amerikanische Truppenpräsenz in Europa. Zur Frage kritischer Verknüpfung währungs- und stationierungspolitischer Zielsetzungen in den deutsch-amerikanischen Beziehungen* (Baden-Baden: Nomos, 1979).

13 *Ibid.* and Joseph R. Biden, Jr, 'Unholy symbiosis: isolationism and anti-Americanism', *Washington Quarterly*, 23: 4 (2000), pp. 7 ff.

14 A favourite question in opinion polls was in the vein of 'Do you think the United States should continue to defend Europe . . . ?'

15 Thus the remark by Kagan ('Power and weakness') that the Americans were doing the cooking while the Europeans did the dishes is rather ridiculous. If one wanted to draw such a comparison, the United States would be doing the cooking but the Europeans would be doing practically everything else. See also Chapter 2, below.

16 See Jessica T. Mathews, 'Estranged partners', *Foreign Policy*, 127 (2001), pp. 48–53; also interview with German Foreign Minister Joschka Fischer, 'Wir sind keine Satelliten', *Die Welt*, 12 February 2002; 'Paris gegen Bushs "Achse des Bösen"', *Neue Zürcher Zeitung*, 8 February 2002, p. 3; and Jonathan Freedland, 'Patten lays into Bush's America', *Guardian*, 9 February 2002.

17 See *The National Security Strategy of the United States of America*, September 2002, pp. 14 f. (www.whitehouse.gov/nsc/nssall.html).

18 See, for example, Jim Hoagland, 'Cooling off after Germany's election', *Washington Post*, 26 September 2002; Susi Schneider, 'Deutschland nicht mit an Bord', *Der Standard*, 23 September 2002. A rather critical issue also arose when the then German Justice Minister, Herta Däubler-Gmelin, compared President George Bush to Adolf Hitler. Bush, she said, was trying to use the conflict with Iraq to divert attention from internal difficulties; Hitler had done this too.

19 Signed in March 1947, this was the first post-war European security pact. An agreement between Britain and France, the treaty was aimed at preventing the possibility of a renewal of German aggression.

20 See pp. 33–7.
21 See Heinrich Schneider, 'Die Europäische Union als Wertegemeinschaft auf der Suche nach sich selbst', *Die Union*, 1 (2000), pp. 14–47; 'Europäische Identität: historische, kulturelle und politische Dimensionen', in Rudolf Hrbek, Mathias Jopp, Barbara Lippert and Wolfgang Wessels (eds), *Die Europäische Union als Prozeß* (Bonn: Europa Union Verlag, 1998), pp. 397 ff.

2

Instability and crises: risks and challenges for European security

This chapter will not consider all possible risks and challenges for European security. It will concentrate only on two broad areas, namely instability on Europe's perimeter, the Mediterranean and the Middle East. Other issues such as the development of Russia, international terrorism and the proliferation of weapons of mass destruction will be dealt with in the following chapter, since these questions are more strongly tied to the development of NATO. Emphasis here will be on the more European aspects, and the chapter will hence include an analysis of initial European reactions to the issues of instability and crises in Europe.

Instability on Europe's perimeter

Instability in Europe is the issue that analysts and practitioners dealing with European security have been most concerned about since the end of the Cold War. Instability implies conflict, either inter-state or more frequently intra-state, and its causes may be disputes over boundaries, minority issues, either within a state or across state boundaries, ethnic or religious strife, economic or environmental disputes or political and/or economic instability.[1] Europeans, but also the United States, became concerned about the issue in the early 1990s for two reasons: the situation in the Baltic states and the break-up of Yugoslavia. The major considerations were that such conflicts might spill over into other European states, that Western Europe would be confronted by large masses of refugees, that Western countries might be drawn into the disputes or that Russia might seize the opportunity to revive imperial ambitions.

The Baltic states

Obviously, after the NATO meetings in Rome in May and in Prague in November 2002, the question of the stability and security of the Baltic states is no longer an acute issue. In fact, with the undisputed invitations to join both NATO and the European Union (at the Copenhagen Summit in December 2002), this issue seems resolved. Nevertheless, it is worth reviewing a problem that was considered to be the most acute and potentially dangerous immediately after the end of the Cold War.

The initial concern was that Russia would not accept the independence of these states and would use extensive force to prevent it from coming about. In fact, some force had been used for exactly that purpose when Mikhail Gorbachev was still in power,[2] but after his successor Boris Yeltsin had taken office, and the Soviet Union broke up in December 1991, independence was accepted.[3] Nonetheless, both Europeans and Americans recognised this as being demanding on Russia in view of the large Russian minorities in the three states,[4] the value of the Baltic ports and the territorial separation of the Kaliningrad area from the rest of Russia, making an exclave of a territory that had been annexed by the Soviet Union after the Second World War and that had acquired considerable military importance for Russia. Americans and Europeans feared that Russia might be tempted to use the minority issue to regain a foothold in these states, either to place them under Russian influence or completely to reintegrate them into Russia. Indeed, talk from Moscow about the country's 'near abroad' and a sense of responsibility for Russians living outside the state's boundaries served to enhance Western concern.[5]

A closer look at why the West was concerned is useful. After all, in view of the psychologically difficult situation for Russia one might have accepted perhaps not the reintegration of the Baltic republics but some form of 'Finlandisation'. The reasons were twofold. For one thing there were moral considerations and these should not to be underestimated, particularly as far as the United States is concerned. The Baltic republics had been independent after the First World War, and 1989 for them was a return not to 1945 but to 1918. Their independence had been sacrificed by a deal between Nazi Germany and Communist Russia, and although they had been under Russian rule for long periods even before 1940[6] they were not, and had never, been an integral part of Russia. There was a feeling that the Baltic states had been betrayed or at least left to their own fate by the West after 1945. Secondly, there was a perception that if Russia intruded into the Baltic republics then this might herald the beginning of a fundamental reversal of all the favourable events since 1989.

But this did not happen, and despite grumbling and occasional threats on the part of Russia the Baltic republics have witnessed a highly positive development. They have established stable democracies, they are advancing economically and they have made commendable efforts to resolve their difficult problems with the Russian minority. Furthermore, they have set up a minimum defence capacity on a co-operative level and have made this available for international peacekeeping in the Balkans; also, of course, with the aim of improving interoperability with NATO forces. Last but not least, they have participated extensively in political and security activities comprising all Baltic Sea states.[7]

The only major uncertainty appeared to be the relationship with Russia. In the years following the collapse of the Soviet Union, Russia had to adjust to the new reality. Thus, for example, although progress was made with regard to the boundary disputes with Russia, they had not been finally resolved as late as 2002.[8] In the early 1990s, more than anything else, the idea of the Baltic states becoming members of NATO seemed unbearable to the Russian leadership. Indeed, here seemed to be one of the 'red lines' drawn by Russia, and the most aggressive threats were made in conjunction with an extension of NATO into this region.[9] Similar objections were not advanced with regard to EU member-ship of the Baltic republics.[10]

As a consequence, the West treated the question of NATO membership with caution. Under the CDU/CSU/FDP government Germany tended to be scepti-cal.[11] However, Estonia was among the first group of countries to be invited to start negotiations on EU membership. Some argued that this could in part com-pensate for NATO membership.[12] The Western countries made efforts to indi-cate to Russia that any moves against the Baltic republics would be considered a serious threat to European stability and hence to Western relations with Russia. The Europeans took pains to create and include the Baltic states in various forms and forums of Baltic Sea co-operation, and the United States emphasised its bilateral relations with the three republics.[13]

As the relationship with Russia improved, the United States began to take on a more pronounced position in regard to NATO membership for the Baltic states. On his European tour in June 2001 – hence, even before the events of 11 September – US President George W. Bush indicated that NATO should be open to all European countries.[14] After the events of 11 September 2001 there were signals that the hard Russian line against Baltic membership had softened.[15] The motive for this change was probably the realisation that compromising on NATO enlargement could secure major benefits for Russia. Not only could it acquire political credit that could be cashed in later, but some sympathy could be obtained for Russia's problems in Chechnya. In the light of the previous experience with opposing NATO membership of Poland, the Czech Republic and Hungary, it did not seem likely that Russian opposition could stop the acces-sion of the Baltic republics to NATO. Moreover, membership might not turn out to be that threatening (or meaningful) if NATO changed as part of the process.

As far as the relationship of the Baltic republics to the European Union is concerned, the Europeans have been much bolder. Already at an early stage such membership was declared not only possible but desirable, and Estonia was among the first group of applicants invited to start negotiations for member-ship. Finally, at the EU Copenhagen Summit in December 2002 all the Baltic republics were invited to commence negotiations for EU membership.[16] There were no negative reactions on the part of Russia.

The Balkans
European and American concern about the south-eastern corner of the conti-nent grew in the course of the 1990s. Both the United States and the European

Union became aware that the Balkans presented a potential security problem for Europe. Hence both got involved; the United States mainly militarily, the Europeans both militarily and economically.

Yugoslavia, for almost a decade after Tito's death in May 1980, had seemed capable of maintaining the cohesion of the diverse and artificial state created by the Treaty of Trianon in 1920. However, by 1991 it was rapidly breaking apart.[17] After an initial attempt by America, Britain and France to hold the state together, the inevitability of its collapse had to be accepted. With some delay the West turned against Slobodan Milosevic, who was determined to uphold the unity of Yugoslavia under Serb domination by brute force. Less than half a decade after the collapse of the Berlin Wall and the defeat of Saddam Hussein, and without the political support of a unanimous UN Security Council, European and American forces were used on European soil. This experience was to have major consequences for European thinking about the maintenance of peace and security in Europe.

Why was there so much concern, even anxiety about what was happening in the Balkans? Would it not have been possible to stand aside and let the various groups in the area resolve the issue by themselves?

While there were some moral considerations, they were least important. Self-determination had the West's sympathy as far as Poland, Hungary or Czechoslovakia and even the Baltic republics were concerned, but self-determination should not lead to fragmentation and destabilisation. In other words, 'Balkanisation' was understood not in its pre-World War I sense of freedom and self-determination for the Balkan nations, but in its later sense of instability. Indeed, destabilisation was the overriding concern of both Europeans and Americans. Even if a 'new world order' seemed too ambitious on a global scale, it was certainly deemed possible for Europe: a continent of stable, peaceful, prosperous and co-operating democracies.

Such a stable Europe could be threatened by the Balkan fiasco in several ways. First, there was the question of the 'bad example'. In this new Europe it was unacceptable to allow such blatant use of force, and this had to be made clear, at least from 1995 onwards. Second, there was some apprehension that outside powers could become embroiled in the Balkan conflicts, not only with the Russians on one side and the Western powers on the other, but even the Western powers might end up on different sides. Third, the Balkan quarrels might spill over into neighbouring states, such as Hungary or Bulgaria, and turn a small fire into a blaze. Last but not least, the conflict and its results could be carried into the Western European countries, not only burdening them with refugees but bringing the conflict into their midst. Hence, after considerable hesitation and uncertainty, it seemed imperative for both the Europeans and the Americans to become engaged in the Balkans in the name of stability and peace, and ultimately also in the name of human rights, on which such peace and stability was to be based.

The United States is involved in the region for three reasons. First, there is the overall American interest in European stability, second, the apparent need for American leadership, as the various crises in former Yugoslavia once more made clear, and, third, an understanding that instability and the loss of Western influence in this region is likely to have implications for the Middle East as well as Central Asia.

Europeans and Americans have few differences in their assessment of the Balkans. The possible challenges, the need to meet them and the necessary measures to be undertaken are seen in a similar vein. Differences on policy details do arise, but the overall aim is seen in practically identical terms; namely to create politically and economically stable democracies in the area. Both sides recognise the dilemma between self-determination and sovereignty/territorial integrity, and both sides tend to dally on the issue.[18] There is also general agreement on the division of labour. The United States has borne a relatively large share of the military effort, particularly in the conflict with Serbia over Kosovo, with a correspondingly determining voice in the conduct of operations. The Europeans, on the other hand, have taken on the (much) larger share of peace-keeping duties, economic reconstruction, development and political stabilisation. Of course, the United States maintains influence by various means: through its military presence, through NATO (even when in practical terms the Europeans take on most of the task, such as during Operation Essential Harvest in Macedonia in autumn 2001 or the subsequent Operation Amber Fox), through the Organisation for Security and Co-operation in Europe (OSCE) and through the United Nations. Nevertheless, in view of the existing consensus and because it is convenient the United States has been content to let the Europeans take a leading role in post-crisis developments. In contrast, the determining American role both in Bosnia and in the Kosovo conflict has left the Europeans somewhat less than content and, in fact, has been one of the motivating forces for the project to create a European rapid reaction force.[19]

The Mediterranean and the Middle East

Next to the Balkans, the Mediterranean and the Middle East are the other major areas in which potential threats to European security are seen.[20] They take three forms: mass migratory pressure from North Africa, threats from one or other North African state, with medium-range missiles, for example, and a major military confrontation in the Middle East directly threatening the Europeans or drawing them into a conflict.

The first of these is not a classical security threat, but it would have security implications if individual European states or the European Union as a whole decided on the use of military means to stave off migratory pressure. The impact would be much more far-reaching if migration could not be stopped or halted in time, with possible repercussions for domestic stability in Europe. This is primarily a European issue, however. It would affect transatlantic relations if it led to serious disruption and destabilisation in Europe.

The second potential threat would affect transatlantic relations immediately because it would have a direct impact on the Europeans and would represent an attack on NATO members. This does not seem like an immediate issue: firstly, because the states one might think of do not yet have the capacity to threaten Europe, and, secondly, because it is not easy to imagine a scenario with rational incentives for these states to confront Europe. Nevertheless, two possibilities need to be taken into consideration. One is whether the new threat of terrorism makes such a development more likely and far more dangerous for the very reason that conduct may not be calculable in established rational terms. The second is how and whether the Europeans might want to react if it became certain that these states (or even groups within these states) were developing weapons of mass destruction and their means of delivery. For example, if a country with some credible nuclear capability harboured international terrorists, a reaction would be considerably more complicated – perhaps impossible – than was the case in Afghanistan after 11 September 2001. The United States is reacting to this new environment in two ways: by including in normal policy considerations the option of preventive action with military force, in order to be able to destroy a WMD capability, and by taking defensive measures, such as developing a limited missile defence system.

Both these routes have been anathema to most Europeans. The Europeans tend to emphasise long-term preventive action in the form of economic development and democratisation. But these efforts have shown least results where it seemed most necessary. As to missile defence, Europeans have tended to insist on the value of the Anti-ballistic Missile (ABM) Treaty of 1972, mainly out of consideration for Russian objections and fear of a renewed arms race.[21] The events of 11 September 2001 as well as the American decision to withdraw from the ABM Treaty (announced on 13 December 2001) and the rather calm Russian reaction may change these attitudes. Europeans will have to start thinking about these issues, and they will have to decide on whether they want to react to them individually, in 'coalitions of the willing' or together in the framework of the European Union.

The third potential threat comes from the Middle East. Again, it is relatively improbable that the Europeans would be confronted by a direct military threat. But there are other risks: the spread of terrorism into Europe, a cut-off of oil supplies, or Europe being drawn into an escalating Arab–Israeli conflict.

The Europeans are aware of these risks, and have in growing measure become a party in the efforts to meet the challenges, for example by the European Union's Barcelona Process involving the Mediterranean states in a dialogue to improve co-operation and economic development, or in efforts to help resolve the Arab–Israeli conflict. With respect to the latter, the contribution of the Europeans has included mediation, such as in the Oslo process and during the escalating crisis in autumn 2001 and spring 2002,[22] and financial assistance for the Palestinians. The latter is intended to ameliorate the disadvantaged and discriminated situation of the Palestinians and to offer them an incentive to accept and support the peace process. It does not seem that enhancing European leverage in the area was a major European motive, but if it was, the result has been limited. Significant influence in the area is wielded primarily by the United States because only it has notable influence on Israel. However, this influence is declining, partly because of the domestic restrictions such as consideration of the American Jewish community, but also because Israeli governments themselves have shown more resistance to pressure. For both reasons American influence among Arabs and Palestinians has declined. The Europeans have not been able to step into this opening, simply because their capacity to influence Israel is even more limited, but also because they have been reluctant to become deeply involved.

The perspectives are thus rather bleak. A division of labour between Europeans and Americans has had only limited success, while joint efforts would put the Europeans under the same restrictions as US administrations with regard to Israel. The only remaining alternative is for the Europeans to pursue their own policies – obviously in consultation and co-ordination with the United States, because the ultimate objective is the same – but having to accept the limitations that this implies.[23]

Crises and crisis management

The crises accompanying the break-up of Yugoslavia in the 1990s have created an awareness among Europeans that they need a stronger, more effective crisis management capability, including military means that could be used either together with the United States or alone if America chose not to act.

Crises in the Cold War period, whether in the transatlantic relationship (for example, the introduction of the strategy of flexible response in the early 1960s or the issue of the Enhanced Radiation Weapon – the 'neutron bomb' – in the late 1970s) or in East–West relations (such as the Berlin crises) were dealt with both bilaterally and within the institutions of the Alliance. The instruments were used without ideological or political preconceptions and as seemed appropriate.

It could be argued that this has changed since the end of the Cold War. Certainly, attitudes and perceptions seem to have changed: because standing together after the decline of the Soviet threat appears less urgent, because there is an American sentiment that the Europeans need to make a more significant military contribution to maintaining continental and global stability, and because the Europeans feel that they should play a bigger role in their relationship with the United States as well as in the international arena. Neither economic nor political differences are any longer mitigated by a clear and undisputed external threat. They appear larger and more fundamental, and when American impatience and dissatisfaction with the Europeans on the one hand and European balking at American leadership on the other are added, the resulting cocktail often makes for a muddy transatlantic relationship.

Attitudes and feelings are important, and they have a definite effect on

US–European relations. As far as the actual procedures are concerned, however, little has changed. As before, both NATO and bilateral relations predominate; less frequently is there interaction between the European Union and NATO or the European Union and the United States. This can be observed in all the European security crises since 1989. After the United States had for a time abstained from intervention in the break-up of Yugoslavia in the early 1990s[24] but the Europeans had failed to resolve the issue, Washington again took on an energetic leadership role that culminated in the Dayton agreement. In this and the following crisis in Kosovo consultations were conducted bilaterally and within NATO, the latter being used whenever the issue of military force arose. After the events of 11 September 2001 NATO played an important political role in that it was used to demonstrate solidarity, but many of the political and military measures were undertaken outside the NATO and EU frameworks, bilaterally between the United States and its main European allies, and multilaterally among Britain, France and Germany.

The explanation for this is quite easy. First of all, NATO, as a military organisation, was not going to be used. It was not suited and not needed, quite apart from the fact that at this stage of the development Afghanistan was just too far out of NATO's traditional area of action, and any initiative by NATO would have raised the question of the Alliance as a 'world policeman'. Whereas some observers in the United States felt that NATO should prove its worth in such a serious situation and on a worldwide scale, most Europeans found such an extension unacceptable. (Once again, the European reaction was paradoxical. While, on the one hand, there were muted complaints about the United States not 'using NATO', on the other it is more than likely that the Europeans – except for the British – would have felt extremely uncomfortable had they been called upon to move rapidly into Afghanistan under the NATO flag.)

The second reason is that the Europeans were neither ready nor capable of acting as a Union. The instruments that were available were used, but they were national. The European Union – be it in the form of its presidency, the Commissioner for External Relations or the High Representative for the Common Foreign and Security Policy – did not play a role. Both the High Representative and the Commissioner have important functions, but they act as a type of 'special representative', either offering good services, as in the Middle East, or employing the economic weight of the Union to achieve a certain political result, for example in Macedonia (although, as a back-up, NATO's Secretary General was also involved in Macedonia, and both Essential Harvest and Amber Fox were NATO operations).[25]

Much the same could be observed on the occasion of the negotiations in the UN Security Council on a resolution on Iraq in October and early November 2002. While France and Britain took on major roles, the European Union remained completely outside. Of course, the European Union has been creating instruments to improve its capacity for crisis reaction, and it can be expected that these instruments and the European Union in general will play a bigger role in the future.[26] Prerequisite to the effective use of these instruments and hence to any enhanced EU role, however, is European political unity. Even better would be assured political unity – not unity that is uncertain and has to be established anew in every crisis, but a regular and institutionalised process that would ensure procedures to arrive at common action. All instruments that the European Union may acquire will be of little avail if this cannot be achieved.

More than a decade after the end of the Cold War the major issue in transatlantic relations is the dichotomy between a highly capable and dissatisfied United States and a much less capable (politically as well as militarily) and equally dissatisfied European Union. The United States has enhanced its military power enormously, has developed a distinctly global view of risks and threats, grants developments in Europe less priority, is disposed to look at the Europeans primarily in the light of their potential 'usefulness' in dealing with what Americans consider the main threats and tends to be less than satisfied with the support it is getting from its allies. By contrast, the Europeans have become more inward-looking, concentrating on Europe, on the European Union and to no small extent on national domestic issues. At the same time, their military capabilities have stagnated or declined while political capability in terms of a single and hence more effective European voice has not grown. Global issues tend to be regarded as a disturbing nuisance. Finally, differences with the United States, be they on trade issues or global threat assessments, are no longer played down or resolved quickly but looked upon as reflecting fundamental differences between a 'European' and an 'American way'.

The European Union: improving crisis reaction capabilities

In the course of the 1990s the European Union made several efforts to improve its ability to react to crises. They included crisis recognition, crisis control and crisis resolution, in both the civilian and the military fields. The instruments were developed in several steps, starting from the Maastricht (1992) and Amsterdam (1997) treaties with the objective of ensuring a more unified approach of the EU member states on foreign policy issues, moving on to more specific issues at the Cologne summit in June 1999, followed by the Helsinki summit in December. They comprised improvements for both the institutional set-up and decision-making procedures. Publicly, most attention was given to the creation of the post of the High Representative for the Common Foreign and Security Policy and the project of a rapid reaction force.[27] Several institutional arrangements were made within the framework of the Council both to assist the High Representative in his work and to foresee instruments to guide decisions on the use of force. These included the Policy Planning and Early Warning Unit (PPEWU), the Political and Security Committee (PSC), the Military Committee (MC), the Military Staff (MS) and a Joint Situation Centre. Attention was also given to developing the capacity to co-operate with other organisations such as NATO and the OSCE. In the framework of the Commission such measures included the Europe Aid Co-operation Office, the European

Community Humanitarian Office (ECHO) and improved interaction between the Directorate General for External Relations and the Council, especially the High Representative.

In the political/civilian sphere activities cover the normal diplomatic range of public statements, *démarches*, suspension of political dialogue, interventions by the presidency, the EU troika or the High Representative, the dispatch of special representatives or fact-finding missions as well as the entire panoply of economic measures (sanctions, suspension of assistance programmes, provision of financial assistance and so forth). In addition, humanitarian aid may be offered, advice on strengthening democratic institutions and the rule of law, human rights observers, border control teams, de-mining assistance, control of refugee flows, evacuation or search and rescue operations.[28] Since the crises in the Balkans in particular have shown that police operations are highly suitable and necessary both in an early phase of a crisis as well as in post-crisis reconstruction activities, emphasis was put on the earmarking and training of police officers, to be provided by the member states.[29] Thus the Feira summit declared that by 2003 a total of 5,000 policemen should be 'identified and made available' by the member states for civilian crisis management. At least 1,000 policemen should be ready for deployment within thirty days, either at the request of an international organisation such as the United Nations or the OSCE or as an autonomous action by the European Union. The functions of such a force would be advice and training, but also normal police work. Further decisions were taken in Nice in December 2000, in Gothenburg in June 2001 (establishing a Council Secretariat Police Unit) and in Laeken in December 2001. By early 2002 the European Union had dispatched about 3,300 policemen, mainly to the Balkans (3,100), but also in advisory and training capacities to Guatemala, El Salvador, South Africa and Algeria. In January 2003 the European Union took over control of 500 police officers active in Bosnia under UN auspices.[30]

A European military crisis reaction force
To meet both the material requirement of improved military capabilities and the desire for an enhanced role, and spurred by what was considered poor performance on the part of the Europeans during the Bosnian and Kosovo crises, the member states of the European Union, led by Britain and France, came to the conclusion that in addition to the political and civilian measures a European military force suitable for crisis management was necessary. Hence the European Security and Defence Policy (ESDP) was developed. This included an effort to improve both civilian and military components, but in practice ESDP is mainly associated with the military components. It can be traced back to the initiative by Prime Minister Tony Blair at Pörtschach, the joint French–British agreement at Saint-Malo, and the EU summit meetings in Cologne in June 1999 and Helsinki in December the same year.[31] Despite the ambitious name, a European 'defence force' or a 'European army'[32] is not implied, and there is little relevance for a European 'defence identity'. What is

meant is the earmarking and commitment of available forces of approximately 60,000 troops, plus air and naval components, by 2003. These would be trained together and could be deployed relatively rapidly (within sixty days) in a crisis situation either within the framework of NATO or – if NATO as a whole does not act – 'autonomously' within a European framework. Deployment within sixty days is, in fact, not particularly 'rapid' and reflects that it will be an *ad hoc* multinational force. Certainly it will not be a rapid reaction force usable in an acute crisis.[33]

As stated above, the European motives are threefold: to acquire a capability to react to a crisis with military means without American participation, to enhance European influence in the political process of crisis management, specifically in the councils of the Alliance, and to meet US criticism of European shortcomings in crisis situations, both in order to secure the American commitment and to offset any American tendency to act unilaterally.

The implications for transatlantic relations concern the relationship between such a force and NATO and can be found principally in three areas: with regard to control, with regard to the decision-making procedure and with regard to the use of 'NATO assets'.

First, in order to achieve the desired objectives, the reaction force cannot simply be a European force at the disposal of NATO. The Europeans must be able to decide for themselves whether and when such a force will be used. However, if European consensus is prerequisite, the force would probably not be used 'outside' or 'separate' from NATO, since many Europeans would object. The word that was found to resolve this, or, better, to combine the two objectives, is 'autonomous': an autonomous European capability. But this has not really settled the issue, as became clear during the EU summit conference in Nice in December 2000, when French President Jacques Chirac called for a European force that would be independent of NATO, although 'co-ordinated' with the Alliance, while British Prime Minister Tony Blair considered this to be, at the very least, a mistaken emphasis.[34] This difference reappeared when in autumn 2002 the French President suggested that the European Union should take over Operation Amber Fox in Macedonia even without prior agreement with NATO (which was blocked by Turkey[35]). Britain rejected the proposal.[36]

Directly related to this is the second issue, namely whether in any crisis situation discussions and consultation would first take place within NATO before any decision was taken on whether NATO as a whole would act, whether the Europeans should act on their own, or whether nothing at all would be done. Of course, it is probable that in most of the conceivable 'real' situations the very first decision to take would not be whether to employ military force. Rather, extensive political consultation would take place and – unless it were an acute crisis – as a first step diplomatic and economic measures would be considered. Since this would be likely to take place both bilaterally and within the Alliance, it is improbable that when the issue of the use of force came to the fore, this would suddenly be dealt with outside of the NATO framework. Under foreseeable circumstances, a decision exclusively within a European framework and an entirely 'independent' use of the force would be likely only if the United States withdrew completely.

Therefore, to some extent the issue appears artificial. Nevertheless, in view of the differing views on it among the Europeans themselves, and between them and the Americans, it remains an important question. From the American point of view the answer seems to be obvious: in any crisis situation affecting European security NATO remains the most effective available instrument and hence the logical forum for consultation and decision making. This becomes even more evident if NATO assets are to be used. In view of the efforts to grant the European Union access to NATO assets,[37] and in terms of intelligence, planning and hardware,[38] this will practically be the case for any significant crisis situation.

While all this is true of any crisis directly affecting European security, the situation may be different for crisis situations outside Europe. In such situations the United States may prefer to act alone or within a 'coalition of the willing'. It seems improbable at this stage that Europeans would want to act independently in a serious situation, but in either case it is difficult to assess what implications such practice would have for the Alliance. If there is overall agreement it might not harm the relationship, but it is difficult to believe that it would not sideline the Alliance to some extent. An Alliance used solely as a 'toolbox' would first lose cohesion, then effectiveness and eventually its importance.

The obvious aim of the United States is to ensure that no serious action with implications for European security can take place without Americans having been heard and having had the opportunity to bring their views to bear and to exert influence on the course of events. It is worth looking at this from the American side to understand that it is not just a question of influence or power. After all, in the course of the past century the United States had to intervene, to the relief of France and Britain, in European wars twice (three times, if you count the Cold War, which would not be unjustified). Even after the end of the Cold War the Europeans were incapable of resolving the problems of a disintegrating Yugoslavia on their own. Europeans, who like to emphasise the impact of history and tradition on political behaviour, should understand that this is no different in the United States.

Indeed, there is hardly any disagreement on this between most of the Europeans and the Americans. To a majority it makes sense to consult first within the framework of NATO before deciding on what should be done. In fact, this may be the best instrument to exert influence on an otherwise perhaps unilateral America. This particularly applies to the smaller member states that, if at all, can make significant influence felt only within the framework of the Alliance, and this is likely to be enhanced with the accession of new members, even more so if the new members have an inclination to follow the American lead.[39] It is primarily France that has a divergent attitude on this issue, not so much because it fears an American veto, which France, like all member states, also has, but because it rejects what it considers to be overbearing American influence. It fears that once an issue is discussed with the Americans in the framework of NATO the former will exert a degree of influence that would almost *nolens volens* turn out be dominant. As a consequence the Europeans would no longer be entirely free in their decisions. Of course, this concern cannot simply be dismissed, as there is some truth in it. On the other hand, in the past the degree of American influence was always also a reflection of European weakness. European weight and influence are likely to grow to the degree to which Europe speaks with one voice, to which it makes a relevant material contribution and, last but not least, to which it provides a conceptual input. In the past, American leadership was consistently related also to political and conceptual inputs and a capacity to quickly and determinedly present useful proposals. All too often, this has been missing on the European side.[40]

The converse of the French concern is American uneasiness about a possible 'European caucus', that is, a situation or even a regular procedure by which the European allies would agree on a common position among themselves before going into the Alliance councils. Such a common position would have considerable weight, but – at least, this is what Americans argue – it would also be highly inflexible, thus confronting the two North American allies with a 'take it or leave it' position. According to this argument, the Alliance would be unable to develop a joint position flexibly in the process of consultation, which would not only be a disadvantage in any specific situation but would soon harm Alliance cohesion.

No doubt there is validity to this argument, but only as long as the Europeans act as independent nation states, negotiating among themselves on an intergovernmental basis and indeed coming up with common positions – if they come up with common positions – that are likely to be carefully balanced, highly sensitive to any change, and hence inflexible. The situation would be different if the Europeans were acting as a single political unit. The European position would then be as flexible or inflexible as the American, and the United States would have to accept and adjust to a new situation: a single European ally rather than a conglomeration of states. But that is a long way off.

The third major issue concerning the relationship between a European military crisis reaction capability and NATO pertains to the possible European use of so-called 'Alliance assets' when acting without the Alliance as a whole. Such use presupposes a decision by the Alliance, and specifically agreement by the United States, in large part because these assets would be American. In terms of hardware the Alliance has few assets – mainly pipelines, some airfields and the AWACS (Airborne Warning and Control Systems) fleet of aircraft. But there are also the 'immaterial' assets such as joint planning processes, an element in which the Europeans are definitely interested. Most of the other components that a European force would lack at this stage and for some time in the future would have to come from the United States, primarily logistical support, intelligence, reconnaissance and communications.[41] The Europeans are deficient in these assets because they were available in the framework of NATO and it did not make sense to duplicate them, but also because they have been reluctant to spend the necessary money to acquire them. It is uncertain whether this will change soon, although there are some indications that the Europeans want to reduce or eliminate their dependence in at least some areas, especially in the area of airlift capacity.[42] Of course, it remains an open question as to how much duplication makes sense if crisis reaction and crisis management are dealt with essentially within the NATO framework. Also, increased European defence expenditure may reduce European expenditure in other areas, for example economic and political reconstruction and stabilisation activities that are essential and where the United States is much less active.[43] Whatever the case may be, and despite all declarations, it is highly unlikely that the United States would permit the use of such assets without maintaining a degree of influence. Again, this is perfectly reasonable: no European country would behave differently.

The capabilities gap

The issue of a growing gap between American and European military capabilities is important for three reasons: because of the psychological effects in the United States, because it raises the question of whether the Europeans will in fact do what is necessary to set up a modern and effective military reaction force, and because it has relevance to the interoperability of European and American forces in NATO.

European military technology in many respects is obsolete, some components are missing altogether, and in any case the structures are outdated. There are several reasons for this. First of all, since the founding of NATO European forces have been orientated towards territorial defence, with only the United Kingdom and France maintaining a limited power projection capability. Airlift capacity, for instance, currently regarded as a major deficiency, was geared to and perfectly adequate for the European theatre. In contrast, US forces are by definition – because of America's geographical position and its role as a world power – geared to power projection over long distances.

Nevertheless, the Europeans have been slow to adjust. Adjustment costs money and did not seem particularly urgent. The 'peace dividend' was high on the domestic agenda, and succumbing to it most attractive. Additional reasons include the fact that the European Union consists of sovereign countries, each with its own forces and overheads, resulting in massive duplication. In other words, the money spent is seldom used most effectively, as it is spread among separate armies. The combined armies of Europe's nations amount to roughly 2 million soldiers, almost one-third more than that of the United States, which in view of the low defence budgets means that a smaller amount is spent per soldier, and a remarkably small proportion is spent on research and development.[44] Indeed, Europeans face the question, succinctly put by NATO Secretary General Lord Robertson, of 'modernisation or marginalisation'.[45]

Moreover the gap between American and European capabilities has been exacerbated by the so-called 'Revolution in Military Affairs' (RMA). This has brought high technology into the military sphere, especially in communications, intelligence, precision-guided munitions and battlefield surveillance.[46] This means that both the interoperability of American and European forces is imperilled and the value of the Europeans as military allies is declining.[47] Again, it is an issue of cost. But even if the various European national defence budgets were to be raised by as much as 1 per cent of GDP, the question remains whether this would suffice to close the gap. Compared with American defence expenditure such an increase would be small – even if the Europeans were to pool their resources, a desirable but unlikely event for the foreseeable future. Moreover, a reorientation of expenditure would also be imperative: away from personnel and more towards research, development and procurement.

At least the Europeans have indicated their understanding of the need to improve capabilities. In 2001 the European Capability Action Plan (ECAP) was initiated by the Laeken European Council to investigate EU military shortfalls. Nineteen panels of experts were to report regularly on the shortcomings and progress made to eliminate them.[48] According to an official report in June 2002 the EU member states had met only 104 of 144 capability targets, missing out on such things as strategic mobility and ability to counter nuclear, biological and chemical threats.[49]

Whereas some moves toward more European co-operation have been made, these were primarily in the area of co-operation among existing forces, not specialisation or division of labour. There are units such as the EuroCorps (Belgium, Germany, France, Luxembourg and Spain), the Multinational Division Central (Belgium, Germany, the Netherlands and the United Kingdom), the British–Dutch Amphibious Force, EuroFor and EuroMarFor (France, Italy, Spain) and the German–Danish–Polish Corps in Szezcin. Some co-operation in research and development also exists, but it tends to be limited to smaller 'coalitions of the willing', such as the Franco-German Tiger combat and support helicopter joint venture as well as the joint British, German and Italian development of the Eurofighter 2000 (Typhoon) aircraft to replace not only the Tornado fighter in air defence but also military pursuit planes (such as the MIG-29, Phantom II or Jaguar). A major project is the development of the A400M transport aircraft (to replace the Transall) in which eight countries are to participate: Germany is to purchase sixty, France fifty, Spain twenty-seven, the United Kingdom twenty-five, Turkey ten, Belgium seven, Portugal three and Luxembourg one.[50]

The conclusion must be that the Europeans have done too little. They have enjoyed the sharp decline of defence expenditures since the end of the Cold War, and have inadequately prepared for new risks. What is worse, many of the European states have also done little to adjust their over-extended welfare systems. As a result they are confronted by growing national debts which together with declining economies at the beginning of this century leave scant room for redressing defence budgets. It is thus a question not just of will but also of capability. Consistent with this is the fact that the necessary reforms of the European Union to cope with both new members and new challenges have not been forthcoming. Whether the attempt to redress some of the military short-comings by closer co-operation with NATO – for example, by using NATO pro-cedures, facilities and equipment – is likely to succeed is uncertain. After all, NATO is made up of the same European member states that are failing in the national and in the EU sphere. Nevertheless, it makes sense to use what already exists rather than duplicating.

EU–NATO co-operation

The problems of control, decision making and the use of NATO assets will become easier to resolve if the political relationship between NATO and the European Union, including the European crisis reaction force, is clarified.[51] This is all the more true if it is accepted that it makes sense to deal with any crisis affecting European stability and security within the Alliance. The Washington communi-qué of April 1999 stated that the Alliance serves, 'as provided for in Article 4 of the North Atlantic Treaty, as an essential transatlantic forum for Allied consulta-tions ... in fields of common concern'.[52] If the Europeans had a significant mili-tary crisis reaction capability at their disposal, not only would a decision for an autonomous European activity become possible but at the same time European influence during the entire decision-making process would be correspondingly greater – provided, of course, that the Europeans agree among themselves.

Once the development of a European military crisis reaction capability was accepted by the Alliance, it seemed reasonable to foresee appropriate forms of interaction and co-operation in the planning processes and the use of Alliance assets.[53] Beginning in the year 2000, joint EU–NATO *ad hoc* working groups were set up to discuss three subject areas: security issues, namely procedures for the exchange of classified information, including intelligence, modalities for EU access to Alliance assets, including issues relating to the Alliance's defence planning system and the possibility of permanent consultation agreements. As a result of these discussions NATO and the EU Council secretariat concluded an interim security agreement governing the exchange of classified information.[54] At the same time it was agreed that experts from the Alliance would contribute military and technical advice to the work of the European Union in meeting the 'Headline Goal' decided upon in Helsinki. In 2001 this co-operation was intensified. For the first time the Secretary General of NATO was invited to attend an EU General Affairs Council meeting on NATO policy. In an exchange of letters between the Secretary General and the EU Swedish presidency, it was agreed to hold at least three EU–NATO meetings at ambassadorial level and one at ministerial level every six months.[55] It was also determined that there should be regular meetings between the NATO Council and the EU Political and Security Committee.

A major difficulty in developing closer relations between the European Union and NATO has been the position of Turkey, and to some extent that of Greece. Turkey was concerned that the ESDP reaction force might be used against Turkish interests, an understandable concern in view of the fact that a majority of the potential crisis areas are close to its territory. Moreover, under previous WEU arrangements Turkey felt that it had better access to possible EU military activities. For more than one year Turkey blocked an agreement between the European Union and NATO on EU access to NATO assets, demanding to be included in the ESDP planning and decision-making processes as an equal participant from an early stage. Turkey based its claims on the previous WEU procedures as well as the Washington summit communiqué of April 1999 in which provision had been made that those NATO members not belonging to the European Union would be involved to the 'fullest possible' extent in an ESDP activity.[56] A further Turkish concern was that Greece might attempt to use the ESDP in a conflict with Turkey, for example over Cyprus. Hence Turkey demanded not simply consultation but participation in all ESDP operations, even when the European Union does not request the use of NATO assets, and especially in operations affecting Turkish security interests or in areas of close proximity.

The compromise finally achieved in trilateral negotiations between Turkey, the United Kingdom and the United States was formulated in the so-called 'Ankara Paper' in December 2001. It contains three main elements. First, it makes reference to Article 17 of the EU Treaty, which states that the Common European Security and Defence Policy must be in harmony with the obligations of those states that are simultaneously members of NATO. Second, the agreement proclaims that 'under no circumstances' may ESDP be used against a NATO member. Third, it is agreed that if a NATO member not belonging to the European Union raises an objection to a planned autonomous operation by the European Union because it is to take place in close geographical proximity to that member or because it feels that its vital security interests are touched upon, consultations between the member and the European Union will take place. A decision on the participation by the state concerned in the planned EU action will then be taken in the light of these consultations.[57] However, it was now Greece that refused to accept the agreement, claiming that the Ankara Paper gave Turkey too great a say in EU defence matters. As a result a number of modifications were adopted at the EU summit meeting in Seville.[58] Since the Ankara Paper declared that the European Union would not undertake military action in any area touching upon the vital interests or in the geographical proximity of a NATO country without consultation, Greece now demanded a corresponding clause concerning NATO action close to an EU member state. The Spanish presidency proposed a compromise emphasising respect for the integrity and sovereignty of all states and declaring 'equality' between EU and NATO defence policy.[59] Greece accepted the compromise formulation, but Turkey insisted that the only valid document was the Ankara Paper.[60] At this point, it became difficult to understand continuing Turkish objections, and there was some speculation that Turkey was holding back to put pressure on the European Union to come up with a date for the beginning of Turkish accession talks. Consequently nothing was changed and the Seville proposal was reiterated at the EU summit in Brussels in October 2002. It was confirmed that 'under no circumstances, nor in any crisis, will ESDP be used against an ally on the understanding, reciprocally, that NATO military crisis management will not undertake any action against the European Union or its member states'.[61]

As a result of these Turkish–Greek differences the European Union could not take over the NATO-led Operation Amber Fox in Macedonia in October 2002 as planned. Belgium and France suggested that the European Union should go ahead without an agreement with NATO, but this was rejected by Britain. As it turned out, earlier speculation about Turkish motives for withholding agreement were probably correct. At the EU Copenhagen summit on 12–13 December 2002 Turkey dropped its objections and finally opened the way for an EU–NATO agreement after it had been informed that Turkey's candidacy would be reviewed at the end of 2004 and, provided Turkey had met set requirements on domestic reform, especially on democracy and human rights, a decision on the beginning of accession talks would follow. An additional difficulty from the Turkish point of view had been overcome by deciding that the ESDP 'Berlin plus' arrangements would apply only to EU members who are either also NATO members or participants in the Partnership for Peace Programme, hence excluding Cyprus and Malta.[62]

As a result of the agreement, the High Representative forwarded a note to the NATO Council detailing the EU decisions of Nice on consultation and co-operation for ESDP activities with partners that are not members of the European Union. The European Union and NATO then decided to prepare a formal agreement on 'strategic co-operation' between the two organisations, including EU use of NATO's planning capacities (to avoid the creation of an extensive separate planning staff by the European Union which would mean duplication and possibly friction), the use of other assets such as AWACS, US satellite data and airlift and the role of the NATO Deputy Commander, a European who could foreseeably be responsible for an ESDP activity.[63] In an EU–NATO declaration of 16 December 2002 it was reaffirmed 'that a stronger European role will help contribute to the vitality of the Alliance' and that, while respecting 'the decision-making autonomy and interests of the European Union and NATO', the 'crisis management activities of the two organisations are mutually reinforcing'. Specifically, it was stated that 'NATO is supporting ESDP in accordance with the relevant Washington Summit decisions, and is giving the European Union, *inter alia* and in particular, assured access to NATO's planning capabilities', as set out in the NAC decisions on 13 December 2002.[64]

Not only with regard to the specific question of EU–NATO co-operation but in very general terms the relationship with Turkey had become an issue between the United States and Europe. The United States sees in Turkey a valuable ally in a critical geo-strategic location between the Middle East, the Caucasus and Central Asia. Therefore it wants to tie Turkey in, with regard to activities within the framework of NATO as well as with regard to the European Union. There can be little doubt that both the United States and Europe have a clear interest in keeping Turkey closely tied to the West, a fact that may even grow in importance in the future. Turkey is an Islamic society, but a secular Islamic state. It is not only allied to the West but at the same time it is the type of secular Islamic country that in Western eyes is desirable, probably even necessary, to maintain stability in the present world order, despite its apparent deficiencies as a democracy.[65] Hence it appears logical that the United States should be interested in upholding good bilateral relations as well as keeping a close and co-operative relationship to Turkey within the framework of NATO. But the United States has also been urging the European Union to consider Turkey for membership.[66] It is uncertain to what extent this can be considered as tactical – the United States simply advocating something in which Turkey is interested. In any case, it is easy for American administrations to make such suggestions without the responsibility of having to live up to them. The members of the European Union have tried to face up to both sides of the issue: an understanding of the importance and desirability of keeping a close relationship with Turkey as well as the prerequisites and consequences of Turkish membership of the European Union.[67]

Conclusion: burden sharing and transatlantic relations

Burden sharing and an improved European military crisis reaction capability are obviously closely related issues.[68] Burden sharing has to do with the influence of the Europeans and it is related to the quality of the transatlantic relationship: with the degree of interaction, co-operation and satisfaction or frustration.

Burden sharing is a material problem, but it is also a problem of perception. The problem of perception is an after-effect of the Kosovo bombing in 1999 and the impression that the Europeans were not providing an appropriate and adequate contribution to the maintenance of military and political stability in Europe (and perhaps elsewhere). This view is particularly prevalent in the US Congress and – even when exaggerated, misinformed or over-simplified[69] – should not be underestimated by the Europeans with regard to its potential implications. It is a long-standing opinion in the US Congress as well as among the American public that the Europeans on the whole are free-riders as far as maintaining security in Europe is concerned, the decisive effort with all the accompanying cost as well as the military 'dirty work' always having been left to the United States.

The reality of this has two components. As far as the military side with regard to peace enforcement is concerned, it is in broad terms correct. It is known that the European contribution to the Kosovo bombing was limited,[70] not because the Europeans were not willing, but because they were not able to make an appropriate contribution, certainly within the given framework that it was to be merely a short expeditionary exercise with low risk and no casualties.[71] The given framework is significant because it indicates that the European NATO members were not inherently incapable of defeating Slobodan Milosevic. At higher risk and higher cost, including what it would have required in terms of support from the European domestic constituency, they could have done it by themselves. However, under the new definition that the West should be able to deal with any crisis of this nature by a high-tech, preferably aerial intervention with very low risks and preferably no casualties – a postmodern democratic approach, not at all to be scoffed at – the Europeans could not keep up with the United States.

All this applies to military requirements and more specifically to the requirements of peace enforcement. However, as far as the political, economic and military requirements of peacekeeping and peace building are concerned, the European contribution is respectable, not only in Bosnia and Kosovo, but throughout the Balkans, and, as it appears, well beyond that. Indeed, the European contribution almost dwarfs that of the United States,[72] and it can hardly be categorised as less important for the common aim of stability and peace. Calling this 'doing the dishes'[73] is silly. After all, long-term stability and conflict prevention depend on it; military intervention at best may solve a short-term problem and may also prepare the ground for longer-term activity, but, without peace building, peace enforcement remains little more than a stopgap measure.

Conceivably, there could be a division of labour between Americans and Europeans along these lines, perhaps even between a NATO Response Force[74] and the ESDP force. There is only one problem with this, and that is that neither the Americans nor the Europeans find such a division of labour acceptable, in which the United States would concentrate on the military and the Europeans on the economic and political tasks. Americans find it unacceptable because they do not want to be stuck with the unpleasant part of the job, which is both more risky, domestically more difficult to carry out and prone to arouse more criticism worldwide, leaving to the Europeans the positive elements, such as economic aid, reconstruction and political stabilisation. The Europeans similarly find such a division of labour less than desirable, even though it is rather comfortable. They have, in fact, proceeded on this basis for most of the 1990s (which partially explains the rather slow adjustment of European forces to new demands). There are two main reasons for European reluctance in accepting such a division of tasks. One is that it would in the long run be unacceptable to the United States (the Atlanticist argument), the other that Europeans are beginning to understand that there is a relationship between the degree of political influence and military capability. The member states of the European Union have repeatedly stated that they want to play a bigger political role, and at least on paper they have recognised that such a role comes at a price.

This means that in fact a similar perspective on the part of the United States and the Europeans can be identified. Both favour an improvement of European military capabilities. However, the United States wants this to happen in the framework of NATO so that the Alliance is better equipped, in terms of both hardware and flexibility, to react to new challenges to stability in Europe and beyond. In fairness it should be noted that, despite the emphasis that Americans in the past have placed on NATO, it is not only a desire to maintain American influence that determines such a policy, but also the conviction that NATO is in fact an available and effective instrument for framing transatlantic co-operation to meet new challenges.

However, the American view of NATO may be changing.[75] First of all, there is a growing American tendency to see the Alliance very narrowly: with regard to its usefulness in combating the threats that the United States considers most important – international terrorism and the spread of weapons of mass destruction – and with regard to viewing possible responses to such threats in large measure in military terms. But there is a second reason for a possibly changing attitude to NATO: the limited military contribution that Europeans are able and willing to make to robust military crisis management. Under such circumstances it appears easier for the United States to avoid the problems of lengthy consensus building and 'war by committee' by acting alone. This tendency was probably encouraged further by the European national rather than joint responses after 11 September 2001. It may thus turn out to be easier to form *ad hoc* 'coalitions of the willing' outside rather than within NATO, from the American point of view, but possibly also from the point of view of some of the Europeans. NATO would be used only as a 'toolbox' and 'provider of services'.[76] The question that arises is how American views and European views and actions – or lack thereof – interact, what effects this will have on NATO, and in turn what effects the changing role of NATO will have on the transatlantic relationship.

Notes

1 See on this the perceptive analysis by P. Terrence Hopmann, 'An evaluation of the OSCE's role in conflict management', in Heinz Gärtner, Adrian Hyde-Price and Erich Reiter (eds), *Europe's New Security Challenges* (Boulder CO: Lynne Rienner, 2001), pp. 219–54; also John C. Garnett, 'European security after the Cold War', in M. Jane Davis (ed.), *Security Issues in the post-Cold War World* (Brookfield: Edward Elgar, 1995), pp. 12–39.

2 See Walter C. Clemens, *Baltic Independence and Russian Empire* (Basingstoke: Macmillan, 1991), pp. 234 ff., and Raymond Pearson, 'Nationalities: decolonising the last empire', in D. W. Spring (ed.), *The Impact of Gorbachev: The First Phase, 1985–90* (London: Pinter, 1991), pp. 98 f.

3 See Georg Klöcker, *Ten Years after the Baltic States Re-entered the International Stage* (Baden-Baden: Nomos, 2001), p. 36; Mark Webber, *The International Politics of Russia and the Successor States* (Manchester and New York: Manchester University Press, 1996), pp. 179–83.

4 About 45 per cent of the population in Latvia, about 33 per cent in Estonia and approximately 8 per cent in Lithuania are ethnic Russians.

5 'Russia is obliged to protect the interests of Russians (*rossiyane*) living in the "near abroad". If their rights are violated, it is not only an internal matter for their country of residence, but also a Russian state matter.' This so-called 'Karaganov doctrine' (named for Sergei Karaganov, an early adviser to Yeltsin), as expressed in 1992, calls for the consistent promotion of Russian national interests. For the text of the decree see *Rossiiskaya gazeta*, 23 September 1995; see also Walter C. Clemens, *The Baltic Transformed: Complexity Theory and European Security* (Boulder CO and Oxford: Rowman and Littlefield, 2001), pp. 182 ff., and Yuri Afanasyev, 'A new Russian imperialism', *Perspective*, 4: 3 (1994).

6 Russia emerged as a major European power under Czar Peter the Great in the eighteenth century and gained control of the territories of Estonia in 1721 as well as of Latvia and Lithuania in 1795. At the end of World War I all three Baltic republics declared their independence.

7 See Anne Haglund, 'Baltic Sea Regional Security and Multilateral Security Co-operation: Towards a Co-operative Security Regime?' (M.A. thesis, Bruges: College of Europe, 2000), and Dieter Mahncke, 'Regional Co-operation: Security Aspects', paper presented at the Dubrovnik Diplomatic Summer School, August–September 2001 (forthcoming).

8 Estonian and Russian negotiators reached a technical border agreement in December 1996 under which Estonia made several concessions, including the acceptance of Russian annexation of two strips of territory. The agreement was provisionally signed in March 1999, but formal signature and ratification were stalled by Russia. Lithuania negotiated a draft treaty delimiting the boundary with Russia, but neither of the two parties had signed the agreement by 2002. In 1997 Latvia signed a border agreement with Russia that has also not been ratified by Russia.

9 See David S. Yost, *NATO Transformed: The Alliance's New Roles in International Security* (Washington DC: US Institute of Peace Press, 1998), pp. 137–9.

10 See Dieter Mahncke, 'Russia's attitude to the European Security and Defence Policy', *European Foreign Affairs Review*, 6: 4 (2001), pp. 427–36.

11 The German government (CDU/CSU/FDP) up to 1998 occasionally displayed an ambivalent attitude. While the Defence Minister, Volker Rühe, repeatedly stated that the Baltic republics were not candidates for the foreseeable future Chancellor Helmut Kohl at the 1997 NATO Madrid summit insisted on mentioning the Baltic countries as potential enlargement candidates. See Yost, *NATO Transformed*, p. 112, and Karl-Heinz Kamp and Peter Weilemann, 'Germany and the enlargement of NATO', study based on the conference 'NATO Enlargement: The Debates over Ratification', held in Washington DC on 7 October 1997 (www.nato.int/ acad/conf/enlarg97/home.htm).

12 See p. 62 f.

13 See Haglund, 'Baltic Sea regional security and multilateral security co-operation'. Since December 1991 all three Baltic republics have enjoyed 'Most Favoured Nation' (MFN) treatment with the United States. The Presidents of the United States, Estonia, Latvia and Lithuania signed a US–Baltic Charter in Washington on 16 January 1998 that forms the basic political document defining US–Baltic relations. The main goals of this charter are to support Estonia's, Latvia's and Lithuania's full integration into European and transatlantic structures and to

establish the general principles and aims of co-operation; see 'A Charter of Partnership among the United States of America and the Republic of Estonia, the Republic of Latvia, and the Republic of Lithuania', Washington DC, 16 January 1998 (www.usemb.ee/charter1.php3).

14 See his speech in Warsaw on 15 June 2001 (www.whitehouse.gov/news/releases/2001/ 06/20010615-1.html). See also the statements by US Deputy Secretary of State Richard Armitage on the occasion of a meeting with the applicant countries in Bucharest, *Frankfurter Allgemeine Zeitung*, 26 March 2002.

15 Thus an article in the *Guardian* claims: 'In a major shift of policy, President Vladimir Putin signalled that Russia might reconsider its long-standing opposition to Nato's eastward expansion in the light of the need to construct a global anti-terrorism coalition.' (Ian Black, 'Russia hints at rethink on NATO: Putin softens line on membership of Baltic states', *Guardian*, 4 October 2001.) On NATO enlargement see also p. 60 ff.

16 See Presidency Conclusions, Copenhagen European Council, 12–13 December 2002 (http://ue.eu.int/en/Info/eurocouncil/index.htm); also *Frankfurter Allgemeine Zeitung*, 13–14 December 2002.

17 See on this Dieter Mahncke (ed.), *Old Frontiers – New Frontiers: The Challenge of Kosovo and the Implications for the European Union* (Berne: Lang, 2001), and Sonia Lucarelli, *Europe and the Breakup of Yugoslavia: A Political Failure in Search of a Scholarly Explanation* (The Hague: Kluwer, 2000).

18 Several considerations play a role here. First, there is the complexity of the ethnic distribution in the area. In most cases it is simply not clear where the lines would be drawn. Second, an attempt to redraw lines would open up new questions, particularly with regard to the Albanians, who are spread out in several countries adjacent to Albania. Thirdly, some European countries may be concerned about 'opening a Pandora's box' that is likely to have an effect on minorities in their own countries.

19 See on this pp. 32–7.

20 Although this may be a mistake, the Caucasus and Central Asia rank much lower on the European list of concerns.

21 See on this pp. 70–3.

22 On 18 July 2001 the EU Foreign Ministers meeting in Rome had proposed sending impartial outside observers as a buffer force that might help stop escalating violence between Israelis and Palestinians and that could assist in the implementation of the 'Mitchell report', drawn up by American envoy George Mitchell, to end the killing. The EU High Representative, Javier Solana, had actually participated in the Mitchell group that issued the report, and both he and other high-level European leaders, such as German Foreign Minister Joschka Fischer, went to the region to try to bring the warring sides together. Fischer underlined in an interview that 'it is also in the European interest to prevent an utterly disastrous scenario. The Middle East is our neighbouring region. We want to get the peace process up and running again.' On 15–16 March 2002 the European Council in Barcelona expressed its concern by adopting a Declaration on the Middle East that not only supported a UN resolution but also called on both sides 'to take immediate and effective action to stop the bloodshed'. In addition, Fischer made several proposals in April 2002. His draft included a two-year time frame for, among other things, a durable cease-fire, the withdrawal of Israeli troops, the creation of a Palestinian state, the dismantling of Jewish settle-

ments and an internationally monitored buffer zone. 'EU ministers debate German plan for Mideast peace', Associated Press, 15 April 2002; 'EU kritisiert Israels Politik', *Frankfurter Allgemeine Sonntagszeitung*, 17 March 2002, p. 1; Presidency Conclusions, Barcelona European Council, 15–16 March 2002; Joschka Fischer, 'Israel wird niemals allein stehen', interview, *Die Welt*, 5 November 2001; see also 'Integre Stimme im Nahen Osten', *Die Welt*, 5 November 2001; Herb Keinon, 'EU Ministers seek greater role in peace process', *Jerusalem Post*, 23 October 2001; Horst Bacia, 'Die Handschrift der Europäer im Nahen Osten', *Frankfurter Allgemeine Zeitung*, 22 September 2001; on Javier Solana see Taylor Simon, 'Middle East policy process tests EU's foreign policy ambition', *European Voice*, 9–15 November 2000, p. 17; Horst Bacia, 'The Solana method, not the Chirac way', *Frankfurter Allgemeine Zeitung*, English edition, 26 October 2000.

23 An obvious limitation is lack of agreement between the Europeans themselves, where attitudes range from the more pro-Arab position of France to the restrictions imposed by the historical legacy on German policy.

24 The European reaction to this was paradoxical. On the one hand, Europeans claimed that here was indeed a European affair that the United States should leave to the Europeans; later there were complaints about lack of American leadership and indeed – mainly from the French side – American unreliability.

25 But Macedonia may turn out to be a case where the European Union can assume a bigger role in military terms, in effect taking over from NATO. See 'Die EU sucht ein aktives Krisenmanagement', *Neue Zürcher Zeitung*, 26 January 2002, p. 7, and pp. 52–5.

26 See pp. 32–7.

27 See pp. 33–7.

28 See on this Cesira D'Aniello, 'Interactions between Common Foreign and Security Policy related to Civil Crisis Management', paper presented to the conference 'Integrated Security in Europe: A Democratic Perspective', Bruges, 16 November 2001, *Collegium*, 22 (News of the College of Europe), special edition, Bruges, 2001. See also 'Enhancing the EU's response to violent conflict: moving beyond reaction to preventive action', International Security Information Service, Conference Report and Policy Recommendations, Brussels, 7–8 December 2000.

29 All these measures were taken within the framework of the Council.

30 See http://europa.eu.int/comm/external_relations/cpcm/cm.htm. See also the speech by Javier Solana at the EU Conference of National Police Commissioners, Brussels, 10 May 2001 (Press Release No. 0084/00).

31 See on this Jolyon Howorth, *European Integration and Defence: The Ultimate Challenge?* (Chaillot Papers 43, Paris: WEU Institute of Security Studies, 2000); also Christopher Reynolds, 'Future Tense? ESDP and the Challenge for Transatlantic Relations' (M.A. thesis, Bruges: College of Europe, 2001), and Gustav Brusewitz, 'Towards a European Defence Capacity: The Franco-British Discrepancy and its Implications for the European Security and Defence Policy (ESDP)' (M.A. thesis, Bruges: College of Europe, 2001).

32 This has, in fact, been expressly denied; see the General Affairs Council, 'EU's Military Capabilities Commitment Declaration' ('This process, without unnecessary duplication, does not involve the establishment of a European army'), Brussels, 20 November 2000 (Press Release No. 13427/2/00, 2308).

33 The limited character of the initiative is also apparent from the fact that it was given

a separate name from CFSP. Cynically, one might say that the reaction force is 'autonomous' within the European framework too!

34 See the report on this by the *Frankfurter Allgemeine Zeitung*, 8 December 2000.

35 See section on 'EU–NATO co-operation' below.

36 See Judy Dempsey, 'France pushes enhanced role for EU force', *Financial Times*, 29 October 2002, 'UK and France clash over defence force', *Financial Times*, 30 October 2002, and 'Frankreich will die EU in Mazedonien in die alleinige Pflicht nehmen', *Frankfurter Rundschau*, 16 October 2002.

37 This was already foreseen in the framework of the Combined Joint Task Force concept (initiated in late 1993, but so far never put into practice, at least under that heading). See on this, for example, Mark Smith, 'NATO enlargement and European security', in L. Aggestam and A. Hyde-Price (eds), *Security and Identity in Europe: Exploring the New Agenda* (Basingstoke: Macmillan, 2000), pp. 71–83; also Johannes Varwick and Wichard Woyke, *Die Zukunft der NATO. Transatlantische Sicherheit im Wandel* (Opladen: Leske + Budrich, 2000), pp. 136 ff.; *NATO Handbook*, pp. 253–5. It was reaffirmed in April 1999 at NATO's Washington summit on the so-called 'Berlin-plus' compromise and divided into four parts: (a) 'Assured EU access to NATO planning capabilities'; (b) 'The presumption of availability to the EU of pre-identified NATO capabilities and common assets'; (c) 'Identification of a range of European command options for EU-led operations'; (d) 'Further adaptation of NATO's defence planning system to incorporate more comprehensively the availability of forces for EU-led operations'; see Article 10 of the 'Washington Summit communiqué', 24 April 1999 (Press Release NAC-S(99)64).

38 See 'Strengthening European security and defence capability', NATO Fact Sheet, 15 December 2000 (www.nato.int/docu/facts/2000/dev-esdi.htm).

39 See, for example, John Vinocur, 'The big winner in the EU expansion: Washington', *International Herald Tribune*, 9 December 2002.

40 There are many examples of this. An impressive one is the Partnership for Peace programme. While the Europeans were calling for an 'extension of stability to the East' (and the Germans specifically for an extension of NATO) a concrete and, as it turned out, very useful proposal was put forward by the United States.

41 See on this the detailed analysis by François Heisbourg *et al.*, *European Defence: Making it Work* (Chaillot Papers 42, Paris: WEU Institute of Security Studies, September 2000).

42 See next section below.

43 See pp. 42–4.

44 See Gilles Andréani, Christoph Bertram and Charles Grant, *Europe's Military Revolution* (London: Centre for European Reform, 2001), also François Heisbourg, 'A view from Europe', *Survival*, 43: 3 (2001), pp. 67–70.

45 See Steven Erlanger, 'Military Gulf separates US and European Allies' (www.mtholyoke.edu/acad/intrel/bush/milgap. htm).

46 See François Heisbourg, 'Europe's military revolution', *Joint Force Quarterly*, spring 2002, pp. 28–32; Elinor C. Sloan, *The Revolution in Military Affairs* (Montreal: McGill–Queen's University Press, 2002).

47 An impressive figure is that whereas the United States has about 250 large transport aircraft, Europeans have a total of seven! Within the framework of NATO's DCI (Defence Capability Initiative, NATO Fact Sheet, December 1999) – unveiled at the Washington summit in April 1999 and intended to encourage the European

members to make a stronger contribution to NATO – arrangements between France and Germany on mutual airlift support (European Airlift Command), as well as between Belgium and the Netherlands on the collective use of their air forces through a Deployable Air Task Force, stood as possible models for future European co-operation. See, however, the rather sceptical view of Kori Shake, *Constructive Duplication: Reducing EU Reliance on US Military Assets* (London: Centre for European Reform, 2002), pp. 13 f. and 19 ff.; Diego A. Ruiz Palmer (Vice-president, European Region, Northrop Grumman International), 'Steps for achieving Transatlantic Strategic Convergence', presented to the NATO Parliamentary Assembly's Economics and Security Committee in Berlin, 18 November 2000 (www.nato-pa.int/archivedpub/speeches/palmer 001118.asp). Most of the fifty-eight categories targeted by DCI were, in fact, not or not fully achieved, and DCI was replaced in November 2002 by the Prague Capabilities Commitment; see below, the section on 'The Prague summit', pp. 65–7.

48 See Annex II, 'Declaration on the operational capability of the Common European Security and Defence Policy', of the Laeken European Council Presidency Conclusions, 14–15 December 2001 (europa.eu.int/council/off/conclu/index. htm). In this case the European institutions played only a general management and co-ordinating role, leaving the actual work of finding solutions to the member states. The working groups analysed how to remedy the shortfalls that have been identified, in particular as regards the following items of equipment: tactical drones but also medium and high-altitude UAVs; attack and support helicopters; protective equipment against nuclear, bacteriological and chemical (NBC) attacks; precision-guided munitions; theatre ballistic missiles; deployable communication modules; strategic imagery; troop transport aircraft; roll-on/roll-off ships and strategic lift cargoes; suppression of enemy air defence systems, etc. Since some of the capability gaps were to be addressed in the longer term through planned procurement pro-grammes, efforts were partially focused on finding interim solutions to meet the Headline Goal by 2003.

49 Final reports from all ECAP panels were required by 1 March 2003. See General Affairs Council Conclusions, 19 November and 13 May 2002 (http://europa.eu.int /comm/external_relations/ cfsp/intro/gac.htm#sd191102); see also Kim Sengupta, 'Delay hits rapid reaction force', *Independent*, 26 June 2002; Katia Vlachos-Dengler, 'Getting there: Building Strategic Mobility into ESDP' (Occasional Paper 38, Paris: European Union Institute for Security Studies, 2002) and Daniel Keohane, 'The EU and Armaments Co-operation' (CER Working Papers, London: Centre for European Reform, 2002).

50 See *Frankfurter Allgemeine Zeitung*, 30 January 2002, pp. 1 and 3. Germany was originally to purchase seventy-three aircraft; see 'Bundeswehr wird nur 60 Militärtransporter bestellen', *Frankfurter Allgemeine Zeitung*, 30 November 2002.

51 See on this Michael Brenner, *Europe's New Security Vocation* (Washington DC: National Defense University, 2002), especially pp. 41 ff.

52 Article 6 of the 'Washington Summit Communiqué', 24 April 1999 (Press Release NAC-S(99)64).

53 This is dealt with in Articles 8–10 of the 'Washington Summit Communiqué' of 24 April 1999. Article 10 states that the allies 'stand ready to define and adopt the nec-essary arrangements for ready access by the European Union to the collective assets and capabilities of the Alliance, for operations in which the Alliance as a whole is

not engaged militarily as an Alliance'. This is further specified with reference to access to NATO planning, pre-identified NATO capabilities and common assets, identification of a range of European command options and the adaptation of NATO's defence planning system 'to incorporate more comprehensively the availability of forces for EU-led operations'. See Brenner, *Europe's New Security Vocation*; also *NATO Handbook*, chapter 4 (ESDI) and 'NATO Statement on the Defence Capabilities Initiative', 8 June 2000 (NATO Press Release M-NAC-D-1(2000)64).

54 See *NATO Handbook*, chapter 4 (ESDI), p. 103.

55 *Ibid.*

56 Washington Summit Communiqué, Washington DC, 24 April 1999 (Press Release NAC-S(99)64); see also Yaprak Alp, 'Turkey's Place in the Newly Emerging European Security Architecture' (M.A. thesis, Bruges: College of Europe, 2000).

57 See Horst Bacia, 'Warten auf das Ja aus Athen. Der Streit zwischen der Türkei und der EU ist noch nicht vorüber', *Frankfurter Allgemeine Zeitung*, 10 December 2001, p. 6.

58 See Paul Taylor, 'Optimism grows on EU–NATO defence deal' (Reuter's), 21 June 2002, and Ian Black, 'Greek row stalls launch of EU force', *Guardian*, 19 June 2002.

59 Daniela Spinant, 'Greece in favour but Turkey against EU–NATO deal', *EU Observer*, 24 June 2002.

60 *Ibid.*; see also Ian Black, 'Turkey blocks deal on new EU rapid reaction force', *Guardian*, 24 June 2002; Sharon Spiteri, 'Turkey not recognising EU presidency Greece deal', *EU Observer*, 2 July 2002 (www.euobserver.com); 'Turkey rejects EU force deal born in Seville', *Kathimerini* English edition, 25 June 2002; 'Gespräche über ESVP gescheitert', *Frankfurter Allgemeine Zeitung*, 25 October 2002.

61 Annex II, Presidency Conclusions, Brussels European Council, 24–5 October 2002.

62 See Horst Bacia, 'Mit Berlin-plus', *Frankfurter Allgemeine Zeitung*, 14 December 2002.

63 See 'NATO agrees to help new EU force', *International Herald Tribune*, 16 December 2002; 'OTAN et UE désormais partenaires', *Le Soir*, 16 December 2002; 'EU und NATO beginnen Gespräche über Grundlagenvertrag', *Frankfurter Allgemeine Zeitung*, 16 December 2002.

64 EU–NATO Declaration on ESDP, 16 December 2002, PR/CP (2002) 142.

65 See Heinz Kramer, *A Changing Turkey: The Challenge to Europe and the United States* (Washington DC: Brookings Institution, 2000), pp. 224 ff. and 236 ff.; also Yasemin Çelik, *Contemporary Turkish Foreign Policy* (Westport CT: Praeger, 1999), p. 79.

66 See Çelik, *Contemporary Turkish Foreign Policy*, p. 80; also 'Wolfowitz: Die Türkei ein Schlüsselland', *Frankfurter Allgemeine Zeitung*, 4 December 2002; Judy Dempsey, 'Washington urges talks for Turkey', *Financial Times*, 11 December 2002; 'EU summit host takes tough line with candidates', *New York Times*, 12 December 2002; 'Washington soutient l'adhésion rapide de la Turquie à l'Europe', *Le Monde*, 11 December 2002.

67 The question has led to a lively debate and some controversy in most of the EU member states. Thus when after the elections the German Chancellor, Gerhard Schröder, expressed a more positive attitude towards Turkish membership, the Christian Democratic opposition accused him of wanting to appease the United States because of previous irritations caused by the Schröder campaign against the American Iraq policy. Whether this was the case or not, there were probably also domestic political considerations; after all, there is a growing electorate of Turkish

origin in Germany. Against the official position of the European Commission and the fifteen EU members' governments, the head of the European Union's constitutional convention, Valéry Giscard d'Estaing, reopened a lively European debate by stating in a newspaper interview that 'Turkey is not a European country, it is a country that is situated near Europe.' He added, 'its capital is not in Europe and 95 per cent of its population live outside Europe'. See Arnaud Leparmentier and Laurent Zecchini, 'Pour ou contre l'adhésion de la Turquie à l'Union européenne', *Le Monde*, 9 November 2002; Jochen Hoenig, 'Giscard: Türkei kein europäisches Land', *Handelsblatt*, 8 November 2002.

68 The following is partly based on a previous essay: Dieter Mahncke, 'Eine gemeinsame europäische Außen- und Sicherheitspolitik. Auswirkungen auf die transatlantischen Beziehungen', in Hanspeter Neuhold (ed.), *Die GASP. Entwicklungen und Perspektiven* (Occasional Paper 4/2000, Vienna: Diplomatische Akademie, 2001), pp. 36–44.

69 Which was certainly often the case in the past; see Thiel, *Dollar-Dominanz. Lastenteilung und amerikanische Truppenpräsenz in Europa*; Andréani *et al.*, *Europe's Military Revolution*.

70 See, for example, Andréani *et al.*, *Europe's Military Revolution*.

71 The US Air Force has about 1,400 aircraft equipped with precision guided weapons, making it possible by laser and satellite to guide 'bombs' from high altitudes accurately into foreseen targets. All other NATO partners together have 2,900 aircraft, but only a small number of these are equipped with PGMs, most of them based on an outdated and weather-sensitive laser guidance system. See Horst Bacia, 'Die schwere Geburt einer neuen NATO', *Frankfurter Allgemeine Zeitung*, 20 November 2002.

72 While in Afghanistan, too, the major part of the military effort was undertaken by the United States, the UN peacekeeping force put in place since the end of December 2001 includes no American participation at all.

73 Robert Kagan, 'Power and weakness', *Policy Review*, 113 (June–July 2002), www.policyreview.org/JUN02/kagan.html.

74 See pp. 65–7.

75 See Chapter 3 below.

76 *Ibid.*

3

The changing role of NATO

Despite difficulties and recurrent crises, the Atlantic Alliance, institutionalised in NATO, is not only still the major instrument for dealing with transatlantic co-operation on European security matters but may also become a forum for policy co-ordination and action beyond Europe. Many expected its demise after the end of the Cold War, but the Alliance has shown remarkable resilience and adaptability, in no small measure thanks to American leadership. The role of NATO has changed and continues to change. But there are questions: first, to what extent this change is a managed and directed change, and second, whether the transformation that is taking place is in fact moving in the desired direction. What new tasks need to be taken care of? Is NATO in fact taking on new tasks, and is it a suitable organisation to do this? What are European and American interests and attitudes, and what effects will a 'new NATO' have on transatlantic relations?

An alliance of multiple functions

Initially, the North Atlantic Treaty foresaw no more than a classical defence alliance, an agreement that the members of the Alliance would come to each other's aid in case of aggression from outside. The commitment appeared less firm than it might have been. While Article 5 of the Washington Treaty states that the 'Parties agree that an armed attack against any one or more of them in Europe or North America shall be considered an attack against them all'[1] – which is, after all, not a weak statement – the subsequent decision on what action to take is less certain, calling on each member to 'assist the Party or Parties so attacked by taking forthwith, individually and in concert with the other Parties, such action as it deems necessary, including the use of force, to restore and maintain the security of the North Atlantic area'.[2]

The objectives of the treaty at the time were twofold: to pool the resources of the allies in defence against a Soviet threat and to tie the United States to

European defence, making clear to the Soviet leadership that any aggression against Western Europe would be sure to bring in the United States.[3] In principle, there was nothing new about these classical objectives. If the Alliance had remained in that status, the idea that it had served its purpose after the decline and disappearance of the Soviet threat after 1989 might have been valid. But within a short period after the signing of the Washington Treaty it became evident that under the specific conditions prevailing in Europe, especially the maintenance and forward deployment of large and ready Soviet forces, a classical alliance with lengthy decision making, extended mobilisation time and complex problems of co-ordinating military forces from different allies would no longer do. Before the resources were put together and the United States had arrived on the scene, Western Europe would have been overrun. But 'this time' the United States did not want to arrive late, as it had done in 1917 and 1941; it wanted to be there before a negative development had come about, and it wanted to be sure that it had a determining voice in the unfolding of events. As a consequence, two developments took place in the period up to 1955, strongly influenced by the Korean War. First, there was the decision on the part of the United States to maintain a significant military presence in Europe *in peacetime.* Second, the decision to set up a standing military organisation with a political as well as military headquarters (first in Fontainebleau, later in Brussels and Mons) and structures for policy co-ordination, an Allied command structure, joint planning procedures as well as joint exercises preparing Allied military forces to react rapidly in case of an attack.[4]

Thus, only a few years after the Washington Treaty had been signed, the Alliance had changed from a classical alliance to something more. Basic and permanent structures for military but also for political co-ordination had been created. The Alliance became an important institution for transatlantic co-operation in two ways. First, Western policy towards the Soviet Union and the Warsaw Pact was, at least to a certain extent and in specific cases, co-ordinated within the framework of the Alliance. An impressive example is Western arms control and *détente* policy.[5] In fact, the most successful examples of a common European foreign and security policy can be found here: in the policies developed since the beginning of the 1970s for the Conference on Security and Co-operation in Europe (CSCE)[6] as well as for the arms control negotiations called Mutual and Balanced Force Reductions (MBFR)[7] and Confidence and Security Building Measures (CSBM).[8] These were decisive developments in the framework of Western *détente* policies and the peaceful conclusion of the Cold War. Not once in all these years did the European or North American allies go into negotiations with the Soviet side without a common position, an achievement seldom noted and appreciated.

It could be argued that this was both imperative as well as comparatively easy during the Cold War because the Soviet Union and communist oppression in Eastern Europe were obvious and, no less important, because of determined American leadership on the Western side. Nevertheless, another, less tangible but by no means negligible factor must be added, namely the extensive day-to-day co-operation taking place within the relatively large bureaucracy of the Alliance, in Brussels as well as at SHAPE. This not only includes a daily feedback to the various capitals of NATO's member states. It can safely be assumed that it also to an extent moulds the civil servants and military officers serving in NATO and influences them when they return to their home countries.

After 1989, practically simultaneously with a debate on whether NATO had now served its purpose,[9] the Alliance once again rapidly took on new tasks. Some argued that this was, in fact, necessary to maintain NATO: 'out of area or out of business'.[10] However, it took on new tasks not because it was seeking a new *raison d'être*, but because the situation in the Balkans was seen as demanding Western action, and because NATO was the most suitable instrument. This became even more apparent as the misguided and unsuccessful activities under the auspices of the United Nations unfolded in the first years of the break-up of Yugoslavia,[11] including the differences that arose among the Europeans.[12]

In fact, first in Bosnia-Herzegovina and then in Kosovo, the Alliance became an instrument of crisis management. The Alliance covered the entire gamut of activities: from diplomacy, such as the frequent visits paid to Slobodan Milosevic by both diplomatic and military personnel throughout this period as well as the negotiations and agreement achieved at Dayton and the negotiations at Rambouillet, through to preventive deployments, such as in Macedonia, to peacekeeping in Bosnia-Herzegovina and ultimately peace enforcement in Kosovo in 1999. Post-crisis reconstruction and stabilisation throughout the Balkans then became a task primarily left to the guidance of the European Union, the OSCE and the United Nations. In Macedonia in autumn 2001 there was a division of labour. While both Lord Robertson from NATO and Javier Solana from the European Union mediated between the Macedonian government and the Albanian minority, the military stabilisation efforts of Essential Harvest and Amber Fox were left to NATO.[13]

The role as a crisis manager, including the 'most demanding' elements, has its basis in the new Strategic Concept adopted by NATO at the Washington summit in April 1999, which 'moved NATO's focus away from territorial defence . . . to a wider security role in Europe'.[14]

Three further 'roles' for NATO need to be mentioned. First, there is the role of the Alliance as an 'extender of stability'. This was its role during the Cold War, but after the fall of the Berlin Wall it took on a new significance. The Central and Eastern European states clamoured to join the Alliance.[15] Apart from discussing the specific effects this might have on the commitments, cohesion and effectiveness of NATO, the Western allies felt that it was crucial to ensure both that no new dividing lines were created and that those countries either unwilling or unable to join would not be left in a 'grey zone of insecurity'. In other words, if the extension of NATO membership provided security and stability to the new members,[16] non-members, including Ukraine and Russia,[17] would need to be involved both in a co-operative relationship with the Alliance and in a broader framework of all-European security. Indeed, this could well be described as the second new role, giving NATO the several functions of serving European security by being a crisis manager, by extending membership as well as by creating a network of co-operative relations. One cannot argue that the Alliance has been unaware of this even if one wanted to claim that it falls short of the optimum. In 1991 it created first the North Atlantic Co-operation Council (NACC) and later in 1997 the Euro-Atlantic Partnership Council (EAPC); the Partnership for Peace programme in 1994, and the special relationships with Russia[18] and with Ukraine in 1997.[19]

A third function is the definition of NATO as a 'provider of services'. Services which NATO could provide are planning capacities, intelligence, command and control and to a limited extent communications and infrastructure. This is not negligible, but one needs to be aware that NATO as such has few assets of its own. Most of them are national contributions, specifically by the United States.[20] The pertinent question, however, is in what manner this particular role might affect the Alliance and its functioning. A provider of services by definition implies that NATO as a whole is not engaged. In that case, services would be available, but only some members of the Alliance, a 'coalition of the willing', would be acting. There might be different reasons for such a procedure, each one with a different effect on the Alliance. The least problematical would be a small group of NATO members acting in the name and with the full support of the Alliance simply because the involvement of all members is not required. An example of this would be an evacuation of European or American or Canadian citizens from a crisis area. Considerably more problematical would be the activities of a group of members with only the tacit or reluctant support of the non-participating members but with a claim to some or all of the NATO services. If hesitation on the part of the non-participating members were to grow, or if such cases were to occur frequently, this could entail considerable strain for the cohesion of the Alliance. With or without such strain, such a procedure could lead to a gradual 'dehydration' of the Alliance, with more and more tasks being taken on by coalitions of the willing with little or no reference to the Alliance.

Thus it is clear that, far from standing still, NATO has developed in a specific and coherent fashion. Some would claim that a detailed and clear programme was lacking. But not only does the Strategic Concept of April 1999 meet this objection to an extent, it is also correct that under rapidly changing and uncertain circumstances it is wise to move forward in a cautious, step-by-step manner. Two issues stood in the foreground in the first decade and a half after the end of the Cold War: the relationship with Russia and the response to Central and Eastern European demands for accession to the Alliance.

Relations with Russia

After the end of the Cold War no small degree of adjustment was demanded of Russia. Not only had it lost its external empire in Central and South Eastern

Europe but, with the collapse of the Soviet Union, its internal empire, acquired over centuries, as well. Russia was in the classical position of a power after a lost war: it had lost both territory and power. It is quite understandable that this situation was difficult, particularly for the old Soviet elites, even more so because it was not a classical defeat with a vanquished army and occupied territory. In addition, the country was faced with difficult economic adjustments, many of which were unsuccessful and most of which brought unemployment and personal hardship.[21] In view of all this, it is hardly surprising that nostalgia, however unjustified, was widespread.

In terms of foreign policy orientation, there were two implications. First, Russian foreign policy was marked – not always but frequently – by 'superpower behaviour', and certainly by a great sensitivity with regard to the way Russia was treated. It demanded to be regarded not as a country that had lost a war and was confronted by major difficulties, but as a superpower with only 'temporary difficulties'. Anything that appeared to be different, such as the first round of NATO enlargement or the bombing of Serbia in 1999, was interpreted as the West exploiting Russia's momentary weakness. The results were threats, certainly insinuations, that the West would live to regret its actions once Russia had recovered, and withdrawal from co-operation in the NATO framework.[22]

Second, there were also some more 'outgoing' (to avoid the term 'offensive') elements in Russia's foreign-policy stance. They manifested themselves in an emphasis on Russia's responsibility for its former citizens living beyond its borders, the creation of the concept of the 'near abroad',[23] and specifically in threatening statements towards the three Baltic republics. A sense of obligation on the part of Russia towards its former citizens is not entirely incomprehensible. What was problematical was the threatening stance towards the Baltic states and the Western fear that Moscow might use Russian minorities as an excuse for interference – or more – in neighbouring countries.

On the whole, both the Europeans and the Americans reacted to this situation with moderation, often paying more tribute to Russian sensitivities than some observers felt necessary. The United States continued to see in Russia its main counterpart in terms of nuclear capabilities and disarmament. As far as this was concerned, Russia in the eyes of the United States remained a superpower, and to some extent American policy towards Russia was dominated by these concerns. The United States was also interested in democratisation, economic development and stabilisation in Russia, but the more active role in this respect was left to the Europeans.[24] Of course, Russia was especially interested in co-operation with the European Union.[25] Not only is the European Union Russia's largest trading partner,[26] but Moscow saw the Union as its gateway to the West and it felt itself on an equal footing with the organisation.[27]

During the Kosovo crisis a useful division of labour developed between the United States and the Europeans. While Russia proclaimed the United States the main culprit and withdrew from co-operation with NATO in the framework of the Permanent Joint Council,[28] the Europeans (and especially the Germans) took pains to maintain close relations with Russia and keep it informed. While this may not have been decisive, it eased the situation and did help to keep Russia involved, eventually allowing Moscow to return to a more co-operative stance.

The adjustment of the Russian foreign policy elite and the process of demo-cratisation and economic development will take time. The point of no return in this process has not yet been reached. The situation in Chechnya and the way Russia is dealing with it remain disturbing. Moreover, the attitude towards crit-icism and a free press – visible in numerous instances – is not an encouraging indication for the development of democracy in Russia. Yet the situation is not without hope. The main issue is not whether the United States and the Europeans will continue to be committed to encouraging a positive develop-ment in Russia, but rather what precise policies are most likely to achieve the desired objectives. Further transatlantic co-operation not in the sense of 'joint ventures' but in the sense of an exchange of experience and information would certainly make sense.

As far as the European Union is concerned a Russian application for mem-bership is not under consideration. Russia is neither economically prepared for such membership nor ready to undertake the extensive adjustments that mem-bership would require.[29] As Russia considers itself to be a great power, it would be reluctant to integrate itself into this larger unit. As far as the European Union is concerned, it would be hesitant over whether a much larger and for many reasons much more problematical country such as Russia would really be compatible with membership.

However, there is no question that both the European Union and Russia are interested in developing a closer relationship, mainly as far as regards economic co-operation. This is portrayed by the Partnership and Co-operation Agreement of 1995 (in effect since 1997),[30] the Common Strategy of the European Union on Russia of June 1999[31] and the Russian reaction to it four months later in the form of the Medium-term Strategy for the Development of Relations between the Russian Federation and the European Union.[32] Russia expects and receives assistance from the European Union, both in terms of aid and trade (almost 50 per cent of Russian foreign trade is with the Union). There also remain certain reservations or inhibitions. Co-operation with the European Union tends to highlight the grotesquely weak economic position of the Russian Federation, which now has a GNP smaller than that of the Netherlands,[33] and thus repre-sents a blow to the self-esteem of a 'great power'. A more important reservation is that Russia apparently has no clear idea and hence no precise position on the enlargement of the European Union: what implications will it have on Russian relations with the applicant countries, what effects will it have on the European Union and what will the results be for Russian and Western influence in general?[34] The only issue that played an important role early on was the ques-tion of access to the Russian exclave of Kaliningrad.

As regards the Russian relationship with NATO, there are both similarities and differences. A major similarity is that here, too, efforts have been made to develop co-operation short of membership. In addition to Russian participation in the Partnership for Peace programme[35] there was the NATO–Russian Founding Act of 27 May 1997,[36] the NATO–Russia Permanent Joint Council (PJC) and the Euro-Atlantic Partnership Council (EAPC). Nevertheless, for a long time – and perhaps still in some Russian circles – the Alliance, unlike the European Union, continued to be seen as an opponent, even an enemy.[37] This was particularly obvious when the issue of NATO enlargement arose.[38] There were several reasons. First and foremost, the Alliance was regarded as the main instrument of American influence and power in Europe and it followed that enlargement signified the extension of that power. Second, NATO was remembered as the Cold War enemy, having been portrayed as a grave threat (although there is little evidence that anybody in the Russian leadership believed this). It may be safely assumed that many Russians still find it difficult to concede to NATO a continuing role in Europe, even though it is declared to be a 'new NATO'.[39]

The situation worsened in March 1999 when NATO decided to bomb Yugoslavia, and Russia as a result suspended its co-operation in the Permanent Joint Council. But since the end of this intervention Russian attitudes seem to be changing. Most significantly, this movement got a boost from the events of 11 September 2001. Seeing an opportunity to draw a parallel between the al-Qaida terrorists and the Chechan rebels, and hence to blunt American and European criticism of Russian activities in Chechnya,[40] President Putin not only expressed his immediate sympathy to the United States but explicitly supported its actions. He defended American and British air strikes in Afghanistan as 'measured and appropriate', granted countries fighting the Taliban the use of Russian air space, and did not object to a growing American military presence in the Central Asian republics that had once belonged to the Soviet Union. Moreover, Russia helped the Americans and British establish contact with opposition Northern Alliance forces, whom it had long equipped and aided. Russia also announced the closure of two sensitive bases left over from Soviet times: the Lourdes electronic eavesdropping station in Cuba and a naval station in Vietnam.[41]

Most important, however, Russia's attitude towards NATO began to change. President Putin called for more significant involvement of Russia in NATO. Wisely, Putin did not ask for full membership, but for a role that would give Russia significant influence, perhaps a right of consultation, preferably before NATO decisions were taken. At the same time, there were signals that while Russia still did not consider further NATO enlargement a good idea, it would no longer oppose it.

These moves seemed significant from the Alliance point of view, and thinking began about how and to what extent Russia could be given a special role that would tie it in, that would meet its wishes, but that would not grant it a veto or even obstructive leverage over NATO decisions.[42] The Western motivation was obvious. Not only is Russia needed as a partner in combating international terrorism but, more important, if Russia is to be encouraged to become a co-operative partner in maintaining peace and stability in Europe, it cannot remain a bystander, but needs to get involved in the process. Furthermore, there is interest in Russia as an economic partner, especially with regard to oil and gas, and in a co-operative Russian attitude as far as Western interests in Central Asia are concerned.

Ultimately, it was decided to change the NATO–Russia Permanent Joint Council from the '19 + 1' format, where the nineteen NATO members would meet Russia after prior consultation among themselves, to a council of twenty members meeting jointly and foreseeing joint decisions on a certain set of issues. On the occasion of a meeting of the Permanent Joint Council at the level of Foreign Ministers in Brussels on 7 December 2001 a NATO–Russia joint statement declared:

> Today we commit ourselves to forge a new relationship between NATO Allies and Russia, enhancing our ability to work together in areas of common interest and to stand up to new threats and risks to our security. We reaffirm that a confident and co-operative partnership between the Allies and Russia, based on shared democratic values and the shared commitment to a stable, peaceful and undivided Europe, as enshrined in the NATO–Russia Founding Act, is essential for stability and security in the Euro-Atlantic area. We have decided to give new impetus and substance to our partnership, with the goal of creating a new council bringing together NATO member states and Russia to identify and pursue opportunities for joint action at twenty.

This was reaffirmed when the PJC met a few weeks later at the level of Defence Ministers:

> Ministers fully endorsed the decision of Foreign Ministers on 7 December to give new impetus and substance to the partnership between NATO Allies and Russia, with the goal of creating a new council bringing together NATO member states and Russia to identify and pursue opportunities for joint action at twenty. Ministers committed themselves to enhance their partnership in the security and military field.[43]

After several months of negotiations in Brussels and Moscow, a formal decision was taken at the NATO summit meeting in Rome in May 2002 to establish a new NATO–Russia Council.[44] The agreement came exactly five years after the signing of the Russia Founding Act, and in fact many of the issues to be taken up for discussion and co-operation had already been foreseen for the Permanent Joint Council. But since the meetings of the PJC tended to be little more than an exchange of views and had given Russia scant opportunity to influence NATO thinking, the Russians had lost interest. This is to be different in the new council, where all members 'will work as equal partners',[45] Russia is seated alphabetically between Portugal and Spain, and the meetings are regularly chaired by NATO's Secretary General. Nevertheless, for the beginning a circumscribed number of topics were determined as subjects for 'consensus building, consultations, joint decisions and joint actions'.[46] These were 'the struggle against terrorism, crisis management, non-proliferation of weapons of mass destruction, arms control and confidence-building measures, theatre missile defence, search and rescue at sea, military-to-military co-operation and defence reform, and civil emergencies' as well as 'other areas'.[47]

In the final discussions it was not considered necessary to reiterate the obvious right of NATO to make its own decisions 'at nineteen' without a Russian veto, although the Alliance had still found it necessary to point this out in its final communiqué at the NATO ministerial meeting in December 2001.[48] Certainly, if agreement is not reached in this forum the Alliance members can withdraw to the North Atlantic Council and take whatever decisions they feel necessary without Russia. However, the situation will be different; Russia would be 'invisibly present at the table' and differences among the members could very well be exacerbated.

Ultimate Russian membership of NATO is not inconceivable, either if NATO develops into the major organisation for the maintenance of stability in Europe, a type of OSCE, or if it turns into an all-European military alliance against extra-European threats (or something of both). Prerequisite to either, however, is the development of Russia into a stable, mature and co-operative democracy, without imperial or hegemonic ambitions, and accepted and trusted by the other Europeans. It is not that the importance of Russia is underestimated; it is primarily a question of whether basic values and approaches are compatible so that closer co-operation with Russia makes sense.

NATO enlargement

Next to the development of a new relationship with Russia, NATO was confronted with the question of how to deal with the now independent Central and Eastern Europe countries (CEECs), some of whom asked for membership of the Alliance (and the European Union), while others seemed to hover in a 'grey zone' of uncertainty between Russia and the West.

The relations between Russia and Central and Eastern Europe during the Cold War were determined by complete Soviet dominance. With full justification the Eastern European states were called 'satellite' states. While they were granted some leeway in their internal affairs, the overall line was clear: domestically, communist dictatorships were to be maintained, and externally the foreign policy line set out by the Soviet Union was to be followed. (In the case of Romania, which maintained an iron-fisted Stalinist regime domestically, a degree of freedom existed in external affairs.)

There were four main reasons for this. The first was simply the reflex of any dictatorship to maintain control. In the case of a totalitarian dictatorship, such control delves into all aspects of daily life. The second reason is that with the end of the Second World War the Soviet Union, in addition to Russia's existing 'internal' empire, had acquired an empire in Central and Eastern Europe, and like any colonial power it wanted to keep it. Related to this, is, thirdly, the security the Soviet Union hoped to gain from these 'buffer states'. This was the main argument the Soviet Union offered for its expansionist policies after 1945, an argument that did not fail to impress President Franklin Roosevelt.[49] Fourthly, the expansion of communism went along well with the ideological preconception of a 'world revolution'; the historical inevitability of the expansion and ultimate victory of Marxism-Leninism.

After 1989 and especially after the collapse of the Soviet Union the newly independent states fell into three groups: the former satellites in Central Europe (Poland, Czechoslovakia, Hungary, Romania and Bulgaria), the Baltic republics (Estonia, Latvia, Lithuania) and the remaining states split off from the former Soviet Union (Belarus, Ukraine, Georgia, Armenia, Azerbaijan, Moldova). Of these, the first two groups soon began to ask for accession to Western institutions, specifically to NATO.

The first round

The issue of NATO enlargement came up relatively soon after 1989.[50] It was Germany that first pushed for extension,[51] primarily with the objective of including Poland, Czechoslovakia and Hungary. Essentially three reasons were put forward: a moral obligation to these states that had resisted communism and Soviet oppression and had played a key role in eventually overcoming it, the necessity of 'extending stability' into this potentially unstable area, and the wish to offer them reassurance and deterrence against a revival of Russian ambitions in the area. All of these reasons were valid and convincing. But for Germany there was a further and probably decisive reason, namely the wish to move out of the front line, in which it had stood throughout the Cold War years. The possibility of gaining not only a friendly state but an ally on its eastern boundary became a major foreign-policy objective. This was particularly understandable in the situation of the early 1990s when no one knew whether the Cold War had really come to an end or how Russia was going to develop. It simply seemed better to be surrounded by friends.

The initial reaction by all allies was cautious. A first response was the creation – as the result of an American initiative – of the Partnership for Peace programme (PfP) in 1994.[52] The purpose of this programme was to defer the pressure for extension and at the same time to offer potential members a framework in which they could begin to co-operate with the Alliance and prepare for future membership. In other words, the pressure was to be ameliorated by offering an intermediate step, a type of 'half-way house'. Combined with this was a further substantial objective, namely to get as many of the CEECs as possible to participate in the partnership programme, both to diminish the potential instabilities in this 'grey area' as well as to invite Russian participation in order to assuage Russian objections to the extension of NATO. In other words, from the beginning there was an understanding that, while not all countries could join NATO, it was important to prevent new instability developing in the region as well as specifically tying Russia in.

The Alliance was not immediately successful in achieving the latter objective, for Russia was slow to join PfP and remained strong in voicing its objections throughout the process of the first eastward extension of NATO.[53] But once the United States decided to support the project of extension – both in view of the strong pressure from the first candidates for membership (which included a Polish lobby in the United States) and the plausible argument that it would indeed be an extension of stability – there were major efforts to mitigate Russian concerns while simultaneously making it clear that the Alliance was not going to accept a Russian veto. Thus, in 1997 during NATO's Madrid summit, Poland, Hungary and the Czech Republic were invited to start formal negotiations,[54] and on 12 March 1999, just before the fiftieth anniversary meeting in Washington in April, these three countries became full members. Russian opposition, fuelled also by disagreement on the developments in Serbia and Kosovo, was staunch, but not decisive.

The next round

For some time after the first round of enlargement, the Alliance proceeded with caution. It declared that it would pursue an 'open door' policy,[55] but was careful not to announce any clear-cut criteria.[56] There were good reasons for this. After all, the decision to enlarge was primarily a political decision. The Alliance was not prepared to set up a list of publicly announced criteria, on the basis of which candidates meeting them could claim membership quasi-automatically. Nevertheless, a set of minimum criteria did exist, first indicated in the *Study on NATO Enlargement* that the Alliance commissioned and that came out in September 1995.[57] In addition to a set of military criteria, such as civilian control of military forces, new members were to be stable democracies, they should have stable relations with their neighbours and their membership should form a contribution to NATO's security and overall objectives.[58] This was developed even further when at the Washington summit in April 1999 the Membership Action Plan (MAP) was set up.[59] The purpose was to reaffirm NATO's commitment to enlargement, but also to continue and deepen co-operation with partner countries by foreseeing annual reviews of aspiring members' development toward NATO requirements, mainly in military terms. NATO insisted, however, that both those elements mentioned in the 1995 *Study on Enlargement* and the progress reviews in the framework of the MAP reflected minimum prerequisites and general moves toward improved military co-operation in Europe and not a list of formal criteria. The final decision would remain a political judgement.

But pressure was mounting, and by the end of 2001 there were nine formal candidates: Albania, Bulgaria, Estonia, Latvia, Lithuania, Macedonia, Romania, Slovakia and Slovenia,[60] with Croatia joining the group in May

2002. The motives were varied but could be found in different forms among all the potential candidates. At the top of the list stood the Article 5 guarantee that NATO promises: protection of their territorial integrity and independence. A second reason was the desire to become a member of a respected Western organisation. Finally, it was believed that getting into either of the two major Western institutions in Europe – either NATO or the European Union – might help to get into the other one also.[61]

At NATO's Washington summit in 1999 the policy of keeping the door open for new members was addressed, but it was made clear that no decisions on this question were to be expected before the Prague summit, foreseen for the end of 2002.

While the issue continued to be discussed in Western circles,[62] hopes in the candidate countries rose steadily and became determining elements for the political orientation of the aspirant states: in terms of their military policies (for example, participation in PfP, adaptation to NATO standards and civilian control), in terms of domestic policy (such as democratisation, the development of civil society and the resolution of minority problems), in terms of foreign policy (such as the resolution of disputes with neighbouring states) and indeed in terms of their entire orientation as pro-Western, co-operative democracies.[63]

The decisive factor was the ebb of Russian opposition. With the events of 11 September 2001, the consistent improvement in Russian–American relations[64] and the establishment of the NATO–Russia Council in May 2002, Russian objections declined to a mere statement that it did not consider NATO enlargement necessary or a good idea, but otherwise quietly accepted the fact. Two motives may have been decisive for the change in the Russian attitude. Primarily, Russia was interested in an improved relationship in order to get Western assistance for its domestic, mainly economic, development. This was not to be had – see the first round of enlargement – if Russia made a big issue of NATO extension without in the end being able to prevent it from happening. The second factor may have been a changed view of NATO: Russia was more involved through the NATO–Russia Council, NATO was becoming more political and the Russians may have calculated that extension might weaken Alliance cohesion.

At the Prague summit in November 2002[65] seven applicant states were invited to begin accession negotiations: the three Baltic republics, Bulgaria, Romania, Slovakia and Slovenia. Three countries that had been among the applicant states – Croatia, Albania and Macedonia – were not invited. However, because nobody had expected the admission of these countries at this stage this did not come as a surprise, nor did it draw much attention.

Enlargement and Alliance objectives

It is worth considering the objectives the Alliance and its member states aimed at with NATO enlargement. Whereas they were relatively evident for the first round, they were less clear for the second. Three, however, seemed to stand out.

First, there was the general idea of 'extending stability'. This implies two related elements: the extension of security that membership in the Alliance gives, and, expected to go along with this external security, a general feeling of security within the new member states that would provide an essential or at least contributing factor to a favourable domestic development. Second, the very promise of membership, bound to certain expectations and criteria, was expected to provide significant encouragement to the development of stable democracies. Indeed, the actual experience in the second half of the 1990s seems proof of this. All the aspirant countries, either to NATO or EU membership, made efforts to develop in the direction of stable democracy, including in particular resolving minority problems and disputes with neighbouring states.[66] In fact, some raised the question whether this leverage would be reduced once a country achieved membership, thus implying that membership should not be granted before a minimum stable development had been attained. Finally, the third objective might be termed a 'negative objective': enlargement to meet a promise and avoid the negative results that might occur if the promise is not met.

A further possible objective, namely to improve the geostrategic position of NATO, rarely mentioned during the first round of enlargement, was also not an argument put forward forcefully, although the membership of Slovenia and Slovakia does away with the geographical isolation of Hungary, in addition to creating a bridge to Italy. Whether this was thought to be important or not,[67] it certainly met one of the early demands the Alliance set for membership, namely that there should be a contribution to overall Alliance security.[68]

A final consideration is the relationship between NATO and EU enlargement. Two notions may be mentioned here. One is that there should be as much overlap as possible with regard to the European members of the European Union and NATO. Obviously, this would have benefits, but it has seldom been a driving argument in the debate. The second idea – largely overcome by the broad extension of both institutions – is that whenever membership of both institutions cannot be offered or cannot be realised simultaneously, membership of at least one of them should be considered. Thus the relatively early membership in NATO of Poland, Hungary and the Czech Republic proved advantageous because in that way these countries could be given the desired ties to the West with the accompanying stability while waiting for the more complex and longer process of EU membership. In reverse, for a while it was argued that EU membership for the three Baltic republics should be speeded up in view of the fact that they would not be able to join NATO for some time because of Russian misgivings; in this way the Baltic republics would be granted a type of 'indirect' security guarantee because NATO would hardly be able to stand aside in the event of a threat to an EU member state.

There is general agreement between the United States and Europe on the need to maintain NATO's cohesion and ability to act.[69] However, this may simply be an obvious and readily repeated political want without knowing what it means in terms of actual enlargement. Achieving consensus among a significantly larger number of members is bound to be more difficult. This is particularly true in view of the fact that the new members have quite different backgrounds and traditions, that they will not have acquired NATO customs and usage, and, most of all, that there will be no clear external threat ensuring cohesion. Enlargement thus may create problems and difficulties that are difficult to foresee.

To some it appeared that the priority the United States attached to the Alliance was declining. Pointing to the need to proceed carefully in the interest of maintaining the cohesion and effectiveness of the Alliance, the United States had insisted on limiting the first round of new members to three. This position seemed reasonable and with the exception of France found favour among the other allies. Later, however, and particularly after the terrorist attacks of 11 September 2001, the United States indicated a much more relaxed attitude to NATO enlargement, in fact beginning to favour a larger number of states. This did not run against European feelings, but for some it seemed to coincide with a more general lack of American interest in the future of the Alliance. It was all the more remarkable that the United States had continued to develop ideas about this future and did, in fact, come up with a number of initiatives at the Prague summit in November 2002.

The Prague summit

The decision on enlargement was expected to be the central issue at the NATO summit meeting in Prague on 21 November 2002. As it turned out, the invitation to seven of the ten applicant states – Bulgaria, Estonia, Latvia, Lithuania, Romania, Slovakia and Slovenia – 'to begin accession talks to join our Alliance'[70] was accepted almost as a matter of course. The ground for this decision had been well prepared, and other decisions moved into the foreground. The Alliance:

> approved a comprehensive package of measures, based on NATO's Strategic Concept, to strengthen our ability to meet the challenges to the security of our forces, populations and territory, from wherever they may come. Today's decisions will provide for balanced and effective capabilities within the Alliance so that NATO can better carry out the full range of its missions and respond collectively to those challenges, including the threat posed by terrorism and by the proliferation of weapons of mass destruction and their means of delivery.[71]

The 'package of measures' included a number of potentially far-reaching elements. First was the creation of a NATO Response Force. This force, to be operational 'as soon as possible, but not later than October 2004', will 'include land, sea and air elements ready to move quickly to wherever needed' and will be 'flexible, deployable, interoperable and sustainable'. While no reference is made to the size of the force, it is expected to be more than 20,000 strong, most of them European. The force is to be a 'catalyst for focusing and promoting improvements in the Alliance's military capabilities'. It is also to be 'mutually reinforcing' with ESDP, 'while respecting the autonomy of both organisations'.

The range of tasks for such a force is evident: equipped, trained, available and rapidly deployable 'wherever needed' to deal with crisis situations, with terrorists (in cases where the use of such a force makes sense) or with those sheltering terrorists. It could also be used for action against anybody acquiring weapons of mass destruction. NATO is now unequivocally ready to go 'out of area'. The concept of rapid deployment within three to seven days would give NATO's member states little time for parliamentary procedure or to get a UN mandate. But rapid availability could well make this force suited to preventive or pre-emptive action.

A second decision was to 'streamline NATO's command arrangements'. There will be two commands: a strategic command for Operations, headquartered in Belgium, and a strategic command for Transformation, headquartered in the United States. The former is to be able to 'generate a land-based Combined Joint Task Force (CJTF) and a . . . standing joint headquarters from which a sea-based CJTF headquarters capability can be drawn'. The strategic command for Transformation will have a 'presence' in Europe and 'will be responsible for the continuing transformation of military capabilities and for the promotion of interoperability of Alliance forces'.

The former Defence Capabilities Initiative (DCI) of 1999 was replaced by the Prague Capabilities Commitment (PCC). This new commitment is firmer and more specific, although it still contains a wide range of capabilities that require improvement: chemical, biological, radiological and nuclear defence; intelligence; surveillance and target acquisition; air-to-ground surveillance; command, control and communications; combat effectiveness, including precision-guided munitions and suppression of enemy air defences; strategic air and sea lift; air-to-air refuelling; and deployable combat support and combat service support units.[72]

With regard to terrorism, an agreed military concept for defence against terrorism was endorsed, including improved intelligence sharing and crisis response arrangements. In addition, commitment was expressed for the full implementation of the Civil Emergency Planning (CEP) Action Plan for the improvement of civil preparedness as well as to the implementation of five nuclear, biological and chemical weapons defence initiatives.[73]

Finally, with regard to missile defence a new NATO Missile Defence feasibility study was initiated and the enhancement of the role of the WMD Centre with NATO's international staff was welcomed.

In sum, two things are striking about the Prague summit. First, it gave the Alliance a new and clear orientation: combating new risks with new forces and new structures. Second, it once more proved energetic American leadership: all the decisions had been developed and prepared in Washington.

An issue that immediately arose was the envisaged relationship between the

NATO Response Force and the European rapid reaction force.[74] The Prague communiqué stated that they should be 'mutually reinforcing', which both NATO's Secretary General and the Chairman of the Military Committee reiterated.[75] One possible difficulty is that certain capabilities, such as Special Forces, would be available only once, either for ESDP or for the NRF. However, since it is unlikely that both forces would be used simultaneously, this seems to be more of a theoretical problem. If the NRF is used, NATO 'as a whole' would be acting, and hence the use of an autonomous European force would be excluded by definition. Nevertheless, co-ordination will be required, for example, when the forces exercise together. At the same time, the NRF will require clearer and quicker steps on the part of the Europeans in modernising and reorganising their forces. This would decrease the 'capabilities gap', make European forces more interoperable with their American counterparts as well as enhancing the value of the European contribution. An obvious difference between the two forces is that whereas the EU force foresees a full range of possible tasks, including combat action for peace enforcement, but will probably concentrate most of its activities on peacekeeping, the NATO Response Force is primarily orientated to rapid military reaction, such as in the case of a terrorist attack. Provided there is adequate co-ordination, the two forces should not be in competition with each other.

New tasks

Maintaining security in Europe by protecting the European allies: that was the task of NATO during the Cold War. After the Cold War NATO developed into quite an effective crisis manager, and enlargement was to extend and solidify the stability and security that NATO offers. But, this achieved, and under the impression of the terrorist attacks on 11 September 2001, the United States has demanded that the Alliance should take on new tasks. These include taking more responsibility for upholding stability on a global scale and specifically combating what Washington considers as the major threats of the future, namely international terrorism and the spread of weapons of mass destruction to 'rogue states' or terrorists.

Combating terrorism

Terrorism is not a new topic. For almost ten years it has appeared regularly in NATO communiqués as a potential problem.[76] However, it was 11 September 2001 that abruptly made everyone aware of the dimensions of the problem. Suddenly, matters of daily routine became dangerous: meetings, football games, visits to a discotheque, public transport or, worse, just going to work or opening a letter. The world was shocked to discover that this event had been carefully and skilfully planned a long time before its execution, that the perpetrators were obscure and in hiding, and that they might strike again, anywhere and at any time. No means were barred, nothing was sacrosanct, not the lives of innocent bystanders and not even their own lives. This was terrorism marked by massive destruction, skilful organisation, secrecy, zealous commitment and absolute recklessness. Uncertainty and fear spread, and it was the worst kind of fear, because the enemy was invisible. It was indeed an attack on the Western system of values with unforeseeable consequences for Western societies.[77]

Overnight it had become clear that the United States was vulnerable: the sole superpower, overwhelmingly powerful in military and economic terms, was confronted by a problem that it could not deal with simply and on its own. It needed the solidarity and support of friends and allies and the co-operation of many more partners all over the globe. Moreover, it became clear to the Europeans as well as to the Americans that the impression of assured security that had developed after the decline of the Soviet nuclear threat was treacherous. The European homeland, as the American, had been considered safe; 'instability' or 'crises' existed only on the perimeter. Now the threat to the homeland had returned.

Thus three things became evident: that the United States needed allies, that the Alliance could demonstrate solidarity, and that everybody was affected. But more than anything else it showed that the Alliance was no longer, as it had appeared throughout the Cold War, only an instrument to assure American protection for Europe. It was a two-way street and indeed a mutual exercise.

Within thirty-six hours after the attack on New York and Washington on 11 September NATO held three emergency meetings, and NATO's Secretary General held a joint meeting with EU Foreign Ministers. On 12 September, for the first time in its half-century history, NATO invoked in principle Article 5 of the Washington Treaty, stating that an armed attack against any member of the Alliance shall be considered 'an attack against them all'. The only condition was that the attacks were directed from abroad. On 2 October the US Co-ordinator for Counter-terrorism presented to the North Atlantic Council the 'compelling' evidence that this had indeed been the case, and Article 5 became fully operative on 5 October.[78]

Acting in unity, America's eighteen allies agreed to grant the United States full use of their air space and access to airfields, ports and refuelling facilities. They accepted an eight-point 'wish list' submitted by the Americans, agreeing 'to expand the options available in the campaign against terrorism'.[79] These were to:

- enhance intelligence-sharing and co-operation on threats posed by terrorism, both bilaterally and through NATO;
- provide appropriate assistance to allies and other states which are or may be subject to increased terrorist threats as a result of their support for the campaign against terrorism;
- take measures providing increased security for the facilities of the United States and other allies on their territory;
- backfill selected allied assets in NATO's area of responsibility that are required to support operations directly against terrorism;

- give access to ports and airfields for operations against terrorism, including refuelling, in accordance with national procedures;
- deploy elements of NATO's Standing Naval Force Atlantic (STANAVFOR-LANT) to the eastern Mediterranean to fill any gaps left by the departure of US forces;
- be prepared to deploy elements of the NATO Airborne Warning and Control Systems (AWACS).[80]

Following these decisions, NATO in addition ordered its Standing Naval Force Mediterranean (STANAVFORMED), a segment of the Alliance's immediate reaction forces, to deploy to the eastern Mediterranean. Within the maritime operation Active Endeavour[81] the purpose was to demonstrate NATO's resolve and solidarity, while releasing American naval vessels there for deployment closer to Afghanistan. Prolonged operations were accomplished through rotation of STANAVFORMED and STANAVFORLANT.[82]

Nobody would have expected that the first time in the more than fifty-year history of the Alliance that Article 5 would be invoked it would be not for the protection of a European ally but for the protection of the United States. NATO took the historic decision to dispatch five AWACS aircraft with US, European and Canadian crews from their base in Germany to protect American air space and release American aircraft for use elsewhere.[83] The United States and Canada had long been training and testing grounds for NATO forces and equipment, but this was the first time NATO assets had been used in direct support of the continental United States. In fact, it was the first time since the American Revolution that the United States had requested and received foreign assistance for domestic security. The number of aircraft was small but of high symbolic value: Europeans were protecting America.

The campaign against the Taliban who had supported Osama bin Ladin and his terrorists will not conclude the issue. The roots of the problem will not have disappeared. They can be found in the frustration with and hatred of Western values and civilisation, not caused but fuelled by Islamic fundamentalism and the Arab–Israeli conflict. It would be foolish to ignore the fact that there is widespread anti-Americanism, indeed 'anti-Westernism', to be found in many of the Islamic countries, both among the leaders and among the population.[84] Islam is not the cause of this, but it is used as justification by the terrorists. This has implications for transatlantic relations. Solidarity was not important only in September and October 2001. It will continue to be important in combating terrorism in the short term and dealing with the underlying issues in the long term.[85] This will be particularly necessary if the terrorists concentrate their attacks on the United States and possibly its institutions outside America. That could decrease the motivation on the part of the 'non-affected' allies, turning the issue more and more into a specifically 'American problem'. Indeed, some allies may seek to maintain a distance from America in order not to be 'infected'. This would amount to blackmail on the part of the terrorists: they would give a tacit promise not to target countries as long as these stayed 'neutral' and kept their distance from the United States.

Apart from putting a potentially fatal strain on the Alliance, there would be concrete effects on European policies in the Middle East. While Israel or the Palestinian issue are not the cause of this new terrorism, the unresolved situation in the Middle East feeds it. Anti-Westernism, the desire for power and criminal instincts are the motivating forces for the leadership, but the situation in the Middle East gives occasion and excuse, and it is the root of much of the anti-Americanism among the masses, particularly in the Arab countries. Resolving the issue has become of even greater urgency than before. Terrorism will not disappear, but it will find less support and hence will become easier to combat.

Political solidarity in the Alliance will not, however, suffice to combat terrorism. It requires increasingly close co-operation among the allies and with other partners both within and outside of the Alliance. The events of 11 September 2001 largely eliminated the classical differentiation between external and internal security. To be sure, setting up and preparing forces specifically for counter-terrorist action will be important. Air-space protection is an area where NATO can play a role. In the past this protection had an outward orientation; now the interior air space also requires protection. But other than purely military means will be more important in combating and overcoming international terrorism: primarily intelligence, police work, and financial co-operation to drain the resources of the terrorists. Co-operation in terms of intelligence, for example, should imply not only the exchange of information, but also co-operation in gathering the information, analysing, interpreting and acting on it.[86] In most of the activities, however, NATO will play only a comparatively small role. It will be suited to quick military action with the new NATO Response Force, it can assure air-space protection, can assist in intelligence exchange and analysis, and it has a contribution to make in analysing threats from the proliferation of weapons of mass destruction and suggesting various means of preparing for and responding to such threats. Most of the other forms of co-operation will take place outside NATO.

Weapons of mass destruction

The spread of weapons of mass destruction bears three potential risks: such weapons (primarily biological or chemical) in the hands of terrorists, such weapons (primarily nuclear) in the hands of a state sheltering terrorists, and such weapons in the hands of 'rogue' states or states threatening Europe or the United States.

The first case is the most complex, since it is likely to be discovered only after the terrorist attack has occurred. Pre-emptive or preventive action may be possible if there are clear or sufficient indications that terrorists are in the process of acquiring or have already acquired such weapons. But the prerequisite would be finding them in time. In such cases elements of a NATO Response Force might be used.

In the other two cases it may be easier to detect the signs of what is occurring and thus have more time to consider counter-measures. Pre-emptive action by, for example, the NATO Response Force would be conceivable to prevent such states from acquiring these weapons or to destroy them in a surprise attack. Here, too, information and time are critical. If such action is not undertaken in time or successfully, the situation changes completely. One would then be confronted by a state possessing weapons of mass destruction and presumably the means of delivery. In other words, any action would risk a major war or at least major destruction and casualties. This is probably the strongest argument for pre-emptive action and, indeed, the NATO Response Force is likely to be a most suitable instrument for such action. At the same time this shows the difficulties. Action would have to be by surprise or at least very short-term, leaving little or no time for debate, parliamentary procedures or getting a UN mandate. Moreover, it is possible that not all members of NATO may agree (as was the case with Iraq at the end of 2002). A 'constructive abstention' would not help if at the same time some national forces were withdrawn from the NRF. In such a situation, action would have to be undertaken by an *ad hoc* 'coalition of the willing', perhaps making use of some of the benefits of the NRF but without the full advantages of a ready, trained and complete force. In addition, it would be more difficult to ensure secrecy and rapidity of action.

Once confronted by a situation in which states have acquired weapons of mass destruction and missiles to deliver them, the only alternatives are civil protection and defence. In the field of civil protection, NATO has significantly stepped up its activities since 11 September 2001. With regard to theatre missile defence the Alliance members are also co-operating closely. Disagreement exists mainly with regard to a more extensive missile defence system for longer-range weapons.

Missile defence

At this point in time, it is quite uncertain when – or even whether – an effective and reliable missile defence system will become technically and financially feasible.[87] In any case, discussion is not about a global system of the Strategic Defence Initiative (SDI) category, but about a limited protective shield against what would presumably also be a limited attack.

The objectives of such a system would be threefold: protection against an actual attack, presumably by a so-called 'rogue state' or 'state of concern' that has acquired a limited number of missiles with nuclear warheads, against a blackmail threat, and to maintain a minimum degree of freedom of action when dealing with such a state. Military measures such as those taken against Iraq during the Gulf War or afterwards would not have been possible had Iraq been in possession of missiles with nuclear warheads against which the allies would not have been able to protect themselves. This supports the proposition that it would not make sense for the United States to develop a defensive system limited to the North American continent. The United States, the Alliance and transatlantic relations would surely be in a more than awkward position if only the European allies were threatened. In fact, the Europeans could be the first to be threatened, for in the foreseeable future none of the 'states of concern' is likely to be developing intercontinental missiles.[88] The threat, rather, would come from medium-range missiles, which those states have already acquired or are in the process of acquiring.

It is all the more surprising that most Europeans tended to be sceptical if not clearly opposed to the project. The initial reaction was indeed somewhat irrational. It was difficult for the European states that had just gained a Europe 'whole and free' and were enjoying the 'peace dividend', in what seemed like a finally peaceful and stable Europe, to accept that the situation was not nearly as stable as it seemed and that new threats to peace were arising. Why question a system that had proved itself and that appeared so stable? Amazingly, even many of the former critics on the left had become supporters of 'mutual assured destruction'. Would it not be better to deal with 'states of concern' by increasing the incentive to co-operate: by political and economic means?

Yet there were also more rational concerns.[89] First, Europeans were concerned about the potential effects the American plans might have on relations with Russia.[90] This referred not so much to the fear of a renewed arms race, which under the circumstances Russia could not even conceive of taking up. Rather, it was concern that the effort to tie Russia into a stable European security system would receive a serious and perhaps fatal blow. However, these concerns have much less grounding after the events of 11 September 2001[91] and particularly after the NATO meetings in Rome and Prague: Russia is in fact being tied into the system.

A second European concern was that a missile defence system would be seen as for the protection of the United States only. The danger in this regard would be that the United States might lean towards a hard line in its policies toward 'states of concern' with little consideration for its allies, which is not entirely inconceivable. This would mean that the Europeans, without any protection against limited missile attacks, would be vulnerable, subject to blackmail and under dual pressure: from the American side, to fall into line with US policies and, from the opposing side, to pursue an opposite course of action. If the Europeans opt for the former, they would increase their vulnerability; if they opt for the latter, they would put the Alliance under considerable strain.

A particular concern often attributed to France may finally be mentioned, namely that a missile defence system would decrease the value of small nuclear forces. However, this would apply only in the probably very long run if numerous states acquired missile defences. As long as only the United States and the European allies and perhaps Russia had such protection this would hardly affect, for example, the French nuclear force, since French missiles are not directed against France's allies and no longer against Russia. In this respect the objections of China make more sense.

Certainly, a solution to what should not have been a problem in the first place is not that complicated. First of all, if a missile defence system becomes technically feasible, it should from the beginning be developed not in a national but in an Alliance framework. That would ensure the inclusion of the European allies.[92] This is, in fact, the intention of US President Bush.[93] But the Europeans would have to finance their share. In any case, it makes sense for the Europeans to enter the debate without prejudice and with competence, technically, financially and politically, including a sober threat analysis. To stand stubbornly behind a wall of rejection will lead to little more than the Europeans being overrun by events.

Secondly, it is sensible to seek co-operation with Russia. The prospects are encouraging, as the developments since September 2001 seem to show. For one thing, Russia is not in a position to compete with the United States in another arms race. Furthermore, Russia also has an interest in such a protective shield. The United States has not been adverse to seeking a co-operative solution.[94] Finally, a limited missile defence would allow further significant reductions of existing nuclear forces, which is in the Russian interest and which could contribute to non-proliferation efforts.[95] This would allow a progressive adaptation of the START agreements and offer a potential advance for arms control.[96]

In all cases, there is an urgent need for co-operation in the area of threat analysis. Even before 11 September 2001 the United States considered the proliferation of weapons of mass destruction, terrorism and international crime to be the major challenges to international stability.[97] Europeans have been much more hesitant, both with regard to defining the problems and even more with regard to consideration of possible measures to be taken. Any common action, however, requires common views on the nature of the threat.

Conclusion: a new NATO?

Since the early 1990s NATO has been called a 'new NATO'. To be sure, it was new in the sense that former enemies were turning into partners, many of them even to allies. Furthermore, there was the proposition that the Alliance was becoming less military and more political, less of an alliance in the traditional sense and more of an organisation for consultation and co-ordination. Surprisingly, this idea was hardly hurt by the Kosovo crisis in March 1999 when NATO for the first time employed military force in earnest. But perhaps the 'new' and more political NATO includes the use of force provided it is for crisis management only.

Paradoxically, the developments after 11 September 2001, which in the first instance showed a politically united and determined Alliance, subsequently led it to appear weaker than before. In the United States a growing tendency towards a more unilateral view of many foreign policy issues seemed to coincide with a certain disenchantment with NATO: the burdens of 'war by committee' during the Kosovo bombing, the disappointment about the meagre

European contribution, enhanced by the widening gap in military modernisation, the nuisance of European criticism on a variety of issues, and the feeling that the United States did not really need the Europeans or could get what it wanted through bilateral co-operation. Finally, there was the increasingly relaxed American approach to NATO enlargement. The United States seemed concentrated on and content with the positive turn in US–Russian relations and seemingly less concerned about what a much larger and more diverse membership might do to the cohesion and effectiveness of the Alliance. If NATO as a unified instrument was no longer as important as before, the question of its effectiveness became less important too.

Similar indicators could be found on the European side. The rapid solidarity shown after 11 September covered up underlying criticism about American unilateralism and leadership. In fact, the opportunity to display solidarity may have been welcome as an offset to the more deep-seated misgivings about American policies. Once solidarity had been demonstrated, it was subsequently easier to criticise. Secondly, the Europeans themselves responded only partly in the framework of NATO and preferred a national setting when it came to concrete military measures. In other words, if the United States preferred bilateral agreements and 'coalitions of the willing' the Europeans had done little or nothing to counter this.

When the seven states invited by NATO at the meeting in Prague join in 2004 NATO will be a much bigger but perhaps also a weaker organisation. There will be twenty-six members at the Council table with different backgrounds, different traditions and different experiences. It seems logical that NATO as a whole might then be less coherent and less manageable. Of course, this may be offset by a pronounced pro-American stance and willingness to follow the American lead on the part of the new members. Paradoxically – considering European complaints, ambitions and projects – the 'new NATO' may be more 'US-dominated' than before. Perhaps this had already become visible at the Prague summit. The less coherent membership, the likely readiness of the new members to follow the American lead, available and forthcoming American leadership and continuing deficiencies on the part of the Europeans may determine the appearance of NATO for some time to come.

But such a development might not obstruct the usefulness of NATO for its members. It would continue to provide reassurance, particularly for its new members. It could serve as a 'provider of services' for 'coalitions of the willing', and it could well serve as a 'legitimiser' for such coalitions when they lack a UN mandate.

The preponderant American influence does not mean and has never meant that the United States is able to put forward and push through any proposal, however unpopular or implausible it may seem. The United States needs support for its position, which frequently takes shape in consultation with the other allies. Ultimately decisions have to be unanimous, and an entirely one-sided or implausible stance would be unlikely to get that degree of support.

Whatever the case may be, two tasks will stand in the foreground. The first is to set up, train and co-ordinate forces that are suited to seek out and counter terrorist activity. The second is developing a framework, a 'philosophy' as it were, for their employment. This essential task will be all the more important if pre-emption becomes necessary. The members of the Alliance will need not only the means and methods to carry out such action, but also a set of political criteria around which political agreement can be built as well as international justification. This becomes even more crucial when force is employed against a state supporting or sheltering terrorists. Under the profound impression of the events of 11 September 2001 the action against Afghanistan received, certainly initially, general and at least tacit support almost on a worldwide scale. But it is uncertain whether such will always be the case. If combating terrorism is a long-term task, and affects everybody, there will have to be a set of criteria by which to judge the measures and on the basis of which consensus can be built, as well as by which the behaviour of others can be judged. Those not acting will have to justify this as much as those acting need to justify their actions.

Clearly, the crucial question is whether and how the cohesion and effectiveness of NATO can be sustained. This may mean mainly two things: that the Alliance may have to restrain its ambitions and that the Europeans must take on more responsibility. However, caution is required. While the Alliance should be a preferred instrument for consultation and the development of a common approach referring to international stability in a broad sense, NATO becoming a military instrument to be used readily on a worldwide scale could put NATO cohesion under considerable strain. The farther away and the more complex the crises to which NATO would be expected to react, the greater would be the differences of judgement among the members of the Alliance. Whether the Alliance would survive such strain is uncertain. As a result, it will be imperative to maintain a clear idea on the objectives, the resulting missions and thus the required shape of NATO.

If this can be done, and if all members recognise the benefits that the Alliance has to offer, NATO may last. However, the future may show a NATO that has evolved into an 'alliance at two levels'. In the background there would be the classical alliance of 1949: a general commitment to mutual assistance and common defence, reserved, however, for only the gravest cases (the 'reassurance function'). In the foreground, and more visible on a daily basis, would be a significantly enlarged and much looser NATO serving as a broad framework for occasional joint action but more often for 'coalitions of the willing'. NATO's bureaucracy would continue working, but would have less of an impact. The use of Alliance assets, already limited, would be less important than the co-ordination of assets on a bilateral basis, making use of procedures and practices of NATO. The Alliance would not have turned into an 'armed OSCE' as some fear, but it would have turned into something rather different from the NATO of the Cold War.

Notes

1 'The North Atlantic Treaty', Washington DC, 4 April 1949 (www.nato.int/docu/basictxt/treaty.htm). It is worth reading this text when in doubt about whether invoking Article 5 for the first time on 12 September 2001 was justified or not.

2 The specific nature of the formulation had to do with an American wish to maintain flexibility as well as with the US Senate that was concerned about its constitutional prerogative of declaring war.

3 This was indeed the beginning of what later came to be known as 'extended deterrence'.

4 See Osgood, *NATO: The Entangling Alliance*.

5 For a more sceptical view on NATO as 'the principal forum for consultation on security matters' see William Hopkinson, *Enlargement: A new NATO* (Chaillot Papers 49, Paris: WEU Institute for Security Studies, 2001), p. 34, although there is, of course, a difference between 'the principal forum' and an important or even very important forum, which is the line of argument taken here.

6 See on this James Macintosh, 'Confidence-building processes – CSCE and MBFR: a review and assessment', in David Dewitt and Hans Rattinger (eds), *East–West Arms Control: Challenges for the Western Alliance* (London and New York: Routledge, 1992), pp. 140 ff.; Pierre Gerbet, *La Construction de l'Europe* (Paris: Imprimerie Nationale, 1999), pp. 376 ff., 442 f.; Web site OSCE (www.osce.org/ docs/english/chronos. htm).

7 A history of these negotiations can be found in Macintosh, 'Confidence-building processes', pp. 128 ff. The official name of the negotiations was Mutual Reduction of Forces and Armaments and Associated Measures in Central Europe (MURFAAMCE).

8 See Dieter Mahncke, *Vertrauensbildende Maßnahmen als Instrument der Sicherheitspolitik. Ursprung – Entwicklung – Perspektiven* (Melle: Ernst Knoth, 1987).

9 For a discussion of this debate see, for example, Yost, *NATO Transformed*, p. 48, and Rob de Wijk, *NATO on the Brink of the New Millennium: The Battle for Consensus* (London and Washington DC: Brassey's, 1997), pp. 11 f.

10 Among them Manfred Wörner, NATO's Secretary General from 1982 to 1988 and an advocate of regional peace enforcement missions for NATO.

11 See Lucarelli, *Europe and the Breakup of Yugoslavia*, pp. 29 ff.; Michael Wesley, *Casualties of the New World Order: The Causes of Failure of UN Missions to Civil Wars* (Basingstoke: Macmillan, 1997), pp. 31–49; Carsten Giersch, *Konfliktregulierung in Jugoslawien 1991–1995. Die Rolle von OSZE, EU, UNO und NATO* (Baden-Baden: Nomos, 1998), pp. 213 ff.

12 See on this Dieter Mahncke, 'Questions to be asked', in Mahncke (ed.), *Old Frontiers – New Frontiers*, pp. 22 f.; Giersch, *Konfliktregulierung in Jugoslawien*, pp. 108 ff.; Lucarelli, *Europe and the Breakup of Yugoslavia*, pp. 226 ff.; Jörg Nadoll, 'Die Europäische Union und die Konfliktbearbeitung in Ex-Jugoslawien 1991–1998. Mühl- oder Meilenstein?' in Klaus Schubert and Gisela Müller-Brandeck-Bocquet (eds), *Die Europäische Union als Akteur der Weltpolitik* (Opladen: Leske + Budrich, 2000), pp. 83 ff.

13 See Horst Bacia, 'Seit Montag tickt die Uhr – am 26. September soll der Nato-Einsatz beendet sein', *Frankfurter Allgemeine Zeitung*, 31 August 2001), p. 6; Lara Griffith

and Michael Meyer, 'After the conflict, the reconstruction', *Guardian*, 27 September 2001. There is consideration, however, that Amber Fox might be taken up by the European Union; see Horst Bacia, 'EU will Führung bei Amber Fox', *Frankfurter Allgemeine Zeitung*, 9 February 2002, p. 5; and 'Italy to command peace force in Macedonia', www.euractiv.com (12 February 2002).

14 Hopkinson, *Enlargement: A new NATO*, p. 1.

15 See on this also pp. 60–5.

16 *Ibid.*

17 For a broader discussion see pp. 55–60.

18 *Ibid.*

19 A Charter on a Distinctive Partnership between NATO and Ukraine was signed in Madrid in July 1997. It not only gave formal recognition to an independent and democratic Ukraine but also created a NATO–Ukraine Commission that consists of the North Atlantic Council and Ukrainian representatives. This body meets regularly and aims for a steady improvement of co-operation.

20 See on this also pp. 33–7.

21 See on this Hannes Adomeit, 'Russische Aussen- und Sicherheitspolitik. Zwischen Anspruch und Wirklichkeit', AP 3091 (Berlin: Stiftung Wissenschaft und Politik, 1999), pp. 19 ff.

22 See Margot Light, John Löwenhardt and Stephen White, 'Russian perspectives on European security', *European Foreign Affairs Review*, 5: 4 (2000), pp. 494 f.; 'Yeltsin: Don't push us towards military action', *Guardian*, 9 April 1999; Michael Andersen, 'Russia and the former Yugoslavia', in Mark Webber (ed.), *Russia and Europe: Conflict or Co-operation?* (New York: St Martin's Press, 2000), pp. 197 f.; Adomeit, 'Russische Aussen- und Sicherheitspolitik', p. 18.

23 See Stephen Foye, 'Russia and the "near abroad"', *Post-Soviet Prospects*, 3: 12 (1995), Washington DC: Center for Strategic and International Studies, www.csis. org/ruseura/psp/pspiii12.html.

24 The Partnership and Co-operation Agreement, signed in 1995, included the covenant on 'common values', such as the promotion of international peace and security, respect for human rights and democratic principles as well as the commitment to economic and political freedoms (see the Preamble and Article 2). The European Union's 'Common Strategy on Russia', adopted in 1999 at the Cologne Council, outlined 'a stable, democratic and prosperous Russia, firmly anchored in a united Europe free of new dividing lines', as 'essential to lasting peace on the continent'. (Annex II, Council of the European Union, Presidency Conclusions: Cologne European Council, 3–4 June 1999, p. 1, Press Release DN: PRES/99/ 1500, 9 June 1999.)

25 For more detail see Dieter Mahncke, 'Russia's attitude to the European Security and Defence Policy', *European Foreign Affairs Review*, 6: 4, especially 'Russia, the EU and NATO', pp. 430 ff; see also 'Joint Statement by President George W. Bush and President Vladimir V. Putin on a New Relationship between the United States and Russia', 13 November 2001 (http://usembassy.state.gov/moscow/wwwhst1.html) as well as the Web site of the European Commission on the EU–Russian relationship (http://europa.eu.int/comm/external_ relations/ russia/intro/index.htm).

26 See Jackie Gower, 'Russia and the European Union', in Webber, *Russia and Europe*, p. 89.

27 For a long time Russia did not quite know what to make of the European integration

process, and to an extent this may still be the case, e.g. with regard to EU enlargement. The more positive Russian attitude towards the European Union is relatively recent; see Mahncke, 'Russia's attitude to the European Security and Defence Policy'.

28 *NATO Handbook* (Brussels, 2001 edn), pp. 84 f.; Light *et al.*, 'Russian perspectives on European security', p. 495.

29 See Chris Patten and Pascal Lamy, 'Economic space and beyond: EU enlargement will help build closer economic ties between Russia and the rest of Europe', *Financial Times*, 5 December 2001.

30 'Agreement on Partnership and Co-operation', signed on 1 December 1995 (http://europa.eu.int/ comm/external_relations/ceeca/pca/pca_ russia.pdf).

31 'Common Strategy of the European Union of 4 June 1999 on Russia' (1999/414/ CFSP), *Official Journal of the European Communities* (L-157/1), Brussels, 24 June 1999.

32 'Medium-term Strategy for Development of Relations between the Russian Federation and the European Union, 2000–10'; this unofficial – and not particularly good – translation can be found under http://europa.eu.int/comm/ external_relations/russia/russian_medium_term_strategy/.

33 According to the *The Economist* the Russian GNP was US$251.1 billion in 2000 while that of the Netherlands was US$369.1 billion; see www.economist.com.

34 See Timofei V. Bordachev, 'The Russian challenge for the European Union: direct neighbourhood and security issues', in Iris Kempe (ed.), *Beyond EU Enlargement*, I *The Agenda of Direct Neighbourhood for Eastern Europe* (Gütersloh: Bertelsmann Foundation, 2001), pp. 50 f. and 59 ff. See also the 'Medium-term strategy for development of relations between the Russian Federation and the European Union, 2000–10', p. 8.

35 Russia signed the required general agreement in June 1994, but did not agree to a PfP Individual Partnership Programme (IPP) with NATO until May 1995. Although practical co-operation commenced with the implementation of the 1995 Dayton Peace Agreement on Bosnia and Herzegovina when Russian troops took part in the NATO-led Implementation Force (IFOR) and in the succeeding Stabilisation Force (SFOR), Russia's military participation in PfP remained limited. See Joseph L. Black, *Russia Faces NATO Expansion: Bearing Gifts or Bearing Arms?* (Lanham MD: Rowman and Littlefield, 2000), pp. 10 ff., and Yost, *NATO Transformed*, pp. 135–7.

36 Founding Act on Mutual Relations, Co-operation and Security between the Russian Federation and the North Atlantic Treaty Organisation of 27 May 1997 (www.nato.int/docu/basictxt/fndact-a.htm).

37 See Horst Bacia, 'Auftauen mit kaltem Wasser. Das Verhältnis zwischen Russland und der NATO auf dem Wege der Besserung', *Frankfurter Allgemeine Zeitung*, 21 February 2001, p. 12.

38 'I reaffirmed that NATO enlargement at the Madrid summit will proceed, and President Yeltsin made it clear he thinks it's a mistake.' President Bill Clinton, Helsinki summit, March 1997, quoted in Alain Pellerin, *NATO Enlargement: Where we Came from and Where it Leaves us* (Aurora Paper 29, Military Analysis Network, 1997).

39 Bacia, 'Auftauen mit kaltem Wasser'.

40 Although some parallels exist, an essential difference lies in transparency and particularly in the way in which Russia has dealt with the problem. This becomes

apparent when one compares how Russian forces are regarded in Chechnya as opposed to how Western forces are regarded in Afghanistan. See on this Markus Wehner, 'Tschetschenien ist nicht Afghanistan. Wie Russland Unvergleichbares miteinander vergleicht', *Frankfurter Allgemeine Zeitung*, 25 January 2001, p. 10.

41 'Hope gleams anew', *Economist*, 3 November 2001, p. 55.

42 See Ian Black, 'Russia hints at rethink on NATO', *Guardian*, 4 October 2001; Horst Bacia, 'Die Runde der Zwanzig', *Frankfurter Allgemeine Zeitung*, 23 November 2001, p. 16; 'Eine Allianz in der Allianz?' *ibid.*, 7 March 2002, p. 12; 'Suddenly, such good neighbours', *Economist*, 10 November 2001, pp. 11–12; 'A new alliance could nudge aside the old', *Washington Post*, 4 November 2001, p. B5; 'NATO and Russia reinventing relationship', *ibid.*, 15 November 2001, p. A42; Stephen Dalziel, 'Analysis: Putin looks west', BBC News, 3 October 2001, http://news.bbc.co.uk /2/hi/europe/1578018.stm.

43 NATO press statement on NATO–Russia Permanent Joint Council Meeting at the level of Defence Minister, held in Brussels on 18 December 2001. See on this Bacia, 'Die Runde der Zwanzig', 'Eine Allianz in der Allianz' and 'Die NATO und Russland in einer neuen Ära', *Neue Zürcher Zeitung*, 8 December 2001, p. 2.

44 See NATO statement, NATO–Russia Council, Rome, 28 May 2002 (www.nato.int/ docu/pr/ 2002/p020528e.htm); also Horst Bacia, 'Verhältnis repariert', *Frankfurter Allgemeine Zeitung*, 14 May 2002; Tony Blair, 'Wenn ehemalige Feinde Freunde werden', *ibid.*, 28 May 2002.

45 NATO statement, NATO–Russia Council.

46 *Ibid.*

47 *Ibid.*

48 Final communiqué, Ministerial meeting of the North Atlantic Council, 6 December 2001 (M-NAC-2–2001–158), www.nato.int/docu/pr/2001/p01-158e.htm, see also Horst Bacia, 'Verhältnis repariert'.

49 See Anthony Beevor, *The Fall of Berlin, 1945* (New York: Viking Press, 2002).

50 The original membership consisted of the United States and Canada, Belgium, Denmark, France, Iceland, Italy, Luxembourg, the Netherlands, Norway, Portugal and the United Kingdom. NATO was extended in 1952 by Greece and Turkey, in 1955 by the Federal Republic of Germany and in 1982 by Spain.

51 This is sometimes forgotten, but see for a similar assessment Ryan C. Hendrickson, 'NATO's open-door policy and the next round of enlargement', *Parameters*, winter 2000–1, pp. 53–66, at p. 55.

52 At the Brussels summit meeting of the North Atlantic Council in January; see *NATO Handbook*, pp. 67 ff.

53 See Yost, *NATO Transformed*, pp. 136 f.

54 See *NATO Handbook*, p. 21; Duignan, *NATO: Its Past, Present and Future*, pp. 76–8; Martin A. Smith and Graham Timmins, *Building a Bigger Europe: EU and NATO Enlargement in Comparative Perspective* (Aldershot: Ashgate, 2000), pp. 53–85. Czechoslovakia had split in 1993, and Slovakia was – because of its domestic developments under Meciar – not invited.

55 President George W. Bush, in a speech in Warsaw on 16 June 2001. At the conclusion of the July 1997 summit meeting in Madrid, NATO had issued a declaration stating that the Alliance 'remains open to new members . . . The Alliance expects to extend further invitations in the coming years', see Madrid Declaration on Euro-Atlantic Security and Co-operation. (NATO Press Release M-1(97)81.)

56 For a comprehensive discussion of the enlargement issue see Hopkinson, *Enlargement: A new NATO*, and Karl-Heinz Kamp, *Die nächste Runde der NATO-Erweiterung. Kriterien und Optionen* (Sankt Augustin: Konrad-Adenauer-Stiftung, 2001).

57 See www.nato.int/docu/basictxt/enl-9502.htm.

58 Defining these objectives for a changing NATO is one of the difficulties; see below, pp. 63–5.

59 NATO Press Release NAC-S-99-66, www.nato.int/docu/pr/1999/p99-066e.htm.

60 In May 2000 these nine had issued a joint declaration at a meeting in Vilnius requesting NATO to enlarge soon and to include a large number of states; see 'NATO Vilnius Statement' at the International Conference in Vilnius, 19 May 2000 (www.nato.int/pfp/lt/current/2000-05-19st.html).

61 See Hopkinson, *Enlargement: A new NATO*, pp. 57 ff.

62 See, for example, both Hopkinson, *Enlargement: A new NATO*, and Kamp, *Die nächste Runde der NATO-Erweiterung*.

63 See the detailed analysis by Kamp, *Die nächste Runde der NATO-Erweiterung*, pp. 17 ff., and Hopkinson, *Enlargement: A new NATO*, pp. 79 ff., who adds the idea of a 'rolling programme' with a number of states being defined as candidates and admitted when certain criteria are fulfilled; he does not consider this option as being very useful, however (p. 84). At the end of January 2002 the US Under-Secretary of State, Richard Armitage, stated that the United States considered all three of the Baltic republics to be 'serious candidates' for membership (*Frankfurter Allgemeine Zeitung*, 24 January 2002, p. 1) and in March he pleaded, at a meeting of the applicant countries in Bucharest, for extensive enlargement (*ibid.*, 26 March 2002).

64 Alexander Vershbow, US ambassador to Russia, talked about a 'fundamentally redefined relationship' and a 'common vision'. (Remarks at the inaugural conference of the Institute of Applied International Research, Moscow, 17 May 2002, www.state.gov/p/eur/rls/rm/2002/ 10312pf.htm.) Focal points of the relationship were stated to be the fight against terrorism, arms control, upgraded NATO–Russia relations, enhanced economic relations and co-operation on the continued development of democratic institutions in Russia. See also Dimitri Rogosin, 'Eine neue russisch-amerikanische Philosophie', *Frankfurter Allgemeine Zeitung*, 3 January 2002, p. 12; Jim Hoagland, 'Bridging the transatlantic gap', *Washington Post*, 17 November 2002.

65 See p. 65.

66 In order to encourage conciliation, Estonia and Latvia gave up territory that had been annexed by Russia. Estonia is considered to have been especially successful in turning the Russian minority into 'loyal Estonian citizens'. Lithuania, with a much smaller minority, from the beginning granted full citizenship to all residents. See above, pp. 24–8 and p. 45 n. 8; Piotr Dutkiewicz and Robert J. Jackson (eds), *NATO Looks East* (Westport CT: Praeger, 1998), pp. 158 f.; also Nils Andren, 'Is NATO an option for ex-neutrals and ex-Soviets on the Baltic?' in Dutkiewicz and Jackson (eds), *NATO Looks East*, pp. 139–67; Jackie Gower, 'The Baltic states: bridge or barrier to the east?' in Martin A. Smith and Graham Timmins, *Uncertain Europe: Building a New European Security Order* (London: Routledge, 2001), pp. 206 f.; Walter C. Clemens, Jr, *The Baltic Transformed: Complexity Theory and European Security* (Lanham MD: Rowman and Littlefield, 2001), pp. 186 f.; James Sperling, *Two Tiers or Two Speeds? The European Security Order and the Enlargement of the European Union and NATO* (Manchester: Manchester University Press, 1999).

67 See also Kamp, *Die nächste Runde der NATO-Erweiterung*.

68 See Hopkinson, *Enlargement: A new NATO*.

69 See Kamp, *Die nächste Runde der NATO-Erweiterung*, p. 13.

70 Prague Summit Declaration, North Atlantic Council in Prague, Press Release (2002)127, 21 November 2002, www.nato.int/docu/pr/2002/p02-127e.htm.

71 *Ibid.*

72 *Ibid.*

73 A Prototype Deployable NBC Analytical Laboratory; a Prototype NBC Event Response Team; a virtual Centre of Excellence for NBC Weapons Defence; a NATO Biological and Chemical Defence Stockpile; and a Disease Surveillance system.

74 This force was first proposed by US Secretary of Defense Donald Rumsfeld at a NATO meeting in Warsaw in September 2002; see 'Washington schlägt NATO-Eingreiftruppe vor', *Frankfurter Allgemeine Zeitung*, 25 September 2002.

75 See, for example, Horst Bacia, 'Keine Konkurrenz. Das Projekt einer modernen NATO-Interventionstruppe nützt auch den militärischen Plänen der EU', *Frankfurter Allgemeine Zeitung*, 5 November 2002.

76 See, for example, ministerial communiqués of 11 January 1994 (M-1(94)3) at NATO headquarters in Brussels (www.nato.int/docu/ comm/49-95/c940111a.htm), of 30 May 1995 (M-NAC-1(95)48) in Noordwijk (www.nato.int/docu/comm/49-95/c950530b.htm) and of 3 June 1996 (M-NAC-1(96)63) in Berlin (www.nato.int/docu/ pr/1996/p96-063e.htm) as well as Yost, *NATO Transformed*.

77 The events since then – in Djerba in Tunisia, Bali in Indonesia or Mombasa in Kenia – have reinforced this evaluation.

78 See, for example, Ian Black, 'NATO convinced by "clear and compelling" evidence', *Guardian*, 3 October 2001; Judy Dempsey, Stephen Fidler and David White, 'NATO sees evidence of Bin Laden's involvement', *Financial Times*, 2 October 2001; 'NATO ruft Büdnisfall aus', *Die Welt*, 2 October 2001. Since then evidence has been found in Afghanistan that bin Laden and his organisation al-Qaida were indeed responsible; see 'Pentagon: bin Ladin-Video in Dschalalabad gefunden' and transcript of Osama bin Ladin's video-tape, *Frankfurter Allgemeine Zeitung*, 13 December 2001. The legitimacy of America's and NATO's actions was further supported by resolution 1378, passed unanimously by the UN Security Council on 14 November 2001, S/RES/1378 (2001).

79 These measures were additional to the non-NATO police investigations and arrests of suspected terrorists conducted by almost all European states, cognisant of the chilling fact that al-Qaida had terrorist cells in about sixty countries around the globe. German police found that many of the plans for the 11 September attacks were concocted in a student apartment in Hamburg, and Spanish police acted on information that al-Qaida activists on Spanish soil had had knowledge of the assaults.

80 *Jane's Defence Weekly*, 10 October 2001, p. 6.

81 www.afsouth.nato.int/operations/Endeavour.

82 *Ibid.*

83 NATO lends a hand with US sky patrol', *Washington Post*, 11 October 2001, p. A18.

84 See, for example, 'Hating America', *Congressional Quarterly Researcher*, 11: 23 (2001).

85 See the rather sceptical view of Klaus-Dieter Frankenberger, 'Wie dauerhaft ist die

neue transatlantische Solidarität?' *Frankfurter Allgemeine Zeitung*, 29 October 2001, p. 12; and of Frank Nienhuysen, 'Militärische Kontinentaldrift', *Süddeutsche Zeitung*, 9–10 February 2002, p. 14.

86 American–European co-operation is crucial when it comes to intelligence gathering and law enforcement aimed at uncovering small, self-contained terrorist cells. Almost three months after the attacks a White House official noted that 'for the first time, we have a real international intelligence network' (*Washington Post*, 3 December 2001, pp. 1 and A12).

87 A large number of publications on this issue is available: see, for example, 'Missile defense: should the US build a missile defense system?' *Congressional Quarterly Researcher*, 8 September 2000; Steven Andreasen, 'The Bush strategic plan', *Survival*, 43: 3 (2001), pp. 79–82; Joseph Cirincione, 'Still kicking: a forecast of the post-Clinton NMD debate' (www.acronym.org.uk/50nmd.htm); Mark Hewish, 'Raising the ballistic shield: the latest advances in ballistic missile defense are emerging', *Jane's International Defense Review*, 9 (2000), pp. 30–5; Michael Krepon, 'Missile defense: not such a bad idea', *Bulletin of the Atomic Scientists*, May–June 1999, pp. 31–3; Krepon, 'Moving away from MAD', *Survival*, 43: 2 (2001), pp. 81–95; Jan M. Lodal, 'For modest defences and low offensive numbers', *Survival*, 43: 3 (2001), pp. 71–4; John Newhouse, 'The missile defense debate', *Foreign Affairs*, July–August 2001, pp. 97–109; Steven Weinberg, 'Can missile defense work?' *New York Review of Books*, 14 February 2002.

88 Although there is some argument that a limited missile defence system would also provide protection against the still limited number of Chinese missiles, at least for some years to come.

89 See also Justin Bernier and Daniel Keohane, 'Europe's aversion to NMD', *Strategic Review*, winter 2001, pp. 41–8; François Heisbourg, 'A view from Europe'; Andrew J. Pierre, 'Europe and missile defense: tactical considerations, fundamental concerns', *Arms Control Today*, May 2001, pp. 3–9.

90 See, for example, Celeste A. Wallander, 'Russia's new security policy and the ballistic missile defense debate', *Current History*, October 2000, pp. 339–44.

91 See, for example, Ivo H. Daalder and Christopher Makins, 'A consensus on missile defence?' *Survival*, 43: 3 (2001), pp. 61 ff.

92 See Lewis Dunn, 'Co-ordinated security management: towards a "new framework"', *Survival*, 43: 3 (2001), pp. 86–90.

93 See US Foreign Policy Agenda (US Department of State), September 2000, p. 2 (Statement by George W. Bush on New Leadership on National Security, Washington DC, 23 May 2000); also 'Bush. Raketenabwehr ist ein heikles Thema', *Frankfurter Allgemeine Zeitung*, 10 January 2001, p. 1; 'Rumsfeld plädiert für raschen Bau eines Raketenschilds', *ibid.*, 13 January 2001, p. 1; Lothar Rühl, 'Abrüstung auf den Stand von 1972', *ibid.*, 4 January 2002, p. 12; Simon Jeffery, 'The anti-ballistic missile treaty', *Guardian*, 14 December 2001.

94 Russia has shown itself highly co-operative and moderate in its reaction to the announcement by President Bush on 12 December 2001 that the United States would withdraw from the ABM Treaty within six months.

95 See the interesting analysis by Joachim Krause, 'The new crisis over national missile defense', *Internationale Politik*, Transatlantic Edition, 2 (2000); see also 'Suddenly, such good friends', *Economist*, 10 December 2001, pp. 11–12; Dimitri Rogosin, 'Eine neue russisch-amerikanische Philosophie', p. 12.

96 See Lodal, 'For modest defences and low offensive numbers', pp. 71–4, and Baker Spring, 'Achieving agreement on nuclear weapons, missile defence and arms control', *Survival*, 43: 3 (2001), pp. 91–4.

97 See, for example, Lother Rühl, 'Von Schurkenstaaten und Schurken-Syndikaten. Das neue Bedrohungsbild für Amerika auf dem Horizont des Jahres 2015', *Frankfurter Allgemeine Zeitung*, 4 January 2001; also speech by President George W. Bush on National Missile Defense at the National Defense University, Washington DC, 1 May 2001.

4

Perspectives:
European security and the future of
transatlantic relations

New risks, new challenges and a new NATO: what does this imply for the development of European security and the future of transatlantic relations? The wider concept of security that has become a focus of academic discussion for more than a decade[1] requires more precision and conclusions on what, in concrete terms, this implies for security policy. What does a clearer definition of our security needs imply for transatlantic co-operation and what institutional implications does this have?

Statements on what kind of order or 'architecture' for European security might be foreseen in the long run have tended to be vague. The most prevalent idea is a Europe 'whole and free', made up of stable and co-operative democracies, bound together in various organisations, such as the OSCE, European Union and NATO. Together these would represent a 'security community', or group of saturated states in which the use of military force to achieve political aims or resolve conflicts is no longer conceivable. It would not be incorrect to call this a 'Wilsonian order', the questions being whether it is a feasible concept: in other words, whether it is more than an ambition, and whether it is supported by concrete policies.[2]

The answer to the first question is that there is no reasonable alternative. A return to a Europe of unfettered nation states is undesirable, and a truly politically united Europe looks less and less realistic. The answer must lie somewhere in between the two, and the only conceivable target is a Wilsonian order. While it is obvious that there is no clear-cut blueprint to be followed, it would be wrong to say that the European states are hovering about more or less aimlessly, as was the case after the First World War. There is an understanding that:

- the development of stable and durable democracies must be fostered in all countries;
- economic development and the creation of acceptable living conditions for all citizens, including perspectives for personal development, are an essential part of this;

- structures for interaction and conflict resolution must exist and be used on a daily basis;
- common interests, values, attitudes and outlooks need to evolve;
- transparency and openness are essential;
- military force must be limited and controlled;
- the order must be encompassing, i.e. all states must be part of and involved in it.

While one may be dissatisfied with the results so far or the speed with which they are being attained, it is difficult to deny that these are in fact the objectives being pursued by the Western European democracies and the United States. The development of the major organisations in Europe, the policies towards Central and Eastern Europe, in the Balkans and towards Russia: all have the same aim, namely to stabilise peace and security in Europe by promoting the development of stable and co-operative democracies. This includes in particular the enlargement of both NATO and the European Union. The principal objective of both is 'to extend stability' in order to ensure a peaceful future for all of Europe.

The United States and the Europeans thus have the same aim. Of course, aims are broad and overarching, and they do not always translate into the same interests or policies. Nevertheless, the United States and the European Union have generally moved in the same direction. At times, there has also been a division of labour. The United States has often tended to concentrate on the military side of things (sometimes *nolens volens*, for example in Kosovo or with regard to the denuclearisation of Ukraine), and the Europeans have emphasised political and economic development. There is no harm in this if it serves the common purpose. The only disadvantage lies in the fact that the European contribution, although essential for peace and stability in Europe, is complex, long-term, makes fewer headlines and hence tends to be underestimated and undervalued in the United States.

The critical issues are of a different nature. They concern the role of the United States in Europe – its reliability and American influence relative to the Europeans – and the future development of the European Union. Without question, many Europeans have a contradictory attitude towards the American role. On the one hand, they have enjoyed and continue to enjoy its benefits, not the least of which is the chance to maintain relatively low defence expenditures and rely on the 'ultimate' American ally if matters deteriorate. On the other hand, they are dissatisfied with American leadership, not because it is taking them somewhere they do not want to go, but as a matter of principle, perhaps pride. This is in itself often contradictory, for when American leadership is forthcoming, as during the Kosovo crisis, there is criticism of it; when it is not forthcoming, as in the first years of the Yugoslav crisis, there is criticism again, now about the lack of leadership and reliability. The fact that the United States is a non-European power (in a geographical if not in a political sense) is irrelevant in this context: the same attitudes would apply to a predominant European power, in fact even more so.

Contrary to occasional indications, American involvement in Europe and in the Alliance has not declined; in fact, in some ways it became more intense as the complexity of the new challenges became more and more visible. US involvement in the preparation for and the decisions of the Prague summit in November 2002 shows this quite clearly. What is more, as both Bosnia and Kosovo have shown, the Europeans continue to rely in no small measure on both American military involvement and leadership.

There are only two solutions, neither of them ideal. One is for both Americans and Europeans simply to get used to living in an imperfect world, in which there is a lead nation that is often dissatisfied with what it feels to be an unfair burden and unfair criticism to go along with that, but which is grudgingly followed. The other is for the Europeans to make a greater political and material effort to redress the imbalance.

However, political leadership in Europe seems unwilling to face up to this alternative. A secondary role, even though important in economic and to a large extent also political terms, appears unacceptable to many, certainly to France, but perhaps also to Germany. Remarkably, Britain seems to have carved out a special role for itself. Based on its long-standing close relationship with the United States and the specific contribution it is able to make in military terms, it has taken on a still clearly junior, but privileged, status in the transatlantic relationship. With the exception of these three, to most of the remaining European countries, more used to adapting to powers larger than themselves, secondary status seems much less of a problem. At the same time, however, none of the European states is really willing to do what would be required to develop a common foreign and security policy. Germany, specifically, is unwilling to spend more on defence, while both France and Britain are unwilling to give up their own, specifically national, roles in favour of a joint European policy. The hard fact of the matter is that the European Union is not a 'union', which is, however, prerequisite to an effective common foreign and security policy, and that few member states, and none of the big ones, with the possible exception of Germany,[3] are willing to make a decisive move in that direction. In sum, we continue to be confronted by a Europe that does not have an effective foreign policy, that is slow in coming up with common positions and that has too little in terms of military capability and political decisiveness to back them up. There is no getting away from it: it all hinges on the ability of the European Union to achieve real political union, and the chances of that are not really improving.

When discussion on the eastward enlargement of the European Union started in the early 1990s, it was recognised that such a move would have to go hand in hand with a significant step towards political unity. This did not happen, as the EU summit in Nice exemplified. The Convention, decided upon in Nice and started in Laeken in December 2001, was an open recognition of the fact: the EU was unprepared for enlargement and it needed a political push forward. But it is quite uncertain whether much more than the usual bit of 'institutional engineering' will come out of it, leading once again to more and more complex institutional set-ups, hence to less clarity, less effectiveness and less legitimacy.[4] Despite the introduction of the euro, the European Union has not yet reached the point of no return. As it enlarges, it may become shallower rather than 'deepening', ending up as a large free-trade area with elements of an internal market and a network of co-operative relations. This is not to be scoffed at, but it will not be a union capable of common action. West European leadership is becoming aware of this and as a way out is beginning to talk about a 'core' of states that might move more rapidly towards union. The problem is only that it is this very core that has not moved forward in the past decade or two.

Thus, if political union is not in the offing, the most likely scenario would be a continuation of the past, namely European concentration on economic and political development, on peacekeeping, and on continuing but modest efforts to improve European crisis reaction capability. Latent and often explicit dissatisfaction with the European role and with American activities would continue.

This would be matched on the American side by continuing dissatisfaction with such limited European capabilities and undervaluation of the European economic and political contribution. From an American point of view this might be quite acceptable. The United States wants the Europeans to improve their military capabilities – not, however, to become an equal and perhaps more difficult partner, but to become a more effective and useful assistant – which is not a particularly strong incentive for Europeans.

All this would be 'more of the same'. But the real issue is that a number of other factors must be added, and that together these may have a more negative effect on the transatlantic relationship than the issue of European defence efforts alone. Such factors exist on both sides of the Atlantic. What is new is that they have become more important on the American side and are no longer offset by the 'glue' of an overarching Soviet threat.

On the American side there is a stronger trend towards unilateralism: the feeling that the United States is strong enough and does not really need its allies; indeed, that these allies have little to contribute and can be a nuisance, with their differing points of view. In addition, there is the desire not to be fettered by multilateral agreements or institutions, be they the International Criminal Court, the Test Ban Treaty or the Kyoto Agreement. And, in a paradoxical way, there may also be a bit of hurt pride after 11 September 2001: the vulnerable and hurt superpower that needed the sympathy of its allies.

Of course, if this is a prevailing feeling, it is wrong on all counts. The United States needs allies, and the economic, political and military contribution of those allies is far from insignificant. There are shortcomings in the military realm, and allies that do not simply follow the lead may be difficult, but in return the United States has a privileged leadership role with numerous benefits in the circle of the most important and economically most powerful democracies in the world. All these have come to understand, perhaps more by experience than by insight, the advantages that can be found in multilateralism. Multilateral agreements and institutions bind you, but they also bind the others. Most important, they set norms and they provide a legal framework for exactly those values which democracies stand for and which they rightly believe should form the foundation for the maintenance of security and order. It would seem that this is also in the interest of the United States, and if that country generally accepts multilateral restrictions it could probably count on greater understanding in such instances where it does not.

On the European side there are the deficiencies that have been referred to: a lack of unity, a lack of political decisiveness, a lack of intellectual leadership, a lack of coherent policies supported by all, and a lack of military capability more suited to requirements of twenty-first-century crisis management. Unfortunately, this goes along with a frequent tendency to complain about not being consulted and heard and an equally frequent tendency to criticise American actions. American policies are not beyond criticism; the problem is that the criticism is often close to being the only activity of the Europeans in specific situations.

But there are also different views, assessments and judgements. The Europeans tend to rely less on military and more on diplomatic efforts, perhaps, one could say, because they have no choice, but also out of conviction. There is no general answer to this: both have a valid role to play. What is important is for the issues to be discussed on a transatlantic level so that a degree of co-ordination and division of labour can be achieved. Such a forum is lacking. Although NATO would be the obvious choice, it does not appear that the Alliance has been able to take on such a function. In fact it may be even less likely to do so as it becomes a larger, but less cohesive and less manageable, institution. Consequently, bilateral relations will become more important again in transatlantic relations.

What this means is that the transatlantic relationship may be facing its first really serious test. That this should happen at the very peak of success would support all those who argued that with the disappearance of the Soviet threat the Alliance had fulfilled its purpose and hence lost its function. As alliances that have served their purpose have disappeared in the past, so NATO would become hollow and meaningless. What we would be witnessing would be not the end, but the return, of history.

This is in the interests of neither the United States nor Europe. But NATO's Prague summit in November 2002 may yet offer the Alliance another chance. Under American leadership and prodding, the Alliance has opened the door to change. It has accepted new tasks and decided to prepare for them with new instruments and procedures. Further developments, however, are needed. The first is a purely European one, namely real and significant progress towards political union. Such a development would meet the problems of enlargement, it would ensure cohesive European policies, it would increase European capabilities, and it would enhance the European voice. It would give Europe identity and reduce European frustration, which is one of the roots of transatlantic disharmony. Compared to that, the modernisation of European military capabilities is both a minor and a secondary issue. Unfortunately, hoping for such a development is not optimistic, it is more and more utopian.

The second development is the modernisation and globalisation of American foreign policy. This may sound surprising, particularly to American ears, but in fact American policy, so enlightened during the past fifty years, has become increasingly parochial. The decline of the Soviet threat has had its effects here too. There is a tendency to emphasise American 'national interest' in its very narrowest sense, forgetting long-term aims and implications. If the United States is willing to shoulder responsibility as a world leader and superpower, it cannot do so by looking at everything from the angle of near-term American interests. An enlightened, long-term and global approach is required, which is also the only way to ensure long-term American interests.

Compared with these two, the third requirement is minor. However, a forum where both transatlantic and global issues can be discussed in depth and on a regular basis is required. To take but one example: when is the Middle East discussed between the United States and the Europeans, except on an irregular and bilateral basis? This is true of most of the other issues at stake. It would make sense to use NATO 'at nineteen' or 'at twenty-six' or more. But it would require good will and active participation on all sides. Perhaps it will come about, but perhaps only when a new threat such as terrorism once again pulls the allies together.

Fifty years of transatlantic co-operation have benefited both sides. It would be foolhardy to put the benefits at risk.

Notes

1 See, for example, Barry Buzan, Ole Waever and Jaap de Wilde, *Security: A New Framework for Analysis* (Boulder CO: Lynne Rienner, 1998), and Adrian Hyde-Price, 'Beware the Jabberwock! Security studies in the twenty-first century', in H. Gärtner, A. Hyde-Price and E. Reiter (eds), *Europe's New Security Challenges* (Brookfield: Elgar, 2001), pp. 27–54.

2 In international relations theory this would be the combination of 'institutionalism' and the concept that democracies do not go to war with each other. See, for example, Robert O. Keohane, Joseph S. Nye and Stanley Hoffmann (eds), *After the Cold War: International Institutions and State Strategies in Europe, 1989–1991* (Cambridge MA: Harvard University Press, 1993); Bruce M. Russett, *Grasping the Democratic Peace: Principles for the post-Cold War World* (Princeton NJ: Princeton University Press, 1993); Michael W. Doyle, *Ways of War and Peace* (New York: Norton, 1997).

3 See, for example, the speech by Foreign Minister Joschka Fischer, 'From Confederacy to Federation: Thoughts on the Finality of European Integration' (Berlin: Humboldt University, 12 May 2000).

4 Excellent examples of this are proposals to somehow involve the national parliaments rather than simply strengthening the European Parliament, or the idea of having the Council select a 'President' rather than strengthening the position of the Commission president.

Part II

Transatlantic responses to global challenges

Wayne C. Thompson

5

European–American co-operation through NATO and the European Union

In a speech to the European Institute in Washington DC in March 1995, Belgian Prime Minister Dehaene stated: 'The Cold War is over now. Very fortunately so, but at the same time ... we have been deprived of an enemy. The glue which kept us together for so long has lost its strength.' With the disappearance of communism in Europe and the disintegration of the Soviet Union, the United States and its European allies faced both a danger and an opportunity. The danger was that that they would drift apart from each other and become absorbed by the regional challenges in their own hemispheres. The opportunity was that they could broaden the partnership they had successfully created during the past half-century and co-operate in confronting other long-standing problems and new threats around the globe. They hesitantly chose the latter, although they have learned that global collaboration is easier to proclaim than to practise.[1]

In the post-Cold War environment, freed from the threat of major warfare and domination by a tyrannical superpower, the partners began to think of security as something beyond the military realm. It includes the use of civilian and economic means to secure other international public goods, such as reducing global warming or poverty in the Third World, protecting mankind from diseases or unhealthy food, or enlarging the European Union eastward in order to strengthen freedom, market economies and democracy.[2]

Although Americans are sometimes more inclined than Europeans to see security primarily in military terms, their leaders have demonstrated willingness to reassess what is required to maintain peace and stability. In April 1995 the US Assistant Secretary of State and later UN ambassador, Richard Holbrooke, stated, 'building a new security architecture for Europe means providing a framework to build democracy, market economies, stable societies, and ultimately a stable and just peace across the continent'. This did not mean that Americans and Europeans faced no external threats. But the dangers of attack by weapons of mass destruction (WMD) or by suicidal terrorists seemed remote.[3]

That changed dramatically on 11 September 2001, when Islamic fanatical al-Qaida terrorists, trained and financed by Osama bin Laden and sheltered in Taliban-ruled Afghanistan, hi-jacked four American commercial airliners and crashed three of them into the twin towers of the World Trade Center in New York and into the Pentagon in Washington, killing more than 3,000 persons. Americans' feeling of invulnerability from outside threats went up with the noxious smoke from the buildings' rubble. Any temptations to pursue a unilateralist – not to mention an isolationist, North America-focused – policy disappeared, at least temporarily. A shaken America looked for help from its friends, and the most steadfast of them were Europeans and the neighbouring NATO allies, the Canadians. They responded with emotion and resolve and Article 5 of the Washington Treaty was invoked.

The President of the European Commission, Romano Prodi, called an emergency session the morning after the terrorist attack. After a moment of silence for the victims, he decided to send 'the strongest possible signal of European solidarity with the American people' and to 'call for a common European approach to all aspects of this tragedy'. In moving language Prodi announced, 'this barbaric attack was directed against the free world and our common values. It is a watershed event, and life will never be quite the same again . . . In the darkest hours of European history, the Americans stood by us. We stand by them now.' In a poll taken a week after the attack, Europeans showed strong willingness to support a US military assault: 80 per cent in Denmark, 79 per cent in Britain, 73 per cent in France, 58 per cent in Norway and Spain, and half in Germany. The European Union called for a three-minute silence on 14 September, and from Finland to Italy, and Berlin to Paris, businesses and stock exchanges, buses and shoppers stopped to honour the dead and reflect upon their world that had changed so suddenly. Speaking a month later, Prime Minister Tony Blair said of this event and its aftermath: 'The kaleidoscope has been shaken. The pieces are in flux.'[4]

US President George W. Bush had reminded an enthusiastic audience at the University of Warsaw on 15 June 2001 of how important Europe remains to the United States: 'All in Europe and America understand the central lesson of the century past: when Europe and America are divided, history tends to tragedy; when Europe and America are partners, no trouble or tyranny can stand against us.' Since 1945 US governments have regarded a united and prosperous Europe as essential for guarding American values, for protecting itself and the rest of the free world against communism and the Soviet Union, for promoting reconciliation and securing West Germany and other post-war democracies in the West, and for providing American access into what has become the largest and richest trading area in the world. This was stated most succinctly and accurately by former Secretary of State George C. Marshall in his 5 June 1947 Harvard Graduation speech, which culminated in the Marshall Plan: 'It is logical that the United States should do whatever it is able to do to assist in the return of normal economic health in the world, without which there can be no political stability and no assured peace.'

The Atlantic community is bound together by more than common vulnerability to physical violence. The partnership straddling both sides of the ocean has brought mutual economic benefit that cannot be overestimated. The EU and US economies are roughly the same size: in 1999 the European Union's gross domestic product (GDP) was US$8.5 trillion, compared with an American GDP of $9.2 trillion. With 10 per cent of the world's population, they have 56 per cent of the world's GDP. They share the largest and deepest economic relationship in the world. At the outset of the twenty-first century, total annual investment and trade come to approximately US$1.5 trillion. Sixty-five per cent of all foreign direct investment (FDI) in the United States stems from the European Union, and about 56 per cent of FDI flowing to the European Union comes from the United States. In 2000 the European Union accounted for 18.3 per cent of world trade (excluding intra-EU trade), compared with 20.2 per cent for the United States. In 1999 24 per cent of the European Union's exports went to the United States, and 20.5 per cent of its imports came from that single country. Together they account for 37 per cent of world trade. Unlike America's trade with Asia, its trade with Europe is balanced.[5]

The United States and European Union are the giants in the many rounds of global trade liberalisation, and when they can reach an agreement between themselves, the rest of the world follows. Despite an ever-present string of disputes that affect only about 2 per cent of the total trade volume – over agriculture, bananas, intellectual property and privacy rights, product safety, service trade, subsidy rules, foreign sales corporations and much more – the economic relationship is sound and is growing.

The very magnitude of the world's most important economic relationship, amounting to US$2 billion per day, deters trade wars. This is why the United States has consistently supported the process of European integration despite occasional flutters caused by fears of 'fortress Europe' or a powerful unified European currency. The two sides deal with each other as economic equals. In world trade diplomacy, and in such international forums as the World Trade Organisation (WTO), the European Union has become a key player and can confidently counter American attacks by charges of its own. Indeed, together they shape the global economic agenda and are increasingly interdependent economically even though there is only limited global co-operation between the two giants in economic matters.[6]

The two sides' military and commercial links progressively tightened since the onset of the Cold War. They were significantly enhanced in the 1990s by deepening foreign policy co-operation, facilitated on the European side by the development of the EU Common Foreign and Security Policy (CFSP). It provides added coherence and focus to America's dealings with Europe and increases the chances that the United States would have the European Union's foreign policy support in an emergency.[7] It also creates occasional tensions with the United States, which must share its pre-eminence in such issues as the Middle East peace process with an increasingly confident, unified and assertive Europe.

Nevertheless, the relationship continues to represent the world's most comprehensive thicket of multilateral ties.

This is an immensely complex relationship encompassing bilateral ties between the United States and individual countries, formal relations between the United States and NATO and European Union (both of which are undergoing far-reaching changes to adapt to an altered international environment), interaction in a growing number of international governmental organisations (IGOs), such as the United Nations, the Organisation for Security and Co-operation in Europe, or the Group of Eight (G-8), and in countless non-governmental organisations (NGOs). When one includes the interaction of private businesses, educational organisations, city and state governments, we see the evidence for Deutsch's description of a 'pluralistic political community'.[8]

Equal, global partnership?

Is this evolving dense network of multilateral links an equal one across the board? President John F. Kennedy had foreseen equality in a 4 July speech at Independence Hall in Philadelphia in 1962, when he spoke of Europe as 'a partner with whom we could deal on a basis of full equality'. At the time, some compared this partnership to a 'barbell', with North America and Canada on one side and Europe on the other, held together by an unbreakable iron rod.[9]

American leadership was accepted without question in the aftermath of the September 11 terrorist attacks, when the United States forged a global coalition of countries and dominated the military effort in Afghanistan to end Taliban rule and root out the al-Qaida network. The foreign-policy spokesman for Britain's Liberal Democratic Party in the House of Lords, William Wallace, has questioned whether the end of the Cold War had changed the American presumption that it is the 'agenda setter' of the partnership:

> The underlying and constant American presupposition is that the United States is a benign hegemon – and that the Western alliance can work well if Europe accepts this hegemon's leadership. The United States now acknowledges the European Union as an economic partner, but the idea of sharing leadership in political and military matters has yet to gain acceptance in Washington.

A 2002 opinion poll sponsored by the Chicago Council on Foreign Relations and the German Marshall Fund of the United States confirmed Wallace's assertion. Two-thirds of Europeans (65 per cent) said they would like to see the European Union become a superpower alongside the United States, although support for this varied widely between the French (90 per cent) and the Germans (only 48 per cent). The vast majority of Europeans believe that superpower status would enable Europe to co-operate more effectively, not to compete, with America. However, only a third of American respondents would welcome superpower rank for the European Union, while 52 per cent would not want to share their unique world position with it. Four-fifths of

American respondents do want Europeans to exert strong leadership in the world.[10]

American leaders are aware that the European Union wishes to be recognised as an equal not only in the economic, but also in the political, realm. Richard Morningstar, US ambassador to the European Union until October 2001, reminded students at the College of Europe in Bruges that Europe is decreasingly dependent on the United States and wants to be treated as an equal partner: 'The US has a wife in every port, and the one in Europe wants to change the rules of the game.' His deputy political counsellor, Peter Mulrean, agrees that political equality is developing, although it will be a long time before it will be fully achieved. In economic terms, 'we have been the two gorillas in the zoo' since the end of the 1980s. But both sides have to get used to what a new political partnership means. Americans have to stop thinking of Europeans as 'junior partners', while Europeans have to get used to being an equal partner, when that time comes. This means not ducking unpleasant questions and not hiding behind others on difficult issues. It means undertaking actions that Europeans really do not want to.[11]

The potential benefit of intensified collaboration among the Atlantic partners to deal with global problems is not in doubt. EC President Romano Prodi summed it up at the time of an encounter with Secretary of State Colin Powell:

> The European Union and the United States have a unique partnership . . . when we work together we can set the agenda on the international scene. Our combined economic and political strengths create a responsibility to co-operate closely in order to find answers to pressing global problems as well as to different threats to regional stability. The two strongest economies of the world and the largest global trading and investment relationship provide many opportunities for our businesses and citizens as well as a responsibility for both sides to overcome differences.[12]

In a speech on 11 June 2001 US National Security Adviser Condoleeza Rice presented her opinion on what the United States and Europe can do through co-operation beyond their borders:

> To help foster open societies with open economies around the world; to help bring peace and health to Africa; to help set an example of multi-ethnic democracy for those lands where difference is still seen as a license to kill . . . one of the defining characteristics of the global age is that no nation – not even a 'hyperpower', if one existed – can reach these goals alone.[13]

The partners' vigorous and multi-faceted response to the global challenge of terrorism after the 11 September attacks, including many partners' willingness to deploy armed forces in Afghanistan, underscored the widening scope of US–European collaboration in the world.

At the outset of the twenty-first century the United States and its European partners find themselves focusing their primary attention on different parts of the globe. Europe is in the midst of a major effort to enlarge the Union and to develop the necessary democratic institutions that could hold old and new democracies together and enable them to be ruled and administered effectively. Much of its energy is absorbed by this effort. The United States has long since completed this process of combining old and new, large and small, states in a constitutional order with functioning institutions. It can therefore look outward. Feeling less vulnerable than its allies to military or other threats emanating from outside North America, the United States emphasised its own hemisphere and elevated Asia in its priorities under the newly elected President George W. Bush. In the cases of both the United States and Europe, the transatlantic relationship was no longer necessarily the component of their foreign policies that was publicly designated as the top priority.[14]

Of course, a country like the United States or an organisation like the European Union can think globally and still devote its primary focus to its own back yard. In a speech on 1 June 2001, shortly before President Bush departed for an important trip to Europe to meet with nervous allies, Condoleeza Rice underscored that the President 'truly believes that good foreign policy starts with one's own neighbourhood'. She referred to the 'democracy summit' in Quebec in early 2001, where thirty-four western hemisphere nations assumed the daunting task of creating a Free Trade Area of the Americas (FTAA) by 2005. The flames that gutted the twin towers and one side of the Pentagon on September 11 at least temporarily weakened this North America-first approach. The United States immediately entered intense negotiations with Canada to create a 'security perimeter' around the two countries by adopting common refugee and immigration procedures and improving controls along their border to prevent the easy movement of terrorists. A primary focus on North America is more difficult to justify when the United States believes it faces deadly threats from outside its own continent and needs to turn to its European and other allies for help. [15]

The distinction frequently drawn between Europe's preoccupation with regional concerns and America's focus upon global issues is not quite as neat and tidy as it might sometimes appear. All European countries in the European Union and most that are not members have worldwide commercial involvements. For instance, countries such as Spain and Portugal, because of their prior colonial empires in Latin America and Africa, play an important role as investors and mediators in these continents. It is no accident that EU links with Latin America tightened and investment increased after Spain and Portugal became members in 1986. The European Union's growing interest in Latin America has increased the frequency of clashes with American policy there. By the beginning of the twenty-first century Spain was investing more in Latin America than was the United States.

Although the United States tends to think globally about problems, it is more inclined than European countries and the European Union to seek regional solutions. By contrast, Europeans may think more regionally when compared with the United States, but they are much more interested in seeking multilateral solutions through international governmental organisations (IGOs), especially the United Nations. Thus they act more globally when seeking to solve problems. In the area of human rights, development assistance or environmental issues Europe clearly thinks globally. Nevertheless, only a handful of EU countries are comfortable with playing a global role. In general, European governments hesitate to act outside their continent unless the problem is close to its perimeter, such as in North Africa or parts of the Middle East, or unless there are powerful historical and cultural links as a result of earlier colonial possession. Thus Belgium is more inclined to become involved in the Congo, Rwanda or Burundi, France in French West Africa or Britain in Sierra Leone.[16]

European hesitancy helps convince Washington that it must still exercise a leadership role in dealing with global problems. However, the United States does not like to act without partners who support its leadership, especially when it comes to the application of military force. Because the American public is not fond of the image of the solitary 'world policeman', Washington almost always tries to enlist allies in order to lend legitimacy to its actions abroad and to acquire added military clout that allies like Britain can offer. The United States' former ambassador to the European Union, Richard Morningstar, noted in a 23 January 2001 speech to the EU Committee of the American Chamber of Commerce:

> the US genuinely wants the European Union to be a strategic global partner, one we can work closely with to address political, security and economic issues of common concern around the world. But being a global player means the European Union will have to take on global responsibilities – this requires financial resources and political will. We hope they can deliver on both.

The ambassador's call finds sympathetic listeners in high places within the corridors of EU headquarters. EC President Romano Prodi said in a speech at the European University Institute in Florence on 9 May 2001: 'We should develop the "new Europe" into a fully fledged global player in world affairs alongside the United States. The "new Europe" should become an effective and more equal partner of the United States in global leadership.' Prodi's use of the word 'should' indicated that the European Union had not yet completed this transformation. Only in the fight against terrorism has Europe declared its willingness to consider acting in any corner of the globe. After the terrorist attacks on the United States the EC president asserted that 'our first priority must be to act in unison' and 'our second priority must be to have specific institutional mechanisms for taking policy decisions . . . We need to develop them fast if we are to be a real force for good in the world now emerging from the tragedy of 11 September.'[17]

Despite their regional focus, which is diminishing slowly, Europeans are less willing to defer to Washington than they once were. This was made clear on the eve of German Chancellor Gerhard Schröder's March 2001 visit to the White

House, whose purpose was to convey to George W. Bush Europe's concern about the new President's apparently unilateralist foreign policy. The chancellor's then top national security adviser, Michael Steiner, justified the chancellor's willingness to serve as such a spokesman. He noted in an interview with the *New York Times*, 'the President's father was dealing with a not fully sovereign Germany, the legacy, if you like, of twentieth-century history. Now Germany is a partner without restrictions, and what we want to address is not the leftovers of the last century, but the future of this one.'[18]

The complexity of US–European co-operation

The transatlantic relationship is intense, multilayered, exceedingly complex, increasingly interdependent, and fraught with fluctuations and frictions. It takes place within several interrelated channels. The United States and all European states conduct bilateral relations with each other. In times of crisis, Washington tends to prefer these bilateral contacts because they bring action and co-operation more quickly than does a complicated evolving structure like the European Union. The same applies to European governments. The German daily *Die Welt* called the anti-terrorist crisis 'the moment of the nation states, the time in which individual European governments turn to the American partner after consulting among themselves'.[19]

The allies interact closely within NATO. The highest political leader in the alliance, the Secretary General, is always a European. But American military leadership is institutionalised through the permanent appointment of an American general as the Supreme Allied Commander Europe (SACEUR). Decisions are reached on the basis of consensus.[20] However, not all European countries belong to this organisation, and not all members participate in the integrated command structure, such as France and Iceland, although they have a part in NATO's political structure. The partners collaborate in a wide variety of international forums, such as the OSCE, the Group of Eight (which includes Japan, Canada and Russia) and, most important, the United Nations. Finally, and of ever increasing importance, the United States has had to adapt to and work intensively with an evolving European Union.

The transatlantic partnership involves the meshing of many different systems of government – the US central government and individual American states, the European Union, its member states and, in some federations such as Germany, states or *Länder*. Thus political authority is dispersed, and there are many points where one or more of the numerous players can veto policies. On both sides of the Atlantic, domestic politics is of vital importance. Negotiators often need to make domestic trade-offs that adversely affect the foreign policies they are trying to pursue. Since all the states involved in this thick network of links are democracies, electoral cycles strongly affect the effort to reach agreements. On the American side, it is often pointed out that Presidents and Congress find it especially harrowing to make bold, potentially unpopular moves within a year of re-election. It is no different in the European Union. For example, President Jacques Chirac made it known that EU agricultural reform was off the table until after the 2002 French presidential elections, and Chancellor Gerhard Schröder implied that the German defence budget could not be raised until after the 2002 Bundestag elections.

The American political system divides power both geographically (between the central government and the states) and within the governing institutions in Washington and the fifty state capitals. This can create diplomatic nightmares for both American and European leaders. For instance, American states have become more and more assertive in global politics and conduct their own foreign policies, particularly in economic and trade matters. Ignoring Washington, the Massachusetts legislature passed a 'Burma Law' in 1996 forbidding the state and its agencies from buying anything from companies or individuals that invest in or trade with Myanmar (Burma), which is under military rule. The same can happen in Europe. Germany's *Länder* have supremacy over certain aspects of immigration policy. Thus they can impede both the policy of the German central government in Berlin and that of the European Union itself.

Europeans must deal with America's large, highly decentralised institutions, which wield power of their own and often seem to be hostile to each other. Separation of powers is particularly troublesome for foreign policy: it is often impossible for a President to produce what he promises to foreign leaders. An American President occupies a central position in the making of effective foreign policy. If he is not personally involved or committed to achieving important foreign policy goals, little gets done. The political system enables persons who are largely unknown in Europe to rise to the highest national political office through a painfully long and complicated electoral system. The unique American selection procedure permits a person to arrive in the White House who has pursued a non-political career as a soldier (Eisenhower), farmer (Carter), actor (Reagan) or governor of a state (Carter, Reagan, Clinton, George W. Bush). It almost always brings to the White House a neophyte in foreign policy; Eisenhower and the first George Bush were the exceptions. Most Presidents learn diplomacy as on-the-job training, learning by doing.

When that President seems to overlook the multilateral dimension of America's dealings with the outside world and the need to engage former adversaries, as George W. Bush appeared to do in the first half-year of his presidency and again in his State of the Union 'axis of evil' speech in January 2002, Europeans react negatively. Although many of the red-letter issues – such as the nuclear test ban treaty, the Kyoto Protocol and the International Criminal Court – had gained prominence during the Clinton administration, Bush's predecessor was able to give the appearance in public that he supported those issues and to put the blame on the Republican Congress for not ratifying them. Bush took more straightforward opposition to policies he thought would damage American interests, and he suffered for it in European public opinion.

In August 2001 polls the *International Herald Tribune* and the Pew Research Center for the People and the Press showed Bush's approval rating among Europeans up to 40 percentage points below that of Clinton. Bush's approval in the United States stood at 45 per cent, in France at 16 per cent, in Britain at 17 per cent, in Germany at 23 per cent, and in Italy at 29 per cent. Almost three in four Europeans were convinced that Bush knew less about Europe than did his predecessor, even though Clinton's opinions did not substantially differ from Bush's on many key issues. Three out of four Germans believed Bush made decisions only with the United States in mind. The sole Bush policy favoured by Europeans was his decision not to withdraw American troops from Bosnia and Kosovo. The low ratings were registered even after Bush had visited Europe twice during the summer and had not succeeded in shifting public opinion concerning his leadership. Not until after the 11 September terrorist attacks did Bush begin to climb in European estimation as a capable crisis leader.[21]

A newly elected President may have little or no experience in foreign affairs and yet have the power to select a multitude of foreign-policy advisers, secretaries and agency chiefs, many with little or no foreign or defence policy background themselves. Such a presidential 'team' appears often to operate in an unco-ordinated way, frequently sending off widely differing signals. This inevitably creates and fuels doubts about American leadership capabilities and the continuity of US foreign policy. The complicated and extensive inter-agency bargaining in Washington confuses many people, European and American alike.

The powerful US Congress can also be frustrating. In the last two decades of the twentieth century Congress underwent significant changes: the seniority system in committees had weakened, and the number of committees and subcommittees proliferated. Also, the work load became so demanding that congressmen and senators are retiring earlier. Therefore, an increasingly high percentage of the legislators are new in Congress. For example, by the mid-1990s half the members of the House of Representatives had entered the chamber after the fall of the Berlin Wall. What these changes did was to take much of the power that used to be concentrated in a few key figures and dispersed it within Congress. In this more decentralised Congress, legislative work has become much more complicated. For instance, more than forty congressional committees and subcommittees deal with the defence budget alone.

In the absence of the kind of strong party discipline that exists in most European parliaments, American congressmen and senators are more protective of their constituents' interests and can safely vote against their party leaders or the President if an issue of great interest in their districts or states is at stake. Thus there is no stable coalition on foreign-policy matters.[22] Nevertheless, the Congress is not as obstructionist and isolationist as it may sometimes seem from across the Atlantic. For example, in the 1990s it supported the United States' entry into the North America Free Trade Association (NAFTA), the World Trade Organisation (WTO) and the enlargement of NATO to include three former communist countries: Poland, the Czech Republic and Hungary. Its unflagging and vigorous support of President Bush's anti-terrorist measures revealed yet again that presidential-congressional unity and the reaching out to allies abroad are the norm in times of crisis.

Complexity on the European side of the Atlantic

One exasperated American official during the Nixon administration described the European Community to be 'as mystifying as the Tibetan theocracy'. William Wallace was more subdued, calling the EU institutional structure 'complex and opaque'. Desmond Dinan attributes this to the 'incremental, often untidy nature of European integration'. The European Union is in the process of steady evolution; it is 'a polity in the making', to use the words of Alberta Sbragia.[23] Ambassador Richard Morningstar put it this way in a speech at the College of Europe on 17 April 2001: 'If we look into the future, we will know what the US will look like. But Europe? It is hard to predict what the relationship will be when we do not know what one part will be.'

Those who deal with Europe must constantly adapt to its changing institutions. It is therefore not simple for Europeans and Americans alike to know precisely who has the authority to make decisions on what exactly is the division of labour among many bodies of the Community, or where the line is between EU competence and that of the member states. This is one reason why the United States still prefers to utilise its bilateral ties with European allies in times of emergency. European countries all have variations of parliamentary systems, which simplify the conduct of foreign policy. Responsibility is clearer than one finds in either the European Union or the United States, and once policy is established by the central government there are fewer obstacles to its implementation. Given party discipline and the fact that a prime minister or chancellor is in office precisely because his party or coalition has a parliamentary majority, it is not easy for its foreign policy to be thwarted by legislative action. Nor does a European government that has negotiated a treaty need to worry as much about ratification as does an American President. There are, of course, some exceptions. In order for Chancellor Schröder to carry out his historic decision to send German military forces to South Asia to support the American and British military action in Afghanistan in 2001 he had to win a majority vote in the Bundestag. Not wishing to see his Social Democratic–Green coalition weakened by having to rely on opposition votes, he combined this vote with a vote of confidence and narrowly carried the day with a two-vote margin.

One of the difficulties of EU foreign policy is created by the presidency of the European Council, which revolves every six months. The member states alternate, and each brings its own perspectives and priorities to its presidency. For instance, the Spanish presidency brought a redirection of attention to Latin America, something in which Finland would have only mild interest. But the Finnish presidency heralded the 'Northern Dimension', with which Spain would not share a strong affinity. Also the member states have differing opinions on how the Community's relations with the United States should be, and this can affect the transatlantic relationship. A country can assume the presidency with a firm agenda but find it hi-jacked by international events. The presidency is so important for setting the EU agenda that the United States and other non-members cannot ignore it. But such a short presidency inevitably creates discontinuity and can disrupt or complicate on-going negotiations.

In determining who really makes decisions in EU external policy, the outsider must decide now among a variety of powerful figures about whom to turn to: the EC President, the EC Commissioner for External Relations, the European Council's High Representative for CFSP, the Trade Commissioner or the Prime Minister or Foreign Minister of the current presidency. A German newspaper wrote what many people already know: 'Neither the European public nor Europe's partners understand the distribution of competencies (if there is one) among the foreign policy representative, Mr Solana, the commissioner responsible for external relations, Chris Patten, and the council president . . . who all travel around the world speaking "in the name of Europe"'. It continues: 'The same applies to operative politics. The European Union has countless commissioners and representatives for special regions or issues, but outside the EU apparatus, nobody knows what powers they have and in whose name they speak'.[24]

Despite the many-headed EU leadership that still exists, this stable of influential EU leaders represents considerable progress toward enhancing the Community's ability to conduct foreign policy. Referring to the jibe Kissinger once made about not having a phone number when he wanted to call Europe, the former Senior Director for European Affairs on the US National Security Council, Antony J. Blinken, argues that there is now a number to call at the European Union, depending on the problem. 'It is true, however, that while each has the receiver in one ear, he also has fifteen European Ministers whispering in the other. As a result, Brussels' executive decision-making authority is circumscribed.' In an interview with the German weekly *Die Zeit* Chris Patten admitted, 'I don't claim for a minute that there will be one single telephone number in the near future, which a Secretary of State Kissinger could dial. Incidentally it's a rather silly question, which Henry Kissinger asked at the time. Which number do you dial if you want to phone the United States?'[25]

Co-operation through NATO

During the Cold War the bedrock of the transatlantic relationship was military security. Faced with a well armed common enemy – the Soviet Union – the United States, Canada and Western Europe had an existential need for solidarity. The attempt to forge a European framework for defence, the European Defence Community (EDC), failed when the French National Assembly rejected the plan in 1954. Great Britain proposed a Western European Union (WEU), ultimately composed of France, Italy, Germany, the United Kingdom, the Netherlands, Belgium, Luxembourg, Greece, Spain and Portugal, with head-quarters in Brussels. But without a command structure, military assets, and a powerful North American partner, it was largely irrelevant throughout the Cold War. The only feasible guarantor of security was the North Atlantic Treaty Organisation (NATO).

During the Cold War there were within Europe rival visions to 'Atlanticism'. The most clearly articulated was that of Charles de Gaulle, who spoke of a Europe 'from the Atlantic to the Urals' that should ultimately take control of its own destiny and make its own decisions without the strong influence of the United States. France's Western European partners did not share his confidence that they could manage their security affairs alone. They also lacked an effective mechanism for exercising co-ordinated European foreign policy. Links among the Foreign Ministries were tightened after 1970 through European Political Co-operation (EPC) within what is now the European Union. Its key features were a commitment to consult, co-operate and agree by consensus on co-ordinated positions and joint action regarding foreign-policy issues of general interest. Nevertheless, member states continued to regard foreign policy as one of their most important prerogatives as sovereign states.

The mutual reliance the transatlantic partners continue to have for each other did not mean that there were no periodic tensions in their relations. Indeed, it often seemed that NATO was 'in crisis' some way or the other. The issues varied and included the importance and manner of conducting *détente* toward the Soviet Union and its Warsaw Pact allies, the deployment of enhanced radiation weapons ('neutron bombs') and Intermediate Nuclear Forces (INF). Nevertheless, for more than half a century, the United States' primary formal link with Europe has been through NATO: Burwell is correct to describe the Alliance 'as the most successful example of transatlantic coopera-tion'.[26]

NATO's commitments and programmes take its co-operation with European allies to the outer limits of Europe and beyond. The Balkans offer an example where the Europeans pulled the United States into active military and political involvement outside the traditional perimeter of NATO but still inside Europe. The United States was determined to remain out of the conflicts raging in Croatia and Bosnia following the unravelling of Yugoslavia in 1991–92. It was the bloodletting in Bosnia and the inability of European soldiers deployed there under UN authority to control the situation that slowly drew a domestically ori-ented President Bill Clinton into more active involvement in Europe, culminat-ing in the Dayton Peace Accord of 1995. After some remarks during the 2000 presidential campaign on pulling out, President George W. Bush assured his audience at Warsaw University on 15 June 2001: 'I know that America's role is important, and we will meet our obligations. We went into the Balkans together and we will come out together.' Thousands of American troops (although only about 15 per cent of the total forces) served alongside other

European and non-European soldiers in the Stabilisation Force (SFOR) in Bosnia-Herzegovina and in the Kosovo Force (KFOR).

Washington maintained this commitment even after launching its major deployment to Asia following in the autumn of 2001. In a 22 November 2001 speech at Moscow's Diplomatic Academy, NATO's Secretary General, Lord George Robertson, compared the new threat of terrorism with the previous pre-occupation with the Balkans: 'The challenges in Kosovo and Bosnia may have seemed far away, but the challenge of global terrorism is not. It threatens us right here at our doorstep. Far more than Kosovo or Bosnia, the attacks of September 11 brought home the lessons of our interdependence.' The fact that he delivered this address in Moscow indicated that he included Russia in that increasingly interdependent and radically changed world.

NATO adds another layer of joint involvement in the Middle East through the Mediterranean Dialogue. Founded in 1994, a security dialogue takes place that aims to strengthen good relations and improve mutual understanding with Algeria, Egypt, Israel, Jordan, Mauritania, Morocco and Tunisia. Co-operation also extends to specific activities in fields such as information and science. In 1997 a Mediterranean Co-operation Group was added. This has overall responsibility for the Mediterranean Dialogue and the conduct of political consultations between NATO member countries and individual Mediterranean participants.[27] As a member of the fifty-five-strong OSCE, the United States along with all European countries engages in formal co-operation with Algeria, Egypt, Israel, Morocco and Tunisia through the OSCE's Mediterranean Partners for Co-operation and with Japan and South Korea through the Partners for Co-operation. The American commander serving as the SACEUR also is the commander-in-chief (CINC) of the US military command of 115,000 soldiers (European Command, EUCOM) that encompasses Europe, Israel, Syria, Lebanon and the entire African continent except Egypt and the Horn of Africa (Sudan, Eritrea, Djibouti, Ethiopia, Somalia and Kenya). Hundreds of US military personnel assigned to this command serve in all corners of Africa.

NATO was always more than a mere collective defence organisation. In 2001 the US ambassador to NATO and later ambassador to Russia, Alexander Vershbow, described the idealistic core of the Atlantic Alliance:

> NATO's founders – like the founders of what today is the European Union – had not only bloody memories but a breathtaking vision. NATO was never just about defending against an external threat. NATO was also conceived as a way of moving erstwhile adversaries from the battlefield to the boardroom, from conflict to co-operation, to so intertwine the security and economic interests of the member nations that war in Europe would become all but unthinkable.[28]

Russia

Both the United States and its European allies regard good relations with Russia as a precondition for stability in Europe. They conduct important bilateral relations with Moscow. They also deal with Russia through a broad range of multilateral channels, such as the OSCE. The Group of Seven wealthiest industrial democracies, which meets periodically to discuss such matters as interest rates and macroeconomic co-ordination, was transformed in the 1990s into the Group of Eight (G-8) in order to include Russia. Both the United States and the European Union conduct summit meetings with the Russian leaders; EU–Russian summits are held biannually. But the most structured dealings occur within NATO.

Issues outside the European theatre have been largely responsible for enhancing the relationship between Russia and the transatlantic allies. Matters of anti-terrorism and countering weapons proliferation were at the heart of the decision to upgrade the NATO relationship with Russia from that of the Permanent Joint Council to the NATO–Russia Council in May 2002. Secretary of State Colin Powell indicated 'the Alliance will retain the right to act on any issue whether or not it has been discussed with Russia'. Nevertheless, a stronger voice has been accorded to Russia in relation to WMD non-proliferation, missile defence, counter-terrorism and crisis management. The new body does not give Russia veto power or a vote in NATO enlargement decisions, and one NATO member can terminate a discussion if it chooses. But President Vladmir Putin, participating in the council's first meeting in Rome on 28 May 2002, confessed that a few years earlier the very idea of his country sitting in such a body 'would have been, simply, unthinkable'. The same could be said of the fact that since 1999 a Russian general serves as a deputy to the SACEUR in Belgium, responsible for Russian soldiers assigned to allied forces in Kosovo and Bosnia. Also Russian *Spetznaz* troops operate with US Special Forces in Bosnia and Afghanistan. The transatlantic allies and Russia entered into a joint enterprise to meet common threats to an extent unparalleled since the end of the Second World War. Referring to the diplomatic realignment since 11 September, Powell asserted: 'Not only is the Cold War over, the post-Cold War period is also over.'[29]

It is within the halls of NATO that both Russia and the United States and the Europeans give many of their most important political signals. For example, it was at NATO Headquarters on 13 June 2001 that President Bush described the need for a different relationship with Russia: 'First we must change our thinking to meet the demands of a new age. The Cold War is over; the Soviet Union is gone; and so is the nuclear balance of terror.' He called on America's allies to work together to deter the new threats of nuclear, biological, and chemical weapons . . . Today, Russia is not our enemy.'

His words had provided the right atmosphere for a successful first meeting with Russian President Vladimir Putin in Slovenia the next day. After the meeting he said: 'I looked the man in the eye. I found him to be very straightforward and trustworthy. We had a very good dialogue. I was able to get a sense of his soul.' He added, 'it indicated to me that we can have a very frank and honest relationship, that there are areas where we can work together.' The following day he showed how much he cared about the European reaction by calling the British and Spanish Prime Ministers and the Polish President to report on his meeting.

The encounter stimulated some scepticism at home, especially on Capitol Hill, about the President's professions of trust toward a former KGB agent. Senate Foreign Relations Committee chairman Joe Biden, a Democrat, said: 'I don't trust Putin; hopefully the President was being stylistic rather than substantive.' Former vice-presidential candidate Joseph Lieberman, also a Democrat, noted that he was struck by Bush's 'very conclusively positive' assessment of Putin after just a two-hour meeting.[30]

Former national security adviser in the Clinton administration, Sandy Berger, argued:

> Yeltsin drew lines in the sand with the West that he could not sustain: 'nyet' to NATO enlargement, 'nyet' to the Balkans. He created for himself zero-sum confrontations, and when the United States and the West held their ground, 'nyet' became 'da' and Russians became bitter . . . Putin does not overplay his hand. He does not draw unsustainable lines in the sand. He does not let himself get cornered.[31]

While Berger seeks to explain why Putin was successful in reaching out to the West, an earlier national security adviser, Zbigniew Brzezinski, asserted on the 15 November 2001 Lehrer Report news hour that Putin's motive is simple: the Euro-Atlantic partnership is 'a smashing success'. Russia does not want to be isolated or allied with China to the south-east or with Moslems in the south. His only alternative was with the West on terms 'we have set'. In late September Putin impressed the German parliament with a speech delivered in German (learned in his days as a KGB officer in East Germany during the 1980s). He asserted that Russia is rooted in European values and 'the Cold War is over'. He concluded his Western European visit by travelling to the headquarters of both the European Union (Russia's main trading partner) and NATO on 3 October for discussions. This historic visit was the first ever to NATO by a Russian leader. While Putin's speech and visits captured the journalists' and public's attention, they basically expressed Russia's prevailing policy of seeking more co-operation and a larger role in Europe.[32]

The bilateral summit in the United States, including a down-home visit to President Bush's ranch in Crawford, Texas, produced no negotiation breakthroughs, but it opened the door to a better relationship between the two countries and with the rest of Europe. The harmony of the two world leaders, symbolised by Bush's invitation for Putin to sit in on his daily national security briefing by CIA Director George Tenet, brought sighs of relief to their European partners. A year later, following the November 2002 NATO summit meeting in Prague, Bush travelled immediately to St Petersburg to meet with Putin in the glittering palace of Catherine the Great to report on NATO's decisions, especially regarding the inclusion of seven new members, all former Soviet allies or, in the case of the Baltic states, former parts of the Soviet Union itself. Hoping to calm domestic criticism in Russia of Putin's acquiescence in the enlargement, Bush publicly said, 'the mood of the NATO countries is this: Russia is our friend. We've got a lot of interests together, we must continue our co-operation in the war on terror.'[33]

The mutual, if unilateral, announcements of drastic reductions in their nuclear warhead stockpiles (the United States by more than two-thirds over the coming decade) broke a long stalemate in arms control and offered reassurance that European fears of a new arms race were unfounded. The American President announced that the US stockpile would be lowered to between 1,700 and 2,200 long-range nuclear warheads, while his Russian counterpart expressed his willingness to reduce his country's number to about 2,000. Considering that on 5 December 2001 both powers completed their reductions in offensive nuclear arms required by the START I Treaty, signed a decade earlier, to just under 6,000 warheads, their commitment to cut their warheads by two-thirds was dramatic. In May 2002 Bush and Putin signed the accord in Moscow codifying their previous pledges to reach their reduction targets by the end of 2012.

Bush had hoped that a deal could be reached on missile defence, but Putin did not agree, despite his softening on the issue in the previous couple of months. The Russian President referred to the 1972 ABM Treaty, which forbade such defences, as central to maintaining stability between the nuclear powers. But when in December 2001 Bush gave the required six-month notice that the United States would withdraw from the ABM Treaty – the first time since 1945 any nation had abrogated an arms control agreement unilaterally – Putin called the decision 'a mistake', but 'it won't be the end of the relationship. ' Defence Minister Sergei Ivanov added: 'Russia is not concerned or afraid regarding its military security.' Bush had calculated correctly that withdrawal from the ABM treaty would not harm US–Russian co-operation and that a new relationship could be built upon a foundation other than arms control. European concern proved to be exaggerated. In December 2002 President Bush announced plans to begin deploying a rudimentary missile defence system to be operable by 2004 and to consist of ten land-based interceptors at Fort Greely, Alaska, and Vandenberg Air Force Base, California, aimed mainly at destroying incoming North Korean missiles.[34]

Both presidents underscored their intention to develop a new partnership for the long term. This new partnership was to be formalised within NATO. In their concluding news conference President Bush said, 'we share a vision of a European Atlantic community while, free and at peace. . . . Russia should be a part of this Europe. We will work together with NATO and NATO members to build new avenues of co-operation and consultation between Russia and NATO.'

This was not empty rhetoric. NATO's General Secretary, Lord Robertson, underscored in Moscow on 22 November that the terrorist attacks against the United States

> oblige us to think afresh about the relationship between NATO and Russia. Because one thing should be clear: if we want to come up with any meaningful response to the terrorist menace, to the proliferation of weapons of mass destruction, and the other new and emerging threats, we need a solid NATO–Russia partnership. . . . The new spirit of co-operation that has emerged between us after September 11 must be made permanent.

Putin stressed his willingness: 'Russia is not standing in line to join NATO, but . . . is ready to develop relations as far as the North Atlantic alliance is prepared for this.'[35]

Partnership for Peace, the Caucasus and Central Asia

Through its Partnership for Peace (PfP) programme, established in January 1994, NATO is linked bilaterally with twenty-seven partners, including Russia. Although some Western European non-NATO countries, such as Finland, Sweden, Ireland and Switzerland, belong, the main focus of activity is former Soviet republics and ex-communist countries in Central Europe and the Balkans. It extends collaboration as far as the oil-rich Caspian Sea and the Central Asian republics and broadens the geographic scope of American–European co-operation.

The purpose of PfP is to expand and intensify political and military co-operation and to strengthen stability and peace, primarily through training forces for peacekeeping operations. Many former communist countries regard PfP as a crucial stepping-stone to full NATO membership, and NATO left the door open for new members at its May 1997 Madrid conference. The participants regularly take part in security co-operation programmes, such as civil emergency operations and annual military exercises. For instance, for the first time Georgia hosted a NATO–PfP military exercise, named Co-operative Partner 2001, in the Black Sea from 11 to 22 June 2001. The purpose of the exercise was to develop naval and amphibious interoperability between NATO and the PfP participants. In this exercise the United States and eight NATO allies engaged in maritime and land training with Azerbaijan, Bulgaria, Georgia, Romania, Ukraine and Sweden. On 15 December 2001 Secretary of Defense Rumsfeld announced that the United States would lift sanctions and resume military ties with Azerbaijan and Armenia, which had granted overflight rights to US warplanes involved in the Afghan war.[3]

The Organisation for Security and Co-operation in Europe
Exchanges of views, as well as joint action, are also possible through the OSCE, whose activity is restricted to Europe defined very broadly to thirty miles from

the Chinese border. The OSCE oversees elections in the Balkans and the former Soviet republics, as well as monitors compliance with UN Security Council resolutions. Its work includes an array of transnational threats, such as trafficking in human beings and small arms, as well as water problems in Central Asia – three countries produce water and two do not have enough of it. It oversees the Conventional Forces in Europe (CFE) agreement. The fifty-five allies conduct formal and informal talks at OSCE headquarters in Vienna and at its more than twenty field missions.

The United States seeks agreement from the grouping of EU members, those countries aspiring to EU membership, and Canada. Co-operation among these countries, which constitute about half the organisation's members, is very good. The EU Common Foreign and Security Policy works very well at OSCE. As a rule, the EU presidency announces the common policy, and the countries clustered around the European Union follow it. Since the United States agrees with these nations on most things, the arrangement is good for both the United States and its European allies. The OSCE co-ordinates its activities with NATO and the European Union and, like NATO, it makes decisions on the basis of consensus. It is an arena where the allies can work with the Russians, who would like the organisation to be the overarching security organisation for Europe. Moscow also believes that it is too active in the Balkans and places too much emphasis on human rights.[37]

On 4 December 2001 representatives of the fifty-five member states from North America, Europe and Central Asia met in Bucharest and unanimously adopted a plan that includes intensified police co-operation and measures to choke off the international financing of terrorist groups. It called on all member countries to abide by the dozen UN resolutions related to fighting terrorism. This action represented a dramatic departure for the OSCE, which has traditionally focused on resolving European conflicts and fostering democracy and human rights in Europe. Although the organisation still has a human rights focus, it helps move American–European foreign policy co-operation to the global stage. By taking an active part in this annual gathering, Secretary of State Powell demonstrated that the American government was committed to opposing terrorism as a member of an international coalition.[38]

Central Asia

America especially, but also some of its key NATO allies who decided to join the war effort against Taliban rule in Afghanistan, became much more involved in the five Central Asian republics as a result of Operation Enduring Freedom, which began within a few weeks of the 11 September attacks. This took place despite evidence that the regimes were repressive semi-democracies with a bad record of imprisoning political dissidents. Before the warming of the United States' and NATO's relations toward Russia in the course of the anti-terrorist campaign, the allies had taken a low-key approach to these former Soviet republics out of deference to Russia, which claimed a privileged role in these states.

The main focus of attention was on Uzbekistan, a nation of 25 million with an eighty-five-mile border with Afghanistan. Of all five republics, it had long sought the most independence from Moscow and had courted friendly relations with Washington despite Russian objections. Quiet co-operation had taken place for several years before the partnership with the United States, and its NATO allies, became public in 2001. This collaboration was intensified after the 2000 attack on the USS *Cole* in Yemen. The bond was made public on 5 October 2001, upon the occasion of US Secretary of State Donald Rumsfeld's visit to Tashkent. The Uzbek government of Islam Karivov granted the United States permission to station ground troops, helicopters, aircraft – including both F-15 and F-16 fighter-bombers operating out of the former Soviet air base in Khanabad – special forces, medical evacuation teams, and 1,000 army troops of the 10th Mountain Division. Facilities were made available to a lower number of troops from other NATO countries, including Britain, France, Germany and Turkey, as well as to Jordan, on their way to deployment in Afghanistan itself. An advanced team of sixty French soldiers was quickly sent.

In January 2002 Kyrgyzstan gave the United States and its allies permission to use one of its air bases at Bishkek. The Pentagon utilises it as a transport hub for air refuelling missions and for reloading cargo from large long-range aircraft into smaller ones for shipment into Afghanistan. It can also accommodate F-15E strike fighters, which can carry heavier bomb loads than the navy jets based on carriers. By the end of 2002 the United States had stationed 1,000 troops at Bishkek, joined by another 1,000 Allied soldiers from Denmark, France, the Netherlands, Spain, Norway, Australia and South Korea. The Russians announced plans to deploy fighter jets at Kant air base in Kyrgyzstan, which may also house a future rapid-reaction force to be created in accordance with a Collective Security Treaty signed by Russia, Kyrgyzstan, Belarus, Armenia, Kazakhstan and Tajikistan. These plans were Moscow's first important military response in Central Asia to the deployment of American-led troops there.[39] Neighbouring Tajikistan was less public in its agreement to co-operate with the United States, but it agreed to grant the use of its air space and emergency landing rights to US soldiers and their allies. The United States also initiated discussions with Kazakhstan for the use of an airfield there.

The development was historic in that it was the first time American ground troops and their allies were sent on a combat mission to areas of the former Soviet Union. Uzbeks were also aware of the dramatic nature of the shift. One of Karimov's former advisers called it 'absolutely colossal'. It represented a bid by Uzbekistan, which has Central Asia's largest standing army but is unable to project its power beyond its own borders, to become the major regional power. This foothold in Central Asia, whether long-term or not, was essential for the joint US–European military effort in Afghanistan. The United States showed every indication of retaining a robust military presence in Central Asia after the cessation of hostilities in Afghanistan. Powell told a House committee on 6

February 2002: 'America will have a continued interest and presence in Central Asia of a kind that we could not have dreamed of before.'[40]

For a long time NATO allies had debated among themselves the geographic limit of their co-operation. Article 6 of the NATO charter contained a clear delineation of NATO's operational area: the members' territory in Europe and North America, Turkey, and any member's islands in the North Atlantic area north of the Tropic of Cancer. Not wanting to be dragged into colonial wars, it was the United States that was most insistent that the alliance be limited to this region. It came up during the Suez crisis of 1956 and France's war in Indochina, when the United States resisted efforts to invoke alliance commitments. However, in the post-Vietnam era American planners began to think about the possibility that European allies would assist Washington in securing such things as vital oil routes. Clinton's second Secretary of State, Madelaine Albright, suggested that NATO should perhaps defend common interests, rather than merely common territory. Europeans and Canadians could not warm to this idea, and the issue of military co-operation 'out of area' had inspired little support.

After Americans and Europeans had gone 'out of area' to fight NATO's first war in the Balkans, NATO gave its backing to the military effort in Afghanistan by declaring Article 5 of the North Atlantic Treaty for the first time. This is not a blank cheque for any alliance member experiencing an attack. Allies can provide any form of assistance they deem necessary to respond to the situation, and that help need not be military. Each ally is responsible for determining what it considers necessary in a particular circumstance. The result was that in so far as military commitments in South Asia were concerned, it was the individual member states that were acting on a bilateral basis with the United States under clear American command. Zbigniew Brzezinski expressed this fact succinctly: 'In the American–European relationship a fundamentally important ingredient continues to be missing: Europe. There is no Europe as such that is joining America in its long-term campaign; individual European states are doing what they can.' Nevertheless, by spring 2002 the United States found its own troops stretched thin in Afghanistan and sought more Allied help. By May 2002 more than two-thirds of America's NATO allies had sent soldiers to Afghanistan, and there were more European forces on the ground than American ones. The Europeans play an even more important role when it comes to long-term efforts to rebuild the war-shattered country.[41] In summary, US/Canadian–European military co-operation (among themselves and with other countries such as Australia) had become truly global despite uncertainty whether this had become a precedent that would extend beyond the fight against terrorism.

Confronted with the terrorist threat, President Bush claimed on the eve of the November 2002 summit meeting in Prague that 'never has our need for collective defence been more urgent'. NATO allies agreed and approved the creation of a joint land, sea and air Response Force composed of 21,000 soldiers equipped with high-technology weaponry and designed for rapid deployment anywhere in the world. To strengthen this new expeditionary role, the President appointed the first Marine general, James Jones, to assume the post of SACEUR in 2003. Lord Robertson emphasised the importance of this shift for America's partners: 'If the Europeans want influence over what the US is doing or planning or thinking, then they've got to be able to be there with them when the time is right.'[42]

At the end of 2002 NATO became involved as an organisation in Afghanistan when Germany and the Netherlands requested and received help from the Alliance in planning for their assumption of command over the International Security Assistance Force (ISAF) in February 2003. This constitutes NATO's first mission outside Europe and North America. The Alliance followed up with expanded aid in the fields of logistics, communications and intelligence gathering and evaluation. This low-key assistance is from NATO's jointly maintained assets and is different from the equipment and capabilities taken to Afghanistan by the troops dispatched by the governments of member states. On 11 August 2003 the Alliance took command of all peacekeepers in Afghanistan, its very first mission outside the Euro-Atlantic area.[43]

US–EU co-operation

Although there was fleeting uncertainty about such daring European innovations as the single market and the Economic and Monetary Union (EMU), the United States consistently supported European integration. In order to help stabilise the devastated European countries politically and to assist in their economic recovery, the United States offered Marshall Plan aid in 1947. However, it insisted that all countries receiving such assistance sit down together and decide as a group how the money should be spent. Thus the United States provided an important initial impetus for a unified Europe and helped strengthen the habits of co-operation that the Europeans have refined over the years.

In response to the offer of Marshall Plan support, the Europeans created in 1948 the Organisation for European Economic Co-operation (OEEC) for making the decisions and the European Payments Union (EPU) for administering US funds. In 1960 the United States and Canada joined the OEEC, which was renamed the Organisation for European Co-operation and Development (OECD), with headquarters in Paris. The OECD provides economic analysis and forecasting for industrialised nations, including estimates of future growth, inflation, unemployment and GDP. It also attempts to co-ordinate members' economic and development aid. It provided a forum for member states to hammer out an anti-bribery convention in international commerce. Later Japan, Australia and New Zealand joined, followed after the end of the Cold War by the Czech Republic, Hungary, Poland, Slovakia and Russia. With only 16 per cent of the world's population, its twenty-nine members produce two-thirds of the world's economic output.

The United States' early and consistent support of European integration has never protected the two sides of the Atlantic from disputes on a wide range of issues. The most venomous were trade disagreements, but the partners also had periodic political controversies over the Middle East, especially concerning Israel and Palestine, Central America, Poland, gas pipelines from Siberia, and such events as the Vietnam War, the Iranian hostage crisis and the Soviet invasion of Afghanistan. Some of these disputes were caused by European efforts to devise policies toward sensitive global issues without discussing them in advance with the United States. Until 1990 most attempts to create institutions that could deal with these disputes in a formal way, such as Henry Kissinger's 1973 'Year of Europe', failed. The only bodies within which Americans and Europeans could sit down together and work out their common problems were such international governmental organisations as NATO and the OSCE.

Nevertheless, consultations between the United States and the European Union have taken place on a regular basis since the early 1970s. Anthony Gardner showed how those dealings evolved by dividing US–EU relations into three eras: *ad hoc* consultations from 1974 to 1990, structured consultations under the Transatlantic Dialogue from 1990 to 1995, and from 1995 onwards more tightly structured consultations covering not only crises but a wide spectrum of global questions, including security, international trade, science, health and the environment, education, development and humanitarian assistance, with a view to joint action. These meetings take place on a variety of levels: summits involving the Presidents of the United States, EU Council and European Commission (EC); Secretary of State and Foreign Ministers of EU member states; American cabinet members with their EC counterparts; American under-secretaries or the assistant secretary of state for European affairs with the EU member states' political directors; Department of State department directors and their counterparts in the member states' Foreign Ministries; bureaucrats at lower levels who work on carrying out policy.[44]

The end of the Cold War brought a downgrading of the security dimension in US–European relations. It increased Washington's conviction that Europe's ambitious reform agenda, such as the Single European Act and the prospect of Economic and Monetary Union, made it advisable for the United States to enhance its consultations and formal links with the European Union and to give renewed support for European integration. In 1989 Secretary of State James Baker advocated closer transatlantic co-operation to keep pace with the dizzying changes in Central and Eastern Europe and with the impressive progress of EU integration, which he saw as an important foundation for economic viability and political stability in Europe. He said: 'we propose that the United States and the European Community work together to achieve, whether it is in treaty or some other form, a significantly strengthened set of institutional and consultative links'. Behind him stood President George H. W. Bush, who had earlier informed EC President Jacques Delors that Washington was ready to work out 'new mechanisms of consultation and co-operation on political and global issues with Brussels'. At the July 1989 G-7 meeting Bush showed his confidence in Europe by explicitly asking it to co-ordinate Western aid to Poland and Hungary. The European partners' ability to take the lead in assisting the new democracies to the east, to whom they were providing the most financial aid, as well as the European Union's influence in the Uruguay Round trade negotiations, strengthened the American appreciation of Europe's political significance, particularly as an essential stabiliser of a united Germany.[45]

Bush's and Baker's calls were seconded by Robert Zoellick, then a key player in the US State Department, and by Commerce Secretary Robert Mosbacher. The Bush team made an even more precise proposal for regular consultations at various levels in order 'to enhance the practice and expectation of joint action, or at least to avoid presenting either side with non-negotiable or surprise positions'. However, the administration made it clear that this 'New Atlanticism' should not diminish the role of NATO and that a tightened US–European link must remain embedded in the Atlantic community. Some Europeans, particularly the French, had reservations about what seemed like dialogue at all levels amounting to a kind of American seat at the European Community table. The result was a weakened 'Declaration on US–EC Relations', signed in Washington in November 1990.[46]

The declaration spoke in terms of common values, principles and traditions, particularly those of democratic government, human rights and market economies. It called for the safeguarding of peace and the promotion of international security. Thomas Frellesen, of the EC's Directorate–General of External Relations, noted that the declaration's objectives 'remain at the core of most EU–US co-operative efforts'. It formalised the exchanges that had taken place informally and sporadically between the US Congress and the European Parliament.[47]

Most important, the declaration created a Transatlantic Dialogue, with a mechanism for regular transatlantic consultations. They centred on biannual summits of the three Presidents (United States, EC, and the six-month presidency of the European Council) alternately in Washington and the European capital of the Council presidency. In 1994 working groups were created to prepare for the next summits. Nevertheless, despite the higher profile of the relationship and the stated intention to breathe new life into the transatlantic link for a changed world after the Cold War, these meetings failed to contribute much to the advancement of US–EU relations. Although regular meetings were also held at lower political levels, there was too little continuity between the biannual summits.

In general, the Transatlantic Dialogue was unable to settle long-standing and tense economic controversies, including strong disagreements in the General Agreement on Tariffs and Trade (GATT). The early 1990s witnessed continuing trade disputes that seemed to overshadow the far larger set of common interests toward the rest of the globe. Some of these problems were dealt with successfully. For instance, the May 1992 'Blair House Agreement', established a gradual reduction of agricultural subsidies, which smoothed the way for concluding the Uruguay Round and the creation of the WTO in 1995. But the Transatlantic Dialogue proved not to be an effective forum for moving beyond talk to action. A deeper, more pragmatic and more structured foundation for co-operation had to be created, one that ironically would combine greater structure with more constructive and non-bureaucratic collaboration: the New Transatlantic Agenda.[48]

The New Transatlantic Agenda

It was in part thanks to the special interest the Spanish presidency showed in revivifying transatlantic relations that the New Transatlantic Agenda (NTA) came into existence on 3 December 1995, after short but intensive negotiations. In order to implement the agreement more quickly, it was not submitted to parliamentary or congressional ratification. Instead it is a non-binding executive agreement rather than a formal treaty.

The NTA has important features that the 1990 Transatlantic Dialogue lacked. In the first place, it is global in scope. It increased the number of mandatory meetings and contained a built-in follow-up mechanism that could assess progress and make adjustments if necessary through the Senior Level Group (SLG) of top officials whose work spans all three of the pillars of the European Union. The SLG prepares the discussions at the summit meetings with the aim of identifying 'deliverables' that can be achieved. Before each new US–EU summit, these officials assess the past half-year and draw up new priorities that could serve as a guide for the next. The SLG monitors the agenda's implementation, and seeks to overcome obstacles that remain. Emphasising that the SLG and other NTA bodies must be more accountable for the work they do, the United States began to refer to the SLG as the Senior Level Co-ordinating Group, or SLCG. The added C signals the higher expectations Washington has of the SLG. The United States also asked that the number of representatives attending meetings at various levels be reduced, especially from the European side, in order to hold participants responsible for following up on the decisions reached in the discussions.[49]

The idea was to make the biannual summit meetings, attended by the United States and EC Presidents and the country holding the presidency of the EU Council, more successful. Unlike summits under the Transatlantic Dialogue, which had low expectations, such meetings under the NTA are intended to create diplomatic momentum, overcome deadlocks, show a sense of direction, and attract public attention to European–American collaboration on important issues. Timetables and agendas are, to a great extent, summit-driven. It was assumed that matters agreed upon in such limelight could not easily be reversed later. Top leaders were supposed to feel the pressure to deliver significant results every six months. The importance of these meetings is shown by the fact that no US–EU summit was ever postponed or cancelled for political reasons. Summits were to be key parts of a vital relationship. Because of on-going discussions on how the summits could be made more productive, no meeting was held at the end of the Belgian presidency in December 2001.[50]

Summits cover a large number of subjects. For instance, the topics discussed at the 14 June 2001 summit in Göteborg, Sweden, ranged from the Balkans, Korea, Colombia, Russia, co-operation in Africa to prevent the spread of communicable diseases, a settlement of the war in Central Africa, support of the peace process in Ethiopia and Eritrea, the spread of weapons of mass destruction, disarmament, control of arms exports and human rights. In Göteborg strategic themes, handed up from lower-level task forces, were adopted, although new priorities always appear in such a dynamic relationship. These task forces also follow up on the meetings. One of the main purposes of this summit was to allow Europeans to size up the new American President, George W. Bush, whose policies since taking office five months earlier, such as missile defence and the refusal to support the Kyoto Protocol on global warming, had caused worry and consternation in Europe.

The European Commission had adopted a communication on 20 March 2001 questioning the wisdom of dealing with such a vast range of issues during a one-day summit. The paper expressed Commission fears that the entire process was becoming too bureaucratic, cumbersome and unwieldy, and it emphasised the need to establish more stringent priorities in order to make the NTA more productive. It suggested a slimming down of the agenda, limiting of strategic themes to such issues as emerging security challenges, globalisation and the multilateral trading system, the fight against organised crime, energy, consumer protection, macroeconomic issues, the fight against poverty in developing countries, and the digital economy. From the US side came the suggestion that the frequency of summits be limited in order to allow more time for preparation and follow-up and to make the summits truly 'action-forcing events'. Washington increasingly had the impression that the summits had become end-of-presidency trappings.[51]

To assist the SLG, a special NTA Task Force was created at the director level to prepare SLG meetings, which meet twice per presidency, and to handle all issues, including foreign-policy ones, which did not require the involvement of higher-level leaders. The Task Force generally meets four times during a presidency. Both bodies include in their discussions a wide range of experts in order to get accurate updates on the state of current problems and to encourage those specialists to think in a transatlantic way as they go about their work. In addition to these high-level bodies, there are many other layers of NTA co-operation, from biannual meetings of Foreign Ministers and commissioners, *ad hoc* consultations at the ministerial level, biannual meetings at the political director level, regular meetings at the expert or working group level, regular dialogue among heads of embassies in selected third-country capitals, and finally at the level of bureaucratic apparatuses. Thus there is room for considerable 'bottom up' input in this process.[52]

The NTA upgrades the level of mutual commitments and identifies four areas for co-operation containing 203 bilateral, regional and global objectives: The first is 'promoting peace and stability, democracy and developments around the world'. This political section included the earmarking of specific countries and regions for attention: Yugoslavia and the work of the War Crimes Tribunal in the Hague; Russia, Ukraine, Eastern and Central Europe; promoting the peace process in the Middle East; sharing responsibilities elsewhere in the world, such as Africa and the Far East; working together in such areas as nuclear non-proliferation, the control of arms transfers and work toward international disarmament; and co-operation in humanitarian assistance, which is of great interest to a cost-conscious United States that until 2002 steadily reduced its foreign aid budget. In 1995 the United States added a USAID representative to its staff at USEU in order to enhance co-ordination of international assistance with the European Union, whose members spend more on such aid than does the United States.[53] The second goal is 'responding to global challenges'. This encompasses such threats as international crime, drug trafficking, mass migration, the degradation of the environment, nuclear safety, disease, and – an issue that took on much more salience after 11 September 2001 – terrorism.

The third and most substantive goal and the one that dealt with the source of most transatlantic tension was that of 'contributing to the expansion of world trade and closer economic relations'. The NTA explicitly links security with commercial relations: the transatlantic 'economic relationship sustains our security and increases our prosperity'. The partners pledged to co-operate in the proper functioning of the WTO, where the two sides have taken more and more of their disputes to adjudication. To show the partners' willingness to tackle some of the most contentious elements of their bilateral trade, both the NTA and Joint Action Plan (JAP) called for a New Transatlantic Marketplace (NTM), intended to do away with trade barriers. It listed fourteen specific problem areas and called for joint study by both sides to facilitate trade in goods and services and to reduce or eliminate tariff and non-tariff barriers. EC trade commissioner Leon Brittan attempted in March 1998 to get NMT off the ground, but it was defeated by the member states themselves at an EU Foreign Ministers' meeting on 27 April 1998.[54]

The Joint Action Plan

The fourth section of the NTA calls for 'building bridges across the Atlantic'. This contains numerous practical proposals aimed at 'deepening and broadening the commercial, social, cultural, scientific and educational ties' among the Atlantic peoples. It calls for strengthening 'people to people' links though internships, scholarships and other forms of educational exchange. The most important of these bridges was the innovative and flexible Joint Action Plan (JAP) that is geared to the most pressing problems and which can be updated when new problems appear. It encompasses the Transatlantic Business

Dialogue (TABD) and other dialogues, which involve CEOs and other top non-governmental leaders in their fields, who meet and identify concrete problems that the nations' political elites need to deal with within the framework of NTA. In other words, JAP adds an important dimension to the relationship by extending it beyond the governmental and into the private sector and civil society. Levine called the TABD, which has developed its own unofficial structure, directors and officers and substantial budget, 'probably the first time in American history that the private sector is determining the substance of future executive or legislative agreements'.[55]

TABD was first proposed by former Commerce Secretary Ron Brown, who believed that international business was at least five years in advance of governments in its thinking about international trade. TABD introduced a 'score card' system of assessing the status of each issue, what still has to be done, and a recommended date for implementation. For instance, its 1998 Mid-year Scorecard Report concluded that American and EU administrations had taken 'significant, concrete action' on about one-third of TABD's recommendations. More than 500 business and government leaders participated in the 1998 TABD conference in Charlotte, North Carolina. They were divided into fifty-two working groups. Demonstrating its flexibility, TABD reduced the number of participants to CEOs and high-level government officials in order to achieve greater efficiency in smaller, less formal meetings. TABD introduced a new atmosphere in transatlantic trade talks by taking much of the combativeness out of its discussions. Cowles concludes, 'the practical, co-operative, results-oriented TABD business strategy has proven successful', and it provided a good example of how the 'bottom up' approach, in contrast to the traditional 'top-down' interaction of US–EU government actors, can work.[56]

William Wallace alluded to the need for popular input into the active governmental co-operation on a wide range of issues. Such collaboration is 'too technically detailed and complicated to make good copy for the press'. He argues that it is even invisible to the public and to most politicians. Thus, when disputes flare up or when co-ordination breaks down, parliamentarians and journalists cry betrayal and foreign interference. 'The gap between transgovernmental co-operation and domestic understanding is as wide within Europe as within the United States.'[57]

There are other 'bottom up' dialogue groups that have sprung to life within the context of JAP and that introduce civil society into US–EU relations. They include the Transatlantic Labour Dialogue, the Transatlantic Legislators' Dialogue and the Transatlantic Civil Society Dialogue. A Transatlantic Small Business Initiative (TASBI) facilitates business partnering. A Transatlantic Donors Dialogue (TADD) brings together private foundations and governmental agencies that finance US–EU people-to-people projects. A Transatlantic Information Exchange Service (TIES) offers an on-line directory of Web links about joint projects and relations. These many dialogues are guaranteed access to leaders and Ministers at summits on a rotating basis, and the relevant

authorities commit themselves to providing them with updates on the implementation of their recommendations. They are also encouraged to develop contacts among themselves.[58]

Christopher Piening called the NTA and JAP 'the first attempt by the
European Union and the United States to identify and tackle an inventory of
objectives perceived by both to be important not only in terms of their bilateral
relationship but also of their roles as world leaders'. Desmond Dinan notes that
this 'political game plan' is heavily weighted with words like 'co-operation',
'reinforce' and 'pursue'. He is not persuaded that NTA has lived up to its expectations. He argues, 'beyond formalizing and making obligatory meetings
among senior officials that had already been taking place on an *ad hoc* basis,
the NTA cannot be said to have substantially improved transatlantic co-
operation'.[59]

Former US ambassador Richard Morningstar found that NTA had become
overly bureaucratised. His deputy political counsellor, Peter Mulrean, agrees
but was a bit more sanguine. Meeting in about twenty sets of foreign policy
forums at the deputy assistant secretary level – that is to say, involving that level
of people who make the day-to-day decisions – the two sides take on substantive issues. There is a strong desire to understand what the other is doing.
According to Mulrean, US officials tell their EU counterparts more than they
would tell others. These discussions span many topics, such as China, Taiwan,
Korea, India, the WTO, Africa, AIDS and human rights. The participants do not
always make decisions at the end of their meetings, but they may offer fruitful
suggestions that will be taken up subsequently. Further, the US ambassador
meets with the EU presidency's ambassador every Wednesday before he joins all
EU ambassadors in the regular weekly meetings on Thursday.[60]

Winand and Philippart have a generally positive view of NTA and JAP and
argue that they upgraded the level of commitments. They carefully analysed
the many commitments made and divided them as follows: 32 per cent are
restricted to the exchange of information, dialogues and consultation; a further
27 per cent consist of encouragement and co-ordination of initiatives; another
35 per cent deal with co-operation, and only 6 per cent involve joint action.
They conclude that the achievements on average were 'between consultation
and co-ordination' and that they fall below the objectives and are 'far from the
generalisation of joint actions suggested by the Joint Action Plan'. However,
they judged the policy output to be 'superior to any previous US–EC record and
to the record of any similar US or EU partnership', except those with immediately neighbouring countries, such as Canada and Mexico for the United States
or Central and Eastern European aspirants to EU membership.[61]

Both the NTA and the JAP widen the scope of the transatlantic relationship
by moving co-operation to the global stage and by dealing with worldwide, not
merely regional, challenges. According to Richard A. Morford, Director of the
State Department's Office of European Union and Regional Affairs, NTA/JAP
keeps non-urgent but important issues on the agenda. By focusing on the

other's problems, NTA/JAP brings differing perspectives to the table in a way that forces the partners to address them. This allows them to survey the extent of the relationship and to see where they are not dealing with things in a parallel manner. In short, NTA and JAP help both sides track the relationship and prod their bureaucrats.

NTA/JAP aimed at results, but it intentionally left out some long-standing disagreements, such as the treatment of 'states of concern', where the resolution of differences was unlikely. The founders of NTA wanted the heightened level of co-operation to be successful and to be popular in citizens' eyes. They hoped that, by creating a framework for a dense network of talks and co-operation, the ultimate achievement would be a revitalised Atlantic spirit and sense of community among Americans and Europeans.

In a speech to the European Parliament on 16 May 2001 Chris Patten said it was a good thing that the NTA shifted the focus of the relationship from consultation to joint action. This co-operation now embraces every area of EU activity.

> And rightly so. No one shares our vision, our history, and our values as much as the United States. With no one else do we have such a wide range of common interests, such a fine-meshed network of co-operation at all levels of society and such a strong economic base to build on. . . . When the US and the EU work together, we set the international agenda. If we are divided, the opportunity for international progress is often lost.

The US Mission to the European Union in Brussels

Politically speaking, Brussels and Washington are very similar towns. Information is widely available and power is relatively broadly distributed. Neither the United States nor the European Union has concentrated power at the top, although the European Union has far weaker central authority and much more powerful member states than the United States. Such decentralisation requires American and European diplomats, businesspersons and lobbyists to aim their activity at many different levels. To be able to do this, both the United States and the European Union maintain missions in each other's capital.[62]

The United States has had diplomatic relations with the predecessors of the European Union since the creation of the European Coal and Steel Community (ECSC) in 1951. It opened an American Mission to the ECSC in Luxembourg in 1956, then broadened its scope in 1961 to include the European Economic Community (EEC) and EURATOM and moved it to Brussels. Thus from the beginning the US Mission has made the kind of structural and functional changes necessary both to adapt to the evolution of integration in Europe and to serve the growing EU priority in American foreign policy. The very name eventually assumed by the office – the US Mission to the European Union

(USEU) – reflects Washington's recognition of the European Union not only as an economic force, but as a political one as well. For instance, in the latter part of the 1990s the USEU was the only US diplomatic office abroad to increase its staff. In 2001 the number of diplomats assigned to USEU had grown to nineteen.[63]

The assignments of the American diplomats in the USEU reveal how the work has shifted from primarily economic tasks to a roughly equal blend of political/security work and economic activity. Ambassador Morningstar indicated that he spent as much time on political/defence matters as on economic affairs. An important consequence of this shift is that the atmosphere changed. The economic relationship between the US and Europe has traditionally been competitive and sometimes combative. It pits the interests of the United States against those of the EU countries. However, in foreign policy the two sides are talking about third countries and overall global objectives. Those aims are quite similar on both sides: the rule of law, respect for human rights, free and open economies, and stability. It is only the tactics for achieving them that sometimes differ. Thus diplomats on both sides must guard against allowing the corrosive dimension of the trade relationship to slip into the political field. 'Foreign policy is not a zero-sum game,' to use the words of Peter Mulrean.

While broadening the range of its work, the mission's personnel have striven successfully to understand how to influence and work with one of the globe's most complicated hybrid, semi-sovereign governmental entities. As Dinan reports, many EU officials complain that Americans do not know much about the European Union. Former US ambassador to the European Union Stuart Eizenstat, who played a key role in infusing a sense of energy into the relationship and shaping the mission into an effective vehicle of American influence, admitted to a journalist upon his arrival in Brussels in the early 1990s that the United States had 'a major problem in dealing with the EC. It doesn't understand quite what it is. There is an information void.' A half-decade later, Dinan concluded that academic study of the European Union was as sophisticated in the United States as in Europe and that American officials and businesspeople are very well informed about how it works. He points to the mission and the EU Committee of American Chambers of Commerce, whose task is to represent the interests of European subsidiaries of American companies, as being among the most effective lobbyists in Brussels.[64]

The European Union is 'one big inter-agency process'. It is not entirely transparent, and overlapping competences of the various players and institutions make it difficult to determine what decisions are made and who makes them. External Relations Commissioner Chris Patten acts for the European Commission and has financial resources at his disposal. The appointment of a High Representative for the CFSP, Javier Solana, whose duties are not clearly defined but who functions within the European Council, helps provide more co-ordination.

The Political and Security Committee (normally referred to by its French acronym, COPS) following the Amsterdam Treaty of 1997 promises to clarify decision making even further. Although still new and understaffed, it is significant in that it is composed of fifteen capable and ambitious ambassadors dealing with CFSP who live and work in Brussels. Before COPS, senior civil servants would fly into Brussels infrequently, meet, and then return home. COPS constitutes a standing committee of senior officials who meet two or three times a week and are on hand to deal with unexpected issues. They are more likely to find consensus and compromise because they work constantly together. Their decisions must go through COREPER, who are responsible for all decisions that are handed up to the commissioners and who remain jealous of their powers. Thus there is still competition and rivalry. Nevertheless, Peter Mulrean calls this innovation 'the Brusselisation of CFSP' and considers it the most significant development in CFSP during the period 1996–2001. COPS 'will increase EU activism in EU foreign policy. . . . It will make things happen.'

American diplomats are still presented with many different officials in Brussels who have a role in the foreign-policy process. These include, in particular, Chris Patten and Javier Solana, who provide a sense of continuity. One interlocutor might be favoured over the other, depending on the issue. For example, Patten, as an official in the Commission, has access to more resources than does Solana, who is more of a co-ordinator. Former Secretary of State Madelaine Albright developed the routine of phoning Patten and Solana every weekend. Her successor, Colin Powell, called Solana daily during the war in Afghanistan and at least weekly in normal times. They also deal with the Foreign Minister of the six-month presidency, despite the constant shifting priorities of the presidencies, because the country occupying the presidency at any one time can stall the agenda. In a crisis, US diplomats talk to every EU player, as well as engaging bilaterally with the most significant EU members on a national basis.[65]

The EC delegation in Washington

The EC's delegation in Washington DC is one of 126 EU diplomatic representations throughout the world and was the first mission that the forerunners to the European Union created anywhere. It originated in 1954 as an information office, led by the lawyer George Ball, who earlier had helped draft the Schumann Plan. It was born of the concern by Europeans, such as Jean Monnet, that American support for European integration would be undermined by the bitter debates in Europe over the European Defence Community (EDC). He feared that the Eisenhower administration and Congress would mistakenly conclude that Europe had lost its ardour for integration.

Since 1964 the Commission has maintained an office in New York, which serves as a delegation to the United Nations. In 1971 the Washington office became a delegation, with full diplomatic privileges and immunities, and its head gained full ambassadorial status in 1990; often this person is referred to in Washington as the 'EU ambassador', which is technically incorrect. It differs from a standard embassy in that it lacks such functions as consular or military affairs; it deals very little with the Pentagon. Its staff of more than eighty continues to serve as an EU informational resource for Washington and the rest of the United States, as well as representing the Commission in its dealings with the US government for all matters within EU competence. It lobbies, maintains contacts with dozens of departments and agencies, develops relationships in Congress, delivers *démarches* through the State Department, gives instructions and reports back to Brussels information of interest to the European Union.

The European Commission's diplomats face the same tangled complex of institutions in Washington as their American counterparts find in Brussels. There is no one office in Washington that co-ordinates US policy toward the European Union. The State Department has the major responsibility for handling daily contacts with the Union, and out of courtesy the EC delegation keeps State informed about its dealings with other US agencies and departments. But the White House, the Congress (which since 1974 has also dealt directly with the European Parliament), the US Trade Representative, USAID, and the Commerce, Treasury and Agriculture Departments all vie for access and influence. At the same time, these often competing institutions deal directly with the embassies of the member states on varying issues. Like the USEU, the EC delegation in Washington is deeply involved in the many parts of the NTA/JAP. In general, both the USEU and its counterpart in the American capital have made an important contribution to US–EU relations.[66]

Conclusion

Transatlantic co-operation is of vital importance for both the United States and Europe, and it takes place in a wide variety of arenas. Nevertheless, it is more effective in some forums than in others. NATO is the forum that offers the United States the greatest opportunity to exercise leadership in Europe. It has served the longest as a channel for exchanging views, reaching compromises and making decisions. The post-Cold War commitments and programmes of the Atlantic Alliance have greatly broadened the scope of transatlantic co-operation by taking it to the outer limits of Europe and into Central Asia to the Chinese border. The decision taken at the November 2002 Prague summit to create a Reaction Force for use anywhere in the world officially ended the previous sanctity of NATO's operational limits within the North Atlantic area.

NATO is more instrumental in drawing Russia into a dramatically changed post-Cold War Europe than is the European Union. It was within the walls of NATO that the former enemies formalised their new partnership, and NATO discussions over such issues as enlargement or warfare in the Balkans are bellwethers for the state of relations between the Western democracies and Russia. NATO's process of enlargement moved more quickly than that of the European Union, so the Alliance played an earlier role in binding smaller ex-Communist states to the West. NATO's preconditions for entry – democratic government, civilian control, respect for minority rights, settlement of border disputes – were significant in keeping the new democracies on a reform course. It was also within NATO that the United States sought and received its most important military assistance in the war against terrorism and diplomatic backing in dealing with Iraq.

Sub-groups of NATO thicken the web of transcontinental multilateral ties. The Partnership for Peace programme and the Euro-Atlantic Partnership Council (EAPC) provide the transatlantic allies with a means of listening to, and communicating with, states in Central and Eastern Europe as well as with friends in Central Asia. NATO fosters joint involvement in the Middle East through the Mediterranean Dialogue, although the European Union is a more useful partner in that region because of its direct involvement in the peace process and the large amount of financial assistance it gives to the Palestinians.

In the 1990s European–US co-operation has intensified in organisational settings other than NATO, and these institutions have facilitated transatlantic collaboration. The United States has learnt to work more closely with its allies through such bodies as the OSCE. The OSCE is a platform for practical co-operation among all European countries and the United States and Canada, and it is an arena where Western allies can work together with Russia. It is a laboratory for the European Union's CFSP and its interaction with US diplomats. It helps move American–European foreign policy co-operation to the global stage. It also assumes some necessary tasks, such as overseeing compliance with the Conventional Forces in Europe agreement, to which the United States is a party.

The United States can never belong to the European Union, as it does to NATO, and its occasional efforts to influence EU policy directly, such as its lobbying the European Union to open accession talks with Turkey, are often resented as inappropriate meddling. However, it is through US–EU co-operation and interaction that the world's largest and most powerful economic relationship is managed. In addition to working with EU initiatives stemming from its Common Foreign and Security Policy, the two sides of the Atlantic have constructed a pragmatic and tightly structured framework in the shape of the New Transatlantic Agenda to systematise their dialogue. The NTA, whose scope is global, and its accompanying Joint Action Plan have tried to identify and deal with objectives found to be important not only in terms of the partners' bilateral relationship, but also in terms of their role as world leaders. The NTA has provided a forum for discussing important common interests, but its most optimistic goals have not been met. Both sides complain that the elaborate process has become too bureaucratised and unwieldy. The semi-annual summits, though useful, have not created the kind of diplomatic momentum to overcome deadlocks and to attract the attention of publics on both sides of the Atlantic to the ways Europeans and Americans can and do collaborate on important issues. At best co-operation has been sporadic.

Nevertheless, the United States and the Europeans have taken on a wide range of substantive issues, and there is a strong desire to continue discussing within the institutions of the NTA and JAP what the other is doing. The NTA and JAP have brought differing perspectives to the table in a way that forces the partners to address them. They have helped both sides track the relationship and prod their bureaucrats. Perhaps most significantly, they have widened the scope of the transatlantic relationship by moving co-operation to the global stage and by dealing with worldwide, not merely regional, challenges.

Notes

1 Dehaene quote in Anthony Gardner, 'From the Transatlantic Declaration to the New Transatlantic Agenda: the shaping of institutional mechanisms and policy objectives by national and supranational actors', in Eric Philippart and Pascaline Winand (eds), *Ever Closer Partnership: Policy Making in US–EU Relations* (Brussels: Lang, 2001), p. 97. Frances G. Burwell, 'Co-operation in US–European relations', in Burwell and Ivo H. Daalder, *The United States and Europe in the Global Arena* (New York: St Martin's Press, 1999), pp. 276–8.

2 Malcolm Chalmers, 'The Atlantic burden-sharing debate: widening or fragmenting?' *International Affairs*, 77: 3 (2001), p. 569. See David Calleo, *Rethinking Europe's Future* (Princeton NJ: Princeton University Press, 2001), chapters 14 and 16.

3 Thomas Frellesen, 'Processes and procedures in EU–US foreign policy co-operation: from the Transatlantic Declaration to the New Transatlantic Agenda', in Philippart and Winand, *Ever Closer Partnership*, p. 317. See John W. Holmes, *The United States and Europe after the Cold War: A New Alliance?* (Columbia SC: University of South Carolina Press, 1997).

4 Prodi quote in EU Institutions Press Release, 12 September 2001. Polling statistics in 'Allies express solidarity and caution' (22 September 2001), p. A19; 'Global grieving: world unites in time of sorrow' (15 September 2001), p. A19, both in *The Washington Post*. Blair quote in 'Slipstream diplomacy', *Economist*, 24 November 2001, p. 55.

5 Trade statistics from EC delegation in Washington publication *Facts and Figures*, others from Charles Grant, 'Euro-muscle', *Washington Post*, 8 July 2001, p. B2.

6 Christopher Piening, *Global Europe: The European Union in World Affairs* (Boulder CO: Lynne Rienner, 1997), pp. 93, 103–4; Desmond Dinan, *Ever Closer Union: An Introduction to European Integration* (2nd edn, Boulder CO: Lynne Rienner, 1999), pp. 531–2, 537–8; Youri Devuyst, 'European Unity in Transatlantic Commercial Diplomacy' in Philippart and Winand, *Ever Closer Partnership*, pp. 283–4, 312; Stephen Woolcock, 'The United States and the European Union in the global economy', and Frances G. Burwell, 'Co-operation in US–European relations', in Burwell and Daalder, *The United States and Europe*, pp. 177–82, 194–5, 285–6.

7 Dinan, *Ever Closer Union*, p. 533; Piening, *Global Europe*, p. 101.

8 K. W. Deutsch *et al.*, *Political Community and the North Atlantic Area* (Princeton NJ: Princeton University Press, 1957), pp. 5–9, 36; Ivo H. Daalder, 'Are the United States and Europe heading for divorce?' *International Affairs*, 77: 3 (2001), p. 554. See Alan K. Henrikson, 'The role of metropolitan regions in making a new Atlantic community', in Philippart and Winand, *Ever Closer Partnership*, pp. 187–205.

9   Piening, *Global Europe*, p. 95; Kennedy in Henrikson, 'Metropolitan regions', p. 208.

10 William Wallace, 'Europe, the necessary partner', *Foreign Affairs*, 80: 3 (2001), p. 20; Craig Kennedy and Marshall M. Bouton, 'The real transatlantic gap', *Foreign Policy*, November–December 2002, pp. 68, 70.

11 Morningstar speech at the College of Europe, Bruges, 17 April 2001; interviews with Mulrean by Alicia Ambos and author, 6 March and 21 June 2001.

12 Prodi in *EU–US News: A Review of Transatlantic Relations*, 2: 7 (2001), p. 3.

13 Rice, 'A mission to build on common challenges', *Washington Times*, 11 June 2001.

14 Wallace, 'Europe', p. 22; Daalder, 'Divorce', pp. 553, 556; Dinan, *Ever Closer Union*, p. 532.

15 'Setting a new perimeter', 22 September 2001, pp. 34–5, and 'Toughening up', 8 December 2001, p. 37, both in *The Economist*; 'US relations change suddenly for Mexico', *Washington Post*, 21 September 2001, p. A32, and 'Fair-weather friends?' *Economist*, 22 September 2001, p. 35.

16 Conversation with Mary Ruth Coleman, Office of European Union and Regional Affairs, US Department of State, 16 November 2001; author interview with Mulrean. Brad Roberts, 'Managing proliferation: a view from the United States', in Burwell and Daalder, *United States and Europe*, pp. 148–9; see also pp. 289–90.

17 Prodi quotes from speeches of 11 and 24 October 2001, EC Press Room.

18 Daalder, 'Divorce', p. 554; Roger Cohen, 'Schröder to visit Bush, bearing Europe's new concerns', *New York Times*, 29 March 2001.

19 'Die USA beobachten ihre europäischen Verbündeten sehr genau', *Die Welt*, 8 November 2001, p. 7.

20 Former SACEUR, General Wesley K. Clark, described NATO as a 'consensus engine'. See his description of how co-operation functions within the Alliance in Clark, *Waging Modern War: Bosnia, Kosovo, and the Future of Combat* (New York: Public Affairs, 2001), pp. 14–15.

21 Daalder, 'Divorce', pp. 561–2. Polling statistics in 'Europeans object to Bush approach on foreign policy', *Washington Post*, 16 August 2001. 'Europäer halten nur wenig von George Bush', *Nordamerikanische Wochen-Post*, 25 August 2001, p. 1.

22 John Peterson, 'Shaping, not making: the impact of the American Congress on US–EU relations', in Philippart and Winand, *Ever Closer Partnership*, pp. 184–6.

23 Nixon quote in Pascaline Winand and Eric Philippart, 'From "equal partnership" to the "New Transatlantic Agenda": enduring features and successive forms of the US–EU relationship', in Philippart and Winand, *Ever Closer Partnership*, p. 39; see also p. 14; Wallace, 'Europe', p. 18 ; Dinan, *Ever Closer Union*, p. 532.

24 Günther Nonnenmacher, 'Equivocally European', *Frankfürter Allgemeine Zeitung*, English edition, 7 November 2001, p. 3.

25 Antony J. Blinken, 'The false crisis over the Atlantic', *Foreign Affairs*, 80: 3 (2001), p. 45. Chris Patten, 'Weltpolitik, warum nicht?' *Die Zeit*, 25 (2001). See Dinan, *Ever Closer Union*, pp. 70–1.

26 Burwell, 'Co-operation', p. 279. Note that the highest-ranking NATO leader is the Secretary General, who is always a European. The SACEUR answers both to the Secretary General and to the US Secretary of Defense. General Wesley Clark explained how the permission to use military force in Kosovo had to come first from Secretary General Javiar Solana: 'Wes, you have the executive order for Phase I of the air campaign. I am giving you the execute order. You will have it in writing tomorrow morning, but this is the order, do you understand?' The SACEUR, whose

deputy is always a European, heads the integrated command structure at the Supreme Headquarters Allied Powers Europe (SHAPE) in Mons, Belgium. The highest military officer who directs the military work at NATO headquarters in Brussels is also always a European, the Chairman of the Military Committee. (Clark, *Waging Modern War*, pp. 14–15, 98, 189; quote on p. 182.) Allies at the NATO summit in Prague in November 2002 agreed to streamline the military structure by creating an operations command in Brussels and a 'transformation' command in the United States.

27 See John Newhouse, *Europe Adrift* (New York: Pantheon Books, 1997), chapter VII.

28 Speech at the Netherlands Institute of International Relations in Clingendael, 23 March 2001.

29 'NATO sets new council, giving Russia a limited role', 7 December 2001, p. A47; 'Powell, Russian discuss NATO', 8 December 2001, p. A22; 'Russia's place', 9 December 2001, all in *The Washington Post*. 'Putin eases stance on NATO expansion', 4 October 2001, p. A1; 'US, Russia recast their relationship', 4 October 2001, pp. A14–15; 'A new alliance could nudge aside the old', 4 November 2001, p. B5; 'NATO and Russia reinventing relationship', 15 November 2001, p. A42; 'NATO explores giving Moscow expanded role', 24 November 2001, and 'Anti-terror war binds US, Russian militaries', 3 May 2002, all in *The Washington Post*. See Paul Flenle, 'Russia in the new Europe', in Fergus Carr (ed.), *Europe: The Cold Divide* (New York: St Martin's Press, 1998). Putin quote in 'NATO gives Russia formal welcome', *New York Times*, 29 May 2002.

30 'Bush gets down to work on a Russia action plan' and 'Bush view of Putin as trustworthy goes too far, Democrats say', both in *International Herald Tribune*, 19 June 2001.

31 Samuel R. Berger, 'Putin's reality trip', *Washington Post*, 15 November 2001, p. A47.

32 'Der Kalte Krieg ist vorbei', *Das Parlament*, 28 September 2001, p. 1; 'Suddenly cosier with the West', *Economist*, 6 October 2001.

33 'A new arms game', *Newsweek*, 24 December 2001, p. 34. Bush quote in 'Putin questions US terror allies', *New York Times*, 23 November 2002, p. A10.

34 Putin quote in Jim Hoagland, 'George and Vladimir have work to do', *International Herald Tribune*, 5 February 2002. Ivanov quote in 'Formal talks on nuclear cuts to begin next month', *Washington Post*, 18 December 2001, p. A24. 'Missile defense to start in 2004', *Washington Post*, 18 December 2002, p. A1.

35 'Bush, Putin announce nuclear arms cuts' and 'Leaders tout spirit of partnership', both in *The Washington Post*, 14 November 2001, pp. A1, A6–7; 'Now, Yalta on the fly', *Newsweek*, 26 November 2001, p. 41; 'A touching of fingertips', *Economist*, 17 November 2001, pp. 25–6.

36 'Azerbaijan, Armenia get break', *Washington Post*, 16 December 2001, p. A26.

37 Author interview with William Scofield, OSCE co-ordinator at the US State Department, 17 December 2001.

38 'Fifty-five nations endorse measures to fight terrorism', *Washington Post*, 5 December 2001.

39 'Rumsfeld tells GIs in Kyrgyzstan to be ready for a long war', 27 April 2002, and 'Russia shows power in Kyrgyz air space', 6 December 2002, both in *The Washington Post*.

40 'US to base troops, planes in Uzbekistan', 'Uzbekistan bets role in region, internal security on US alliance. Collaboration against Taliban is chance leader can't lose'

and 'US operated covert alliance with Uzbekistan', all in *The Washington Post*, 6, 9, 14 October 2001. Powell quote in 'Footprints in Steppes of Central Asia', *Washington Post*, 9 February 2002, pp. A1, A16. The Bush administration also asked Congress to lift trade restrictions against eight former Soviet republics to reward them for their help in the fight against terrorism. ('New trade relations sought for eight countries', *Washington Post*, 6 January 2002.)

41 'A new Age of Solidarity? Don't count on it', 2 November 2001, and Ronald D. Asmus, 'United we'll stand', 6 May 2002, p. A21, both in *The Washington Post*. Unpopular in Europe before the attacks, Bush impressed European leaders after 11 September by his measured tones and his determined and successful effort to build an impressive international coalition, including many Muslim states, to support his government's military course of action. Chancellor Schröder praised the American leadership team as 'intelligent, not just clever'. He had become a more trusted leader with a respected team of advisers, especially Secretary of State Colin Powell. ('Schroeder ready to provide anti-bioterror forces', *International Herald Tribune*, 18 October 2001, p. 1.)

42 Bush quote in 'In blunt words, Bush threatens Hussein again', 21 November 2002, p. A18, and Robertson quote in 'After NATO's year of identity crisis, a defining meeting', 4 November 2002, both in *The New York Times*. General Jones is the first SACEUR to have been born in Europe. Born in Paris, where he spent much of his youth, he is fluent in French.

43 'NATO quietly slips into Afghan mission', *Washington Post*, 12 December 2002, p. A36.

44 Gardner, 'From the Transatlantic Declaration', pp. 83–4. See his full-length study entitled *A New Era in EU–EU Relations? The Clinton Administration and the New Transatlantic Agenda* (Aldershot: Avebury Press, 1996).

45 Gardner, 'From the Transatlantic Declaration', pp. 84–5; Winand and Philippart, 'Equal partnership', pp. 42–4; Dinan, *Ever Closer Union*, p. 536; Piening, *Global Europe*, p. 109.

46 Winand and Philippart, 'Equal partnership', pp. 44–5.

47 Frellesen, 'Processes', pp. 319–20; Gardner, 'From the Transatlantic Declaration', pp. 85–6.

48 Gardner, 'From the Transatlantic Declaration', pp. 86–9; Dinan, *Ever Closer Union*, pp. 537–8; Winand and Philippart, 'Equal partnership', pp. 47–8.

49 Author interview with Richard A. Morford, Director of the State Department's Office of European Union and Regional Affairs, 17 December 2001.

50 Eric Philippart and Pascaline Winand, 'Ever closer partnership?' in Philippart and Winand, *Ever Closer Partnership*, pp. 77–8, 392–6, 424.

51 Communication of 20 March 2001, http:/europa.eu.int; Blinken, 'False crisis', p. 45; interview with Morford. Summits mix both harmony and discord. The May 2002 summit tilted heavily in favour of harmony to emphasise Europe's support of America's war against terrorism. ('US, EU reduce trade tensions', *Washington Post*, 3 May 2002.)

52 Frellesen, 'Processes', pp. 321–7. Frellesen notes that the set-up for the EU–US foreign policy dialogue closely follows the framework of the CFSP. Eric Philippart, 'Assessing, evaluating and explaining the output of US–EU relations', in Philippart and Winand, *Ever Closer Partnership*, pp. 59, 79; see also p. 396.

53 Pascaline Winand, 'The US Mission to the EU in Brussels, the European Commission

delegation in Washington DC and the New Transatlantic Agenda', in Philippart and Winand, *Ever Closer Partnership*, p. 116. For increase of US foreign aid see 'US wakes from twenty-year slumber in development field', *Financial Times*, 25 March 2002, p. 6.

54 Woolcock, 'Global economy', p. 199. NTM in Maria Green Cowles, 'Private firms and US–EU policymaking: the transatlantic business dialogue', in Philippart and Winand, *Ever Closer Partnership*, pp. 260–1, and Dinan, *Ever Closer Union*, p. 541.

55 N. Levine, 'A transatlantic bargain', *Journal of Commerce*, 10 May 1995, p. 6A; Piening, *Global Europe*, 108–12; Winand and Philippart, 'Equal partnership', p. 49.

56 Cowles, 'Private firms', pp. 259–65. According to the *Financial Times* of 3 March 2003, interest in the TABD dramatically dropped since it had failed to remove transatlantic trade barriers. Its Brussels office was closed, its Web site was not being updated and staff was deserting its Washington office.

57 Wallace, 'Europe', p. 32.

58 Philippart and Winand, *Ever Closer Partnership*, pp. 409–11.

59 Piening, *Global Europe*, p. 111; Dinan, *Ever Closer Union*, pp. 541–2.

60 Author meeting with Morningstar in Bruges, 17 April 2001; author interviews with Mulrean.

61 Winand and Philippart, 'Equal partnership', pp. 46–55, 450; see also pp. 106, 130–47, 360–2. Gardner, 'From the Transatlantic Declaration', p. 90. See Jörg Monar (ed.), *The New Transatlantic Agenda and the Future of EU–US Relations* (London: Kluwer, 1998).

62 Winand, 'US Mission', pp. 122–3.

63 *Ibid.*, pp. 107–13; author interview with Mulrean.

64 Eizenstat quote in Winand, 'US Mission', p. 121; see also p. 125. Dinan, *Ever Closer Union*, pp. 532–3; Daalder, 'Divorce', p. 555.

65 Mulrean interviews. *The Economist* called Solana 'a great schmoozer, his tendency to embrace his interlocutors has given new meaning to the phrase "hands-on diplomacy"'. ('Charlemagne Javier Solana', 17 November 2001, p. 52.)

66 Author interview with Willy Helin, EC delegation's Director of Press and Public Affairs, Washington DC, 17 December 2001.

6

American–European global co-operation

The opening of the New Transatlantic Agenda emphasises that the United States and the European Union share 'a common strategic vision of Europe's future security' and the 'indivisibility of transatlantic security'. This remains largely true, and they co-operate extensively on the global arena in a wide variety of forums. Their collaboration can be bilateral, such as the individual European nations offering military contingents to assist the US military effort in Afghanistan in 2001. It can be within NATO, such as the 1999 war in Kosovo, although the range of co-operative areas within the Atlantic Alliance is limited principally to military and security affairs and excludes such fields as development assistance, human rights and trade in non-military goods. When contentious questions arise, such as levying sanctions or dealing with states of concern, co-operation (or conflict) is more likely to occur outside the NTA context. Finally, the partners work together in a host of international governmental organisations, such as the United Nations.

Dialogue among the allies occurs on an *ad hoc* basis in the wings of a wide variety of multilateral meetings. Discussions take place between the European Union's Troika and the United States before many UN events. For instance, the United States co-ordinates with the fifteen EU ambassadors in an effort to pursue common approaches in the UN General Assembly. Americans and Europeans meet on the periphery of such gatherings as the World Conference on Women and the Social Summit. The European Union's presidency is responsible for the daily conduct of CFSP and keeps in touch with American officials and informs the other EU partners of these conversations.[1]

The United Nations is important for America's European partners, who contribute far more to the UN budget – 37 per cent of the overall budget and 39 per cent of the peacekeeping costs – than does the United States, which pledged in a compromise with the United Nations in January 2001 to contribute 22 per cent of the total budget, down from 25 per cent, and 25 per cent of the peacekeeping costs, down from 31 per cent. Also, Europe's payments were never in arrears, in contrast to the United States', which withheld a portion of its dues for years until Washington's renewed need for international support following the 11 September 2001 terrorist attacks prompted the House of Representatives to release $582 million of the $862 million owed. This decision was a reflection of how the international political landscape had changed since the terrorist strikes. It reminded the United States that such international organisations are useful when America is in crisis. In the words of Representative Tom Lantos, the top Democrat on the House International Relations Committee, 'as President Bush, Secretary Powell and our nation's diplomatic corps begin to secure the concrete commitments required to wage this battle against terrorism, they must take advantage of every forum available to reach out to the nations of the world'.[2]

The United States' image was tarnished by its inclination sometimes to treat the United Nations as a nuisance, by its deliberate provocation of withholding a portion of its annual dues, and by the early Bush administration's insistence that certain high-profile treaties should not apply to the United States. The cumulative effect of these policies came on 3 May 2001, when the United States was voted off the UN Human Rights Commission in Geneva for the first time, and France, Austria and Sweden won the three seats allotted to the West. Although the reasons are complex, and include the fact that the United States had still not confirmed its UN ambassador and refused to campaign hard for its seat, its European allies tipped the scales in the vote. There was disgruntlement over Washington's refusal to ratify treaties that would forbid land mines or set up an International Criminal Court. In short, America's seeming disdain for multilateralism had eroded its influence in the world body.[3]

Unilateralism and multilateralism

Multilateralism has an important place in American foreign policy although the United States' power and respect for its own sovereignty sometimes allow it to act unilaterally when its principles and convictions are at stake. Powell expressed this in these words: 'We believe in multilateralism. But when it is a matter of principle, and when the multilateral community does not agree with us, we do not shrink from doing that which we think is right, which is in our own interest, even if some of our friends disagree with us.'[4]

At the same time, unilateralism has deep roots in American history, and it is a source of tension and disagreement between the United States and its European allies today. George Washington warned in his 'Farewell Address' against 'entangling alliances', especially with European nations. The Monroe Doctrine unilaterally put the western hemisphere off limits for foreign exploitation and colonisation. President Woodrow Wilson's Fourteen Points were proclaimed unilaterally, but nevertheless they played an important role in ending the First World War and in the Versailles peace conference that followed. The Truman Doctrine, that drew a line to prevent the spread of communism after the Second World War, was declared unilaterally. President John F. Kennedy unilaterally declared the United States would cease all nuclear testing in the atmosphere if the Soviet Union did the same, and President George H. W. Bush announced in 1992 that the United States would unilaterally stop nuclear testing of all kinds, a policy that has not changed. In a disorderly world that was and is still organised and shaped by sovereign states, the power to act alone is a necessary attribute of that sovereignty. This is not isolationism; this is an option of a sovereign country that has maintained the power to act alone when it believes it must do so. The United States seeks to maximise its freedom of action in order to cope with the exterior threats it faces and to serve its values.[5]

This determination is strongest in the US Congress, although some key senators, such as Richard Lugar, who again became chairman of the Foreign Relations Committee in 2003, are regarded as committed 'multilateralists'. The emphasis on freedom of action is also prominent among segments of every presidential administration. The differences are generally about means, not ends, and they differ from issue to issue. For instance, in the second Bush administration, Secretary of State Colin Powell was widely held to be a multilateralist, whose true colours became apparent when the United States needed to create the broadest possible coalition in the latter part of 2001. By contrast, Bush himself, as well as Defense Secretary Donald Rumsfeld and his deputy, Paul Wolfowitz, were reputed to have stronger unilateralist inclinations. Perhaps the most outspoken unilateralist in the Bush administration was Under-Secretary of State for Arms Control and International Security Affairs John Bolton. In the fall of 2000 he had expounded his view in a *Chicago Journal of International Law* article. He distinguished between 'Americanists', who try to preserve US sovereignty and flexibility, and 'globalists', 'each tightly clutching a favourite new treaty or multilateralist proposal' that binds the United States in a web of agreements. He continued, 'every time America is forced to bend its knee to international pressure, it sets a significant, and detrimental, precedent for all of the others'. Which ones have the upper hand depends on the scenario and what kinds of threats face the United States at any one time. Bolton's views carried some weight in the Bush administration's decisions, unpopular in Europe, not to seek ratification of a half-dozen important treaties. Nevertheless, former national security adviser for the first President Bush, Brent Scowcroft, spoke of the second President Bush's narrowed choices after the 11 September attacks: 'I think he sees clearly that he doesn't have a chance to succeed unilaterally. The only way he can be a success is multilaterally.'[6]

Like its European partners, the United States remains committed to countless multilateral agreements such as those governing world cultural property rights, copyrights, food standards, fisheries, WMD proliferation and the law of the sea. It works constructively with its European and other partners in dozens of International Governmental Organisations (IGOs). It is a signatory and continued supporter of the Conventional Forces in Europe (CFE) agreement, which, in the words of the German weekly *Das Parlament*, 'remains the most essential instrument of arms control in Europe'.[7] It is true that the United States is able and willing to act unilaterally more frequently than most of its European allies. However, as sovereign states, European nations sometimes do so when their national interests seem to require it. For example, France unilaterally announced in 1995 that it would test nuclear warheads in the Pacific despite the worldwide outcry that ultimately forced it to stop.

Bush's use of the term 'axis of evil' in his 29 January 2002 State of the Union address implied the threat of unilateral military action against Iraq, Iran or North Korea, accused both of acquiring WMD and of maintaining ties with international terrorist groups. This unfortunate phrase elicited a thunder of criticism in Europe. For example, French Foreign Minister Hubert Vedrine branded it 'simplistic'; German Foreign Minister Joschka Fischer reminded America that its partners are not 'satellites' and Chris Patten feared that Washington was going into 'unilateralist overdrive'. Secretary of State Powell responded by arguing, 'this suggestion . . . that the United States is acting uni-laterally and not consulting with our European partners simply could not be further from the truth'.[8]

The highly publicised international treaties that George W. Bush announced his administration would review, revise, reject or withdraw from are important. Although they constitute a small percentage of the international agreements to which Washington and its allies adhere, they took on considerable symbolic significance, as Europeans saw their challenge as clear evidence that the new President was concerned only with American interests and had little under-standing of Europe. Virtually all of the problems surrounding US support of these agreements had their roots in earlier administrations and therefore reflect more than fleeting concerns.[9] One of Bush's senior aides noted that the contro-versial issues were ones 'in which the president was reflecting fairly widely held views in his party, and which the Clinton administration didn't really believe in . . . The prior administration left us a couple of land mines . . . and we rather inartfully stepped on all of them and paid a political cost.' Nevertheless, Bush's questioning of them created particular ire in Europe, in part because of the undiplomatic, even occasionally aggressive, language he used in speaking of them.[10]

A very political President, Bush mixed statements about the contested trea-ties with domestic political issues. For example, in explaining why he opposed UN efforts to regulate the global small arms trade, he cited the second amend-ment of the US constitution granting citizens the right to bear arms. The proper interpretation of this constitutional amendment is passionately debated in the United States, and it is not surprising that Europeans would harbour deep dislike of it. The President's curt dismissal of the Kyoto Protocol as 'dead' was unfortunate, and it shocked allied countries, where concern over the damaging effects of greenhouse gases is great. Because of the outcry that followed, the word 'dead' was quickly dropped from his speeches referring to Kyoto, but his policy was lauded by some American energy industries, which were very supportive of his presidency. Some Americans also applauded his reference to the damage the protocol would do to the American economy at a time of recession, although, as will be discussed later, public opinion in the United States on the subject of global climate change is generally in line with that in Europe.[11]

Some Europeans even worry that Bush's rejectionism would undermine the entire system of international agreements that had created order and stability after the Second World War. Post-war Europeans are more steeped in the multilateral tradition than are Americans because of their work on European integration. To cite information from the EC delegation in Washington, 'the EU's multilateral activities are a natural extension of the Union's own example of integration through pooled sovereignty'. Europeans also lack the power most of the time to resort successfully to the unilateralist option. Partly for this reason, they tend to believe that all problems are best resolved through a process of dialogue rather than confrontation. The aim of foreign policy should be to construct international regimes based on common norms and binding treaties. There is also a strong belief, shared by most Americans, that international challenges such as global warming, migration, weapons proliferation, or terrorism, cannot be solved by unilateral approaches alone. Finally, while European nations sometimes act unilaterally, especially toward each other, they lack the power and influence individually to do it as frequently on the global stage as the United States.[12]

The United States almost always tries to enlist allies when it sends its soldiers into harm's way. However, many Americans are also inclined to think of the potential costs and problems created by multilateralism, for example having to conduct warfare with eighteen allies who can veto important military decisions. Also, the United States values its sovereignty more than do most European states in the throes of continental economic and political integration. When it acts unilaterally, it often does so, not to exercise power over others, but to prevent outside countries and groups from asserting power over the United States. For example, the US Senate rejected President Wilson's brainchild, the League of Nations, because of the possibility that such an international body could drag the United States into a war it did not want to fight.[13] At the same time, an American threat to act unilaterally can help persuade the key members of the United Nations to take their multilateral responsibilities seriously. This was the case in 2002 when the UN Security Council was challenged to back up its Chapter Seven resolutions, adopted eleven years earlier, requiring Iraq to destroy its weapons of mass destruction. The US position was credible since it did indeed have the military capability of fighting Iraq without the United Nations and with a coalition of those allies willing to join the action.

It would be incorrect to argue that Americans all agree on the best methods for exercising American power in the twenty-first century. It is a matter of considerable debate whether a unilateral or multilateral approach is best in general or in dealing with a specific problem. Robert Kagan made perhaps the most dramatic argument on this subject in an article published in 2002 and entitled

'Power and weakness'. He posits an 'essential truth': 'The United States and Europe are fundamentally different today.' They no longer share the same view of the world because they do not agree on the role of power. Because of their positive experience in constructing an integrated Europe (an achievement he lauds) through patient negotiation and good will, Europeans regard the world in terms of Kant's perpetual peace and expect the entire world, including the United States, to settle problems by means of discourse, diplomacy and accommodation. By neglecting their military capabilities 'they see the world through the eyes of weaker powers', and this affects their strategic judgement. By contrast, the United States, which did not share the Europeans' experience in sacrificing sovereignty to create a supranational body like the European Union, recognises the anarchic Hobbesian side of the international environment that must sometimes be dealt with by military force. 'Europe's military weakness has produced a perfectly understandable aversion to the exercise of military power.' 'Europeans oppose unilateralism in part because they have no capacity for unilateralism,' but they present their multilateralism as 'proof of their greater commitment to certain ideals concerning world order'. Kagan therefore calls most Europeans 'principled multilateralists', in contrast to most Americans, who are 'instrumental multilateralists'. He argues that Americans like to have allies and approval for their international actions. But their preference for multilateral action, when it is possible, is at its core pragmatic.[14]

Some American commentators object to Kagan's implication that their countrymen's views on multilateralism are accurately expressed by some leading members of the Bush administration. Stephen F. Szabo points out that much of America's military leadership still embraces the 'Powell Doctrine', which is grounded in a clear reluctance to apply force unless it is overwhelming and limited in time. He also objects to the charge that Europe is militarily weak, pointing out that European NATO outspends Russia, China and Japan combined in terms of defence expenditures and that European allies very well understand the role of military force in backing diplomacy, as they proved in Bosnia, Kosovo and Afghanistan. A public opinion poll in 2002 conducted by the Chicago Council on Foreign Relations and the German Marshall Fund revealed that American and European support for multilateral institutions and the use of force is very similar. Asked if the United Nations should be strengthened, 77 per cent of Americans and 75 per cent of Europeans said yes. With regard to military power, 80 per cent of Europeans and 76 per cent of Americans agreed that armed force should be used to uphold international law. A majority on both sides of the Atlantic supported an invasion of Iraq as long as it was sanctioned by the United Nations.[15]

Without such UN backing, war against Iraq was very unpopular throughout the continent, especially in Germany, where most respondents disapproved of military action regardless of the scenario. This was made apparent in the September 2002 Bundestag elections, when Gerhard Schröder's government won a narrow re-election victory by adamantly opposing Germany's involvement in an eventual war in Iraq. He took this stance, which caused serious American–German tensions, without consulting his European partners. It was the first time since 1945 that a leader of one of America's allies won an election by campaigning against US policy.[16]

Kagan was correct that there are very few pure unilateralists or multilateralists in the United States. Joseph S. Nye, Jr, former chairman of the National Intelligence Council and an assistant secretary of defence during the Clinton administration, is a prominent example of the many 'pragmatic multilateralists'. In a much-discussed 2002 book, he warned of the political price the United States must pay if it pursues a foreign policy that 'combines unilateralism, arrogance, and parochialism'. The problem, he explains, is that 'our desire to go it alone may ultimately weaken us'. He continued: 'Learning to define our national interest to include global interests will be crucial to the longevity of our power and whether others see the hegemony as benign or not'. He describes the large measure of 'soft power' that an economically dynamic, culturally appealing and technologically progressive America wields; it could erode if Washington seemed not to know or to care about the concerns of other countries. 'The United States could squander this soft power by heavy-handed unilateralism'. As a former high Pentagon official he does not diminish the importance of military power. But he emphasises that, in the globalised world we all inhabit, 'military power cannot produce the outcomes we want on many of the issues that matter to Americans'. His conclusion is important in the debate over how the United States should use its unique power today: 'Any retreat to a traditional policy focus on unipolarity, hegemony, sovereignty, and unilateralism will fail to produce the right outcomes, and its accompanying arrogance will erode the soft power that is often part of the solution.'[17]

Contentious treaties and non-proliferation

The United States is very sensitive to any international agreement that appears to undermine its sovereignty. Nevertheless, the Clinton administration supported the idea of US participation in an International Criminal Court (ICC) drafted in Rome in 1998. The goal was to create a permanent court in The Hague to succeed the *ad hoc* tribunal established by the UN Security Council to try indicted war criminals from former Yugoslavia and Rwanda. The European Union finds this Rome Statute 'possibly the most significant achievement of international law since the founding of the UN'.

Fearing that such a tribunal would be too vulnerable to political manipulation, America's allies, led by Western European nations who formed the core of the 'Like-minded Group' that guided the negotiations to completion, did not accept Washington's condition that the new court be a tool of the UN Security Council, in which the United States has a veto. Some American leaders fear that persons who resent or oppose the foreign policy of a superpower could stage politically motivated trials of US soldiers and government officials and that the court's judicial decisions could become legal precedents that would affect law in the United States and perhaps even define new kinds of crimes that would be unacceptable in American jurisprudence. The European Union found it understandable that the United States would have concerns over possible prosecution of its military personnel, given America's global military presence. But it believed the statute makes such abuse unlikely. Perhaps the most important safeguard is the principle of complementarity elaborated in Article 17 of the Rome Statute; this specifies that only if the domestic judicial system in a signatory state cannot or does not properly investigate or prosecute an alleged crime would the ICC have the right to take up the case and prosecute the accused.

President Clinton signed the treaty three weeks before leaving office, knowing that the Senate would not ratify it. He hoped that by signing it the United States could continue to press for an American exemption from its provisions. The Senate voted seventy-eight to twenty-four in December 2001 to block US participation in the court, whose creation was triggered in April 2002 when sixty countries had ratified it. The Bush administration's response was swift: in May it formally renounced the new court and pledged to seek agreements throughout the world barring US citizens from being extradited to the ICC. The President's hand was strengthened by a new law, from which NATO and other allies were exempted, threatening countries with a loss of military aid unless they excluded Americans found in their territory from being handed over to the ICC. Supporters of the court, like Senator Christopher Dodd, called the President's decisions 'irresponsible, isolationist and contrary to our vital national interests', and a *Washington Post* editorial decried the promised worldwide campaign as 'showboating'. Europeans largely agreed. Undaunted, the administration placed intense pressure on the United Nations, threatening to shut down UN peacekeeping missions unless Americans were immune from ICC prosecution, and on its EU allies. The latter finally accepted a compromise in October 2002 that American military personnel and diplomats (but not American peacekeepers after a one-year period) would be exempted from prosecution and that individual EU states could also sign agreements with the United States granting such exemption, which the administration still found inadequate. The United States found itself in embarrassing company, with only Israel and countries like China, Iran, Iraq, Libya and Sudan on its side in this matter. The lament expressed in a *Washington Post* editorial was true: the message sent to the world was that 'the United States holds international treaties and institutions in contempt and is unwilling to be bound by rules it expects other nations to accept'.[18]

An example of the difference between the American emphasis on national security in an era of new threats and the European concern for international treaties and law was the transatlantic controversy on the treatment of Taliban and al-Qaida prisoners at the US naval base at Guantanamo Bay, Cuba. Washington categorised them as 'unlawful combatants', a status that initially denied them the protections of the Geneva Convention relative to the

Treatment of Prisoners of War. Ultimately responding to the protests of its European allies, President Bush announced that the Geneva protections would be granted to Taliban fighters (since Afghanistan had signed the convention in 1949), but not to al-Qaida terrorists.[19]

In the 1995 Joint Action Plan of the NTA, the transatlantic allies committed themselves to work together to achieve a host of non-proliferation initiatives. They included the nuclear Non-proliferation Treaty (NPT), the Comprehensive Test Ban Treaty (CTBT), a revision of the 1972 Convention on Biological Weapons, a treaty banning anti-personnel land mines and an extension of the Missile Technology Control Regime (MTCR), created in the mid-1980s to prevent the spread of missile technology. MTCR required close co-operation with North Korea through the Korean Peninsula Energy Development Organisation (KEDO), since North Korea was a leading proliferator of missiles. To the exasperation of many Europeans, the United States had by 2002 still refused to ratify some of these agreements. The exceptions are MTCR, as well as NPT, which was extended indefinitely, thanks largely to the unified efforts of the United States and its European allies. Work with North Korea was deferred for three months in the spring of 2001 while the Bush administration reviewed its policy toward the communist state. While Europeans backed these initiatives, despite some flaws and imperfections, as important steps in the direction of international stability and a less dangerous world, the administration of President George W. Bush, with strong backing in the US Senate, which has the sole authority to ratify treaties, pursued a policy of accepting only those agreements that were judged to serve American national interests, including its economic interests.

Nevertheless, when the focus is broadened, from a few important treaties that came into transatlantic cross-fire in the last years of the Clinton administration and in the first year of the Bush administration to a larger context of creating an arms control regime and preventing the spread of weapons of mass destruction, the record looks better. The United States participates in all the multilateral efforts dealing with the proliferation problem, and its contribution goes far beyond military opposition to the spread of WMD. In some efforts, such as preventing the leakage of WMD from the former Soviet Union, it is the driving force. In general, transatlantic collaboration is well suited to the task of managing the spread of dangerous weapons.

The partners formed the so-called 'Western Group', which was instrumental in creating and implementing the foundations of a global arms control regime based on the NPT, the Chemical Weapons Convention (CWC), which came into force in 1997, and the Biological and Toxic Weapons Convention (BWC). Roberts asserted, 'today, no other group of countries – and indeed no single country – has the capacity to carry forward the multilateral effort'. Moreover, differences among the allies often apply to compliance and implementation questions, not to the basic objectives of the treaties themselves. Compliance is left up to the signatory states themselves. When actions need to be challenged, states can draw on findings of the International Atomic Energy Agency (IAEA) in Vienna and the Organisation for the Prohibition of Chemical Weapons (OPCW) in The Hague, which were created for that reason. But ultimately countries must turn to the UN Security Council to ensure compliance.[20]

Transatlantic disagreements have been particularly sharp in deciding how to induce Iraq to comply with its international treaty obligations and UN Security Council resolutions concerning Baghdad's destruction of WMD. After a lively debate within the Bush administration, the President delivered an effective speech to the UN General Assembly on 12 September 2002 reminding the international body that it risked irrelevance in its important duty of maintaining world peace if it did not rise to the challenge of enforcing its own Chapter Seven resolutions regarding Iraq's military build-up. He demanded that Iraq dismantle its chemical, biological and nuclear weapons programmes or face the prospect of war.

After almost eight weeks of tenacious and skilful diplomacy, spearheaded by Colin Powell, with the British playing a crucial role in helping to find common ground among disagreeing Council members, the UN Security Council unanimously approved a tough new disarmament mandate for Iraq, threatening 'serious consequences' if President Saddam Hussein did not scrap his weapons programme. This was a dramatic diplomatic victory for President Bush, who is frequently accused of acting unilaterally. There can be little doubt that his persistent threats to disarm Hussein with or without the United Nations prompted the Security Council to act. However, the outcome resulted from the realisation that allied help was highly desirable. It was also a victory for Secretary of State Powell, who carried the day within the Bush Cabinet to seek a multilateral solution to the problem of Iraq.[21]

In its Prague summit meeting in November 2002, NATO issued a statement of 'full support' for the UN resolution on Iraq. In a departure from its military effort in Afghanistan, the Bush administration decided that it would like the Alliance to shoulder some of the burden of warfare. The President asked the NATO allies to consider offering a wide range of military assistance, including combat troops and noncombat support, in a possible war against Iraq. In return for Turkey's pledge of support (which was later retracted, since it was contingent upon UN backing), President Bush personally contacted European leaders to lobby for early EU accession talks with Turkey. This effort was widely regarded as inappropriate and counterproductive meddling in EU affairs. It demonstrated how American influence in Europe can best be exercised through NATO, not the European Union. French Industry Minister Nicole Fontaine asserted, 'it's certainly not up to the President of the United States to interfere in something so important and which mainly concerns Europeans'. In the end the United States and Britain, supported by 200 Polish troops, went to war against Iraq without UN, NATO or Turkish backing. Hostilities commenced on 19 March 2003, Baghdad fell on 9 April, and the successful Operation Iraqi Freedom officially ended on 1 May. NATO, which in April had agreed to take over the peacekeeping operation in Afghanistan, offered technical assistance to the Poles, who oversee one of the occupation zones in Iraq between the Americans and British. In addition, Italy, Spain, Denmark, Bulgaria, the Netherlands and Ukraine provided troops to help police post-war Iraq.[22]

As in other fields, American non-proliferation policy is pursued both bilaterally and multilaterally. The most important bilateral co-operation is between the United States and Russia. Europeans watch and generally applaud this US–Russian reduction effort as long as it does not threaten to lead in the direction of total nuclear disarmament, as this might affect the nuclear forces of the United Kingdom and France. At the same time they universally condemn any perceived attempt by the United States to undermine the arms control achievements negotiated with Russia.

The Bush administration's strong support of a missile defence system against a limited missile attack, which is not designed to protect against a country with as high a number of launchers as Russia, creates anxiety among Europeans. As an official European Commission publication, *EU/US News*, expressed it: 'The EU legitimately wants to ensure that this will not negatively affect the international stability and our own security.' Although the United States sought to alter the ABM Treaty only in consultation and, if possible, complicity with Russia, Europeans were nervous. The *EU/US News* had written further of a unilateral scrapping of the ABM Treaty:

> Europe, having been directly exposed at the heart of the Cold War, cannot but view with concern the consequences of such a move, and calls on the United States to abide by its international obligations, while negotiating amendments to the ABM Treaty with Russia, to avoid upsetting the strategic equilibrium and prevent a renewed arms race.[23]

President Bush's announcement of the US intention to withdraw was made with reference to the dangers posed by terrorists gaining access to WMD. Osama bin Laden had sought to acquire nuclear materials and had conducted long discussions with Pakistani nuclear scientists about nuclear, biological and chemical weapons. Bush argued: 'Suppose the Taliban and the terrorists had been able to strike America or important allies with a ballistic missile? Our coalition would have become fragile . . . We must protect America and her friends against all forms of terror, including the terror that could arrive on a missile.' Unhappiness with the decision was expressed not only in Europe but also in the US Senate, but the administration proceeded nevertheless.[24]

Through the Nunn–Lugar Co-operative Threat Reduction Programme, enacted in 1991, the United States sought to address the dominant international proliferation peril: the huge stocks of Soviet nuclear, biological and chemical weapons. American money and technological expertise were contributed to a joint Russian–US effort to destroy or safeguard weapons of mass destruction in Russia. In the first ten years of co-operation 5,700 nuclear warheads were separated from missiles, many of the warheads were dismantled and the highly enriched uranium or plutonium was safely stored. More than 30,000 tactical nuclear weapons were gathered and placed into storage, and thousands of former Soviet nuclear scientists found employment through the programme. Both countries ratified the Chemical Weapons Convention mandating destruction of all chemical weapons. Forty thousand metric tonnes of these weapons were stored awaiting destruction. Nunn–Lugar supported this, as well as the control of Soviet biological weapon stocks. The programme was a success. In 2001, the year it was scheduled to come to an end, the American government had lowered its budget for it to $403 million, down $40 million from the level in fiscal 2001. In the wake of President Bush's warming with the Russian President, however, he pledged more funds to help Russia gather and destroy nuclear and chemical weapons. In addition to Nunn–Lugar, the US Energy Department oversees an impressive programme of laboratory exchanges with an aim of improving the security of nuclear materials in Russia, and the State Department oversees all the various efforts to prevent proliferation through collaboration with Russia.[25]

America's European partners took the general position that the United States is better able to deal with Russia on such things as so-called 'loose nukes'. But they were involved in the effort to deal with the legacy of Soviet nuclear power in the post-Cold War era, especially the denuclearisation of Ukraine. In January 1994 the United States entered a trilateral agreement with Ukraine and Russia whereby Ukraine renounced its nuclear status and handed its nuclear warheads over to Russia. To facilitate the deal, the United States gave some security assurances to Ukraine, as well as some economic aid. Washington was assisted in this effort by the European Union, which entered a wide-ranging economic co-operation agreement with Ukraine that would not take effect until Ukraine renounced its nuclear weapons. Thus the transatlantic partners dealt jointly with the problem. Washington would have liked more European help in the Nunn–Lugar process. However, a kind of division of labour had developed. The European partners funded efforts to enhance the security of Russia's nuclear power plants and civilian nuclear fuel and waste facilities through the TACIS programme. They joined the United States and Japan in establishing in 1994 an International Science and Technology Centre (ISTC) in Moscow. Its purpose is to redirect the research of former Soviet engineers and scientists, who worked on missiles and nuclear weapons, into peaceful directions.[26]

Britain, France, Germany and Italy were part of the Global Partnership against the Spread of Weapons and Materials of Mass Destruction, launched in June 2002 by the Group of Eight (G-8). This US$31 billion programme pledged to help dismantle Russian arsenals. However, Russian financial accountability and co-operation proved difficult. A 2002 Russian parliamentary audit revealed that US$270 million in nuclear disarmament assistance was unaccounted for, and the Russian authorities were not willing to allow free access to the destruction sites. Also cause for concern is the possibility that Western funding for stockpile reduction allowed Russia to spend more on new nuclear programmes, such as its construction of forty naval nuclear missiles and the modernisation of both its naval nuclear forces and fleet of Tupolev-160 bombers, the backbone of its airborne nuclear attack forces.[27]

Most non-proliferation efforts take place in a multilateral setting that brings American and European partners together. The major venues for this collaboration are NATO and the United Nations, with its many specialised organisations, such as the International Atomic Energy Agency (IAEA) in Vienna and the OPCW in The Hague. In May 2000 a Weapons of Mass Destruction Centre was established in NATO headquarters in Brussels to co-ordinate and intensify consultations on disarmament and non-proliferation issues. It builds on the discussions that took place in NATO's Defence Group on Proliferation. Specially designed to facilitate collaboration of Americans, Canadians and Europeans, the new centre has approximately a dozen people, including one American. According to the centre's Canadian director, Ted Whiteside, the United States has done a good job of reminding Europeans that the missile threat is growing and that they are actually more vulnerable to it than is America. President Bush expressed this view on 15 June 2001:

> We must confront the shared security threats of regimes that thrive by creating instability, that are ambitious for weapons of mass destruction and are dangerously unpredictable. In Europe, you are closer to these challenges than the United States. You see the lightning well before we hear the thunder. Only together, however, can we confront the emerging threats of a changing world.

By calling their attention to this unpleasant fact, Europeans have become more inclined to look closely at the American reasons for missile defence and have acquired more understanding of the programme's rationale.

The focuses of the WMD Centre are both political – to serve allied objectives in this field – and the defence response to proliferation – missile defence, force protection, inspection, and generally the ability to defend soldiers from all sorts of WMD. One of its major goals is to ensure that intelligence and information on WMD are shared within the Alliance. The command structure at SHAPE in Mons also has its own proliferation experts. Twice a year all nineteen NATO ambassadors meet with proliferation specialists to discuss the problems. NATO's experts also maintain links with other IGOs working on proliferation issues, such as the United Nations, the IAEA in Vienna and the OPCW in The Hague. They consult with the Russians, with whom they have formulated confidence-building measures (CBMs) on nuclear proliferation.[28]

Comprehensive Test Ban Treaty

Transatlantic friction in the proliferation field became visible to the general public after George W. Bush took office. One of the decisions the new administration had to make was whether to seek ratification of the 1996

Comprehensive Test Ban Treaty (CTBT), which the Senate had rejected in a close (fifty-one to forty-eight) partisan vote in 1999. The United States had unilaterally renounced nuclear testing in 1992 and has continued to observe its own ban. One reason it could do so is that it knows how to conduct 'zero yield' tests, which produce no nuclear chain reaction, and computer-modelling, non-explosive tests. Both are permitted by the CTBT. Nevertheless, they argue, the United States might have to test its nuclear weapons in the future to ensure their reliability and safety.[29] This is disputed among experts.

The Senate majority and the Bush administration argued that the treaty is impossible to verify. Indeed, it is difficult to distinguish an earthquake from a nuclear test under five kilotonnes, and tests under one kilotonne can be confused for a large chemical explosion. They also point to India's and Pakistan's entry into the ranks of nuclear powers as demonstrating that the agreement cannot halt proliferation. In November 2001 Osama bin Laden repeated to a Pakistani journalist what he had claimed for years: that his movement had already acquired nuclear and chemical weapons. Although his claim to have atomic arms could not be verified and is disputable, designs of crude radiological ('dirty') nuclear weapons gathered in abandoned al-Qaida quarters in Afghanistan indicated that his group might have made greater strides toward producing nuclear arms. Such a bomb could be constructed by taking highly radioactive material, such as spent reactor fuel rods, and wrapping it around conventional high explosives. It kills not by its explosive force, but by creating a zone of intense radiation. Since it requires no testing, the CTBT would not prevent such a bomb from being created, tested and used.[30]

Washington announced in early 2001 that it would no longer help pay for the preparation of on-site inspections, although it would assist in the financing of an international monitoring system. In November 2001 it boycotted a UN conference to ratify the treaty, arguing that it had firmly decided not to ratify CTBT, and that the meeting was convened to discuss ratification. Although 161 countries had signed the treaty and eighty-five had already ratified it, its provisions specify that it cannot go into force until all forty-four countries that are capable of developing nuclear weapons ratify it. A host of nuclear countries, including China, India, Pakistan, North Korea and Israel, had not done so. The timing of America's decision not to attend the conference stunned its European allies, given President Bush's determined efforts to forge a sturdy coalition to fight terrorism after the 11 September attacks. They strongly supported this treaty, as the United States had explicitly pledged to do in the NTA.[31]

Non-nuclear treaties: small arms and biological weapons

The United States also departed in 2001 from its allies' efforts to tighten controls on the illegal export of small arms and on biological weapons. Meeting at the United Nations on 21 July 2001, the United States and more than 140 other countries accepted the world's first agreement to curb illegal trade in small arms, a loose category of weapons extending from hunting rifles to shoulder-fired rockets. However, the United States incurred the anger of the EU partners and many more countries by blocking two provisions that would have restricted trade to rebel groups and regulated civilian ownership of military weapons. American representatives argued that the accord, which is not legally binding, would stymie legitimate revolution against tyrants. John Bolton, Under-Secretary of State for arms control, also used the unfortunate and (for Europeans) unpersuasive argument that 'the United States will not join consensus on a final document that contains measures contrary to our constitutional right to keep and bear arms'. An editorial in *The Washington Post* expressed justified puzzlement at this line of argumentation: 'the draft UN plan . . . doesn't come close to infringing on the Second Amendment'. Many Europeans would share the newspaper's suspicion that 'the Bush administration seems to have chosen to use the UN conference as a way to pander to the National Rifle Association, anti-UN zealots and far-right conspiracy theorists'.[32]

In the NTA the partners on both sides of the Atlantic pledged their co-operation in revising the 1972 Biological Weapons Convention (BWC), to which the United States adheres, in order to make it more effective. This seemed logical for the United States, which had been the first country to forswear such weapons unilaterally. Also the American people later experienced anthrax attacks in the aftermath of the 11 September terrorist attacks and knew how psychologically devastating such substances can be. However, the allies found that their general agreement on the aims of a treaty did not necessarily extend to how compliance should be ensured.

A meeting in December 2001 to strengthen the treaty's enforcement mechanism broke up in anger after the United States had proposed to end the conference's mandate; it could not be reconvened until November 2002, when negotiators again failed to resolve the dispute on inspections. The State Department argued that the enforcement mechanism being discussed would not prevent rogue states from developing or acquiring biological weapons if they were determined to do that. American negotiators contended that among the 143 countries, including the United States, that had signed and ratified the 1972 accord, some, including Iraq and Iran, had nevertheless violated it. Washington also objected to a clause that would have allowed foreign inspections of suspected biological weapons sites. The American representatives argued that this could be misused to gain access into private US bio-technology companies, which are the world's leaders, and steal trade secrets. America's partners were unable to persuade Washington that this fear was unfounded. American negotiators insist that the United States remains committed to countering the biological threat, but they propose voluntary co-operation instead of a rigid inspection regime. The break-up of the meetings fuelled European complaints – muted since the 11 September attacks – that Washington was disregarding its partners' needs and was again acting unilaterally, despite its pleas for allied support in the campaign against international terrorism. Many Europeans no doubt agreed with a bitter statement from the Federation of American Scientists terming the American action as 'sabotage' and saying that European diplomats 'privately accused the US of deceiving them'.[33]

Co-operation and tensions on many fronts

Under the rubric of the NTA the European Union and the United States co-operate on many fronts, and that produces both progress and friction. Perhaps no issue created more friction in the final years of the Clinton administration and the first years of the Bush White House than the environment, a field in which Europeans are unmistakably globally involved. The partners pledged to 'work together to strengthen multilateral efforts to protect the global environment and to develop environmental policy strategies for sustainable worldwide growth. We will co-ordinate our negotiating positions on major global environmental issues.' Numerous working groups were formed around specific topics. In some cases, these efforts have been successful. For example, the partners co-operated to set up and assist the operating of regional environmental centres (RECs) in the newly independent states of the former Soviet Union. The RECs manage grant programmes to non-governmental organisations, act as intermediaries between the public and governments, and provide information and training on environmental issues.

However, in March 2001 Europeans were dismayed by President Bush's unilateral declaration that the Kyoto Protocol, which seeks the worldwide reduction of carbon dioxide emissions (greenhouse gases) in order to stop global warming, was 'effectively dead'. A warning signal had been given when a November 2000 round in The Hague collapsed. American and European negotiators disagreed over the right to trade or purchase 'pollution credits' in case a country did not meet a pledge to curtail its emissions. According to former ambassador Richard Morningstar, President Clinton had been promised before he had signed the protocol that such credits would be a part of a final agreement. There was a sense of betrayal on both sides.[34]

Bush explained, 'we will not do anything that harms our economy because first things first, are the people who live in America. That's my priority.' That kind of reasoning from the leader of a country that has 4 per cent of the world's population but emits 25 per cent of the greenhouse gases was intolerable to many Europeans (and to many Americans as well). Sweden's environment Minister, Kjell Larsson, said Bush's action 'sabotages many years of hard work'. Her French counterpart branded it 'suicidal and irresponsible'. The EU Commissioner for the Environment, Margot Wallstrom, asserted, 'this is not some marginal environmental issue that can be ignored or played down'. EC President Romano Prodi said, 'tearing up the agreement and starting again would be a tragic mistake'. A Pew Research Center poll in August 2001 showed that the citizens of the largest European countries agreed: In Britain 83 per cent disapproved of Bush's decision, in Italy 80 per cent, in Germany 87 per cent, and in France 85 per cent. A poll in 2002 revealed that the American public was almost as critical of the Bush administration's policy as were Europeans. Fifty per cent of Europeans and 46 per cent of Americans considered global warming a 'high-priority threat'; only 17 per cent of Americans and 8 per cent of Europeans thought it was not important. In the poll both Americans and Europeans gave President Bush their lowest rating for his handling of the global warming topic. A stream of European leaders journeyed to Washington to attempt to change the President's mind, but to no avail. Josef Joffe, editor of the German weekly *Die Zeit*, wrote that the American government could have levelled good arguments against the imperfect accord that would have been shared by some Europeans, but instead Bush had summarily dismissed the protocol. That performance would cause Bush to fail a course in basic diplomacy.[35]

The US Senate was on record concerning its requirements for a global warming treaty. The 1997 Byrd–Hagel Resolution stated that the United States should sign no treaty unless it also committed the rest of the world, including developing countries. The Energy and Climate Policy Act of 1999 also mandated that a treaty must be a long-term effort on a global basis. Most US senators agreed that the protocol was flawed, but many of them sharply disagreed with the President's refusal to negotiate an improved alternative pact with America's allies. On 1 August 2001 the Senate Foreign Relations Committee adopted a resolution by a bipartisan nineteen-to-none vote calling on Bush to return to the bargaining table with specific proposals. But when 160 nations gathered in Marrakesh, Morocco, in November 2001 to adopt the protocol, America's representatives brought no proposals to the talks and refused to accept the final agreement, despite the fact that it belatedly created a trading programme that allows major industrial polluters, such as the United States, to buy carbon emission credits. This refusal to climb aboard seemed especially puzzling at a time when the United States was trying hard to hold together a large international coalition to fight terrorism. Dutch Environment Minister Jan Pronk spoke for the European partners when he noted, 'after the events of September 11th, if there is any reason for the United States to call for international, global approaches, it should also join a global approach to the existing global problem of climate change'.[36]

Nevertheless, the United States does not obstruct the implementation of the protocol and remains officially committed to working with the European Union and other Kyoto signatories to find market-based approaches and new technology to halt detrimental planet change. Over half the states in the United States have adopted mandatory or voluntary programmes for reducing carbon emissions, including Bush's home state of Texas. These efforts stem in part from frustration over the deadlock that exists on the issue between the administration and Congress. New Jersey environmental official Bradley M. Campbell expressed the discontent this way: 'We're obviously very concerned that the federal government seems to be abdicating its responsibility.' There is considerable support in the US public, governments and legislatures for halting global warming, and the door remains open for the United States to join its European partners in the Kyoto Protocol in the future. EU leaders welcomed President Bush's proposal in February 2002 to use tax credits to encourage companies and individuals to limit greenhouse emissions, but they argued that the Kyoto treaty was still the best response to global warming.[37]

According to Philippart and Winand, the most dynamic, uncontroversial and successful sector of the NTA concerns development co-operation and humanitarian assistance, areas of global European commitment. Co-operation in sub-Saharan Africa outside these fields is low-key and reactive. The European Union and its member states account for about 55 per cent of the world's overseas development assistance (ODA). With an ODA budget of US$27.4 billion in 1999, the European Union outspends the United States, which allotted $9.1 billion the same year. President Bush closed the gap somewhat by raising US spending on foreign assistance by 50 per cent. Together they have provided humanitarian assistance in the Horn of Africa, Sierra Leone, South Eastern Europe, Central America and elsewhere. In addition to collaboration on conflict prevention, food security and health, the partners have jointly tackled the spread of the three major communicable diseases – HIV/AIDS, malaria and tuberculosis – especially in Africa, where 70 per cent of the world's HIV/AIDS cases are found. At their May 2000 and June 2001 summits the partners agreed to accelerate their collaboration. At their December 2000 summit, the partners agreed to redouble their efforts to make pharmaceuticals more accessible to the afflicted in poor countries. They started a Global Fund for their combined efforts, to which the United States is the largest contributor. This fund was called to life very quickly, having been announced in May 2001 and become operational in January 2002.[38]

The Middle East figures prominently in the NTA: 'We will work together to make peace, stability and prosperity in the Middle East a reality.' The United States has always been very concerned about the area, and now the Europeans are taking an increasing interest of their own. This is especially true given the growing Muslim minorities in many European countries, especially in France and Germany. However, Solana explained that it goes beyond that: 'The Middle East for us is a question of values, is a question of responsibility. But it is also a question of security. The security of that part of the world is fundamental to our own security.'[39] Nevertheless, it is not easy for the European Union to forge a unified position on this area. Europeans disagree among themselves on such matters as sanctions again Iraq, although they agreed in 2001 that it should not be the next military target after the war in Afghanistan was completed.

The Bush administration welcomed an EU role in the Israeli–Palestinian conflict, but this had not always been the case. A European country that is not a member of the European Union, Norway, played an enormously helpful role in the peace process by facilitating the 1993 Oslo agreement in the absence of American representation. By 2001 this had broken down. The European Union is the largest donor to the Middle East peace process, providing US$2.3 billion from 1994 to 1998 and about US$350 million to the Palestinian Authority in 2000–01. In 2002 this amounted to nearly US$20 million per month. These funds are carefully monitored to guarantee that they are used for basic services. As the provider of the most financial assistance to the Palestinian authority, the European Union wants a significant political role for itself, and it gets Arab encouragement for this. But Israel is reluctant, in part because most European governments appear to be more pro-Palestinian than is the United States. The 2002 Chicago Council on Foreign Relations/German Marshall Fund poll revealed that a clear divergence in European and American opinion on the Middle East does indeed exist: 72 per cent of Europeans support a Palestinian state, while only 40 per cent of Americans do, despite the fact that in 2002 President Bush publicly advocated such a state. Also Americans expressed far warmer feelings toward Israel than did Europeans. The Israelis trust the Americans more and receive hefty financial and military support from the United States. This enhances Washington's role as a mediator. Chris Patten, who along with Solana is one of the few EU politicians welcome in Israel, noted a further difficulty: German policy toward Israel and Palestine often differs from that of the British or French, for well known historical reasons. For instance, newly elected Chancellor Gerhard Schröder said in November 2002 that Germany has a 'moral duty' to protect Israel and would therefore send Patriot anti-missile systems to Israel if war against Iraq were ever to break out. 'The security of the state of Israel and its citizens is extraordinarily important to us,' he stressed.[40]

Europe consistently supports American efforts to overcome the crisis in Palestine. EU leaders were exasperated by what they saw as American inactivity during the early months of the Bush administration in trying to find a solution to the complicated conflict. EU Foreign Ministers meeting in Rome on 18 July 2001 proposed sending impartial outside observers as a buffer force that might help stop escalating violence between Israelis and Palestinians and that could assist in the implementation of the 'Mitchell Report', drawn up by American envoy George Mitchell. High-level political leaders, such as Solana and German Foreign Minister Fischer, went to the region to try to bring the warring sides together and to prevent Palestinian leader Yasser Arafat from being marginalised when the Israeli government was restricting his movement. In February 2002 Solana even flew to Riyadh to discuss ideas on how to stop the violence in Palestine.

One EU official said just hours before the 11 September terrorist attacks in the United States that his colleagues were in 'despair at the lack of American engagement' in the crisis. Two months later, Solana still believed that America was 'traumatised' by the terrorist threat from al-Qaida and was too preoccupied to get embroiled again in the messy search for peace in the Middle East. He was gratified by Bush's endorsement of the idea of a Palestinian state. However, Washington's Arab allies, especially Saudi Arabia and Egypt, probably influenced that shift in American policy more than did the Europeans.[41]

The European Union is under no illusions that it could deal with the Middle East alone and knows that it can at best play a supporting role. Solana noted: 'We will not solve the problem. To solve the problem, the active presence of the United States with the European Union is fundamental. The Israelis will not be moved by the Europeans.' Nevertheless, Europe's support is important for Washington. In the autumn of 2002 the Bush administration was more assertive about getting the European Union, the United Nations and the Russians more involved in forging a common approach to a peace settlement. They formed the so-called 'Quartet', composed of Secretary of State Powell, UN Secretary General Kofi Annan, and the envoys of Russia and the European Union. This group discusses several approaches to peace, including the 'road map', a three-phase, three-year US proposal that would end in full Palestinian statehood by 2005. Although they might differ on nuances, such as how to handle Yasser Arafat, both sides agree on the basic steps to peace and on the messages sent to both sides in the conflict. An adviser to Chris Patten, Anthony Cary, noted that Americans and Europeans generally agree on the ultimate solution: a Palestinian state neighbouring an Israeli state with secure, defensible borders. 'At the end of the day, we want the same result.'[42]

The NTA's Joint Action Plan calls on the transatlantic partners to 'work together to reduce the risk of regional conflict over the Korean peninsula, Taiwan and the South China Sea'. This accurately reflects the fact that the United States and European Union have common interests in Asia to prevent the outbreak or spread of war in the region. However, they have vastly different commitments. The United States is fully engaged, with roughly 100,000 troops (almost as many as are deployed in Europe) and the Seventh Fleet in the region. There are 37,000 on the Korean peninsula alone. By contrast, Europe is more detached and focuses primarily on trade. The European Union is the largest investor in China, and it provides considerable development assistance to Asian nations. Patten, who was Britain's last governor in Hong Kong, admits that this economic engagement does not have the same meaning for the Chinese as does the US Seventh Fleet. 'But we are everything but unimportant in the political calculation of the Chinese.'[43]

Europe is also more willing than the United States to concentrate its China trade on the mainland and not to sell advanced weapons directly or indirectly to Taiwan. When the Bush administration offered in April 2001 to sell Taiwan two diesel-powered hunter-killer submarines as the centrepieces of a US arms package, Germany and the Netherlands immediately objected. They had not been informed of the sale, are the only countries aside from France and Sweden which have the technology for such boats, and refused to approve of the sale. In fact, the United States had not built a diesel submarine in four decades. Europeans regarded this as one of many examples of the new administration taking unilateral action without discussion with allies.[44]

When the United States hammered out a 'Framework Agreement' in 1994 to provide North Korea with assistance in developing peaceful atomic energy in exchange for a termination of Pyongyang's nuclear weapons programme and freezing its plutonium processing, the Europeans were not happy. France and Germany complained that the compromise had undermined the Non-proliferation Treaty by being too lenient and that not enough concessions had been extracted. There was irritation that the Americans negotiated the agreement and then asked Europe, South Korea and Japan to climb aboard and help pay for it. Further, the two power plants North Korea was to get from South Korea were US-designed, with the Europeans having no opportunity to have their designs considered. Nevertheless, the European Union ultimately accepted the Korean Peninsula Energy Development Organisation (KEDO), the mechanism established to implement the US–North Korean Framework Agreement; EURATOM and KEDO reached an agreement that went into force in 1997, and the European Union is represented on KEDO's board.[45]

The European Union enjoys good working relations with both Korean governments. The Swedes, who had the EU presidency in the first half of 2001, had maintained diplomatic relations with North Korea throughout the Cold War and had long played an important monitoring role along the demilitarised zone (DMZ). On 1 March 2001 Germany became the twelfth EU member state formally to recognise North Korea, something the United States has not done. Declaring its desire to support the reconciliation process between the two Koreas, the European Union decided to establish diplomatic relations with Pyongyang on 14 May 2001, a few days after a trip by a high-level delegation to the North Korean capital.

The European Union enthusiastically supported the 'sunshine policy' of reconciliation between both parts of Korea, culminating in the South Korean President's trip to Pyongyang in 2000 for the first-ever summit meeting between the two Koreas' leaders. However, shortly after George W. Bush came into office, he brusquely told South Korean President Kim Dae Jung during a White House visit that the United States would not quickly resume missile talks with North Korea. The United States was determined to build a missile defence system directed precisely against such states of concern as North Korea, which had test-fired a missile over Japan in 1998. It test-fired missiles again in February and March 2003.[46]

From 1996 to 2001 the European Union had given the Korean peninsula €300 million in order to provide an impulse for reconciliation between north and south. With the knowledge of the Bush administration, an EU delegation that included Patten, Solana and Persson travelled to Pyongyang on 2 May 2001, where they were warmly received. The Europeans intended 'to express support for the peace process started by South Korean President Kim Dae Jung'. They also voiced their concerns about North Korean missiles and were given an assurance by Kim Jong Il that the 1999 two-year moratorium on ballistic missile launches would be extended by an additional two years, a pledge he repeated during a trip to Moscow in August.

Many American conservatives accused the Europeans of meddling, a charge that they rebuffed. In the words of Commission spokesman Gunnar Wiegand, 'there is no rivalry or divergence between us and the US. Our efforts are not to replace but complement the role of the US.' The journey had the desired effect of getting the talks with the North Koreans back on track. After a fierce internal debate the Bush administration decided to 'undertake serious discussions' with Pyongyang. During his February 2002 visit to Korea, Bush called Kim Dae Jung's sunshine policy 'visionary'. This was in spite of North Korea's refusal to respond to Seoul's overtures in more than a symbolic way, to permit IAEA inspectors into the country to verify its compliance with its nuclear agreements, or to curtail its sale of missiles to other countries.[47]

US–North Korean relations were thrust back into the deepfreeze in October 2002 when North Korea confessed that for several years it had been conducting a covert programme to develop nuclear weapons. This admission had come after an American diplomat confronted North Korean leaders with US intelligence information that Pyongyang was attempting to acquire large amounts of high-strength aluminium needed for equipment to enrich uranium for atomic bombs. At the same time the North Koreans boasted that they had 'more powerful things' as well, meaning chemical and biological WMD. This admission caused a severe setback for KEDO, which decided in November to suspend shipments of fuel oil that had been made under the 1994 agreement. In December North Korea shocked the region by announcing that it would restart work at three abandoned nuclear power plants, whose spent fuel could be processed into weapons-grade plutonium. It removed surveillance cameras from its nuclear power facilities, put there in 1994 to prevent the plants from being used to enrich plutonium.

The United States foreclosed military options from the start. Any attempted military strikes against the North's nuclear facilities could spark retaliation that could kill hundreds of thousands of civilians in Seoul, located only 30 km south of the Demilitarised Zone. Also the Bush administration was positioning the US military for a possible war against Iraq and could not contemplate serious military action in two theatres. While South Korea maintained a policy of continued engagement with North Korea, the United States announced that there could be no substantive discussions with Pyongyang until it had agreed to dismantle its nuclear weapons programme. Nevertheless, President Bush's policy remained the same: 'I believe we can deal with this threat peacefully, particularly if we work together.'[48]

Conclusion

Although the United States usually seeks multilateral solutions to international problems, unilateralism has always been an important characteristic of American foreign policy making and is a source of transatlantic tensions. The attitude that the Bush administration has shown towards either reviewing, revising or withdrawing from some major treaty commitments has exemplified this problem. With backing in the US Senate, which has the sole authority to ratify treaties, Bush pursued a policy of accepting only those agreements that were judged unmistakably to serve American national interests, including its economic interests. Europeans are more committed to multilateralism because of their involvement in the integration process on the continent and because of their more limited power. They are inclined to prefer dialogue and engagement with potential adversaries rather than the US predilection for containment and confrontation.

Policies outside of the European theatre have tended to represent areas of friction in the transatlantic relationship. The United States has called upon the Europeans to follow its lead and has berated them for inadequate burden sharing. For their part, the Europeans have struggled to find a united view on foreign-policy issues and continue to seek an effective mechanism for the Common Foreign and Security Policy. They have demonstrated a wariness to follow a US-led agenda of issues, and they have sought to chart a course of action that, whilst not antagonistic to the United States, is at least independent. There is clearly a long way to go before US–European global co-operation can accurately be described as a partnership.

Notes

1 Thomas Frellesen, 'Processes and procedures in EU–US foreign policy co-operation: from the Transatlantic Declaration to the New Transatlantic Agenda', in Eric Philippart and Pascaline Winand (eds), *Ever Closer Partnership: Policy Making in US–EU Relations* (Brussels: Lang, 2001), pp. 329–30.

2 William Wallace, 'Europe, the necessary partner', *Foreign Affairs*, 80: 3 (2001), p. 22; 'House approves UN payment', *Washington Post*, 25 September 2001, p. A13.

3 'UN removes US from Rights Panel', 4 May 2001, 'Revolt at the UN', 7 May 2001, and Jeane Kirkpatrick, 'European allies are behind US defeat at the United Nations', 9 May 2001, all in the *International Herald Tribune*. The United States regained its seat on the UN Human Rights Commission in 2002.

4 'France upbraids US as simplistic', *International Herald Tribune*, 7 February 2002, pp. 1, 4.

5 Michael J. Glennon, 'There's a point to going it alone', *Washington Post*, 12 August 2001, p. B2; Ivo H. Daalder, 'Are the United States and Europe heading for divorce?' *International Affairs*, 77: 3 (2001), p. 560.

6 'A general who paints', 20 October 2001, p. 36, and 'A leader is born', 22 September 2001, p. 33, both in *The Economist*. Bolton quote in 'ABM treaty may be history, but deterrence doctrine lives', *Washington Post*, 16 December 2001, p. A37. Snowcroft quote in 'Bush seeks European support', *Washington Post*, 7 November 2001, p. A18. A December 2001 poll in five continents revealed that large majorities of elites believed the United States was mostly acting unilaterally in the fight against terrorism after 11 September, whereas 70 per cent of American opinion makers said it was acting multilaterally. Only 27 per cent of European elites believed the United States was 'overreacting' to the crisis. ('Divergent views of US role in world', *Washington Post*, 20 December 2001, p. A34.)

7 'Ein dauerhaftes Klima der Sicherheit für alle Regionen des Kontinents', *Das Parlament*, 20 July 2001. Karsten Voigt, who co-ordinated German–American affairs in the German Foreign Ministry, wrote that the United States exercises 'a mix of selective multilateralism with occasional recourse to unilateral action'. ('The labor pains of a new Atlanticism', *Transatlantic Internationale Politik*, 2/2000, p. 7.)

8 'France upbraids US as simplistic'.

9 Karl K. Schonberg argues that a new consensus in American foreign policy developed during the Clinton administration that de-emphasised the United Nations and other multilateral bodies and meant that the establishment of a post-Cold War international order would be subordinated to the maintenance of regional peace and stability on an *ad hoc* basis. Liberal internationalism lost ground. See 'Paradigm regained. the new consensus in US foreign policy', *Security Dialogue*, 32: 4 (2001), pp. 439–52.

10 Quote in 'Bush seeks European support'. William Drozdiak, 'G-8 leaders praise "new" Bush', *Washington Post*, 23 July 2001, p. A18.

11 Jim Hoagland, 'The danger of Bush's unilateralism', *Washington Post*, 29 July 2001, p. B7.

12 Daalder, 'Divorce', p. 561.

13 Glennon, 'Point'.

14 Robert Kagan, 'Power and weakness', *Policy Review*, June–July 2002, pp. 3–28; quotes on pp. 5–6, 10–12; also Kagan, 'Multilateralism, American-style', *Washington Post*, 13 September 2002. His slightly expanded argument is presented in his book, *Of Paradise and Power: America and Europe in the New World Order* (New York: Knopf, 2003). In a less hard-hitting article David C. Gompert also argues that Europe's global role is impeded by its lack of military capabilities: 'The European Union wants a voice without capabilities. The United States would welcome European capabilities but not necessarily a distinct voice.' ('The EU on the world stage', *Transatlantic Internationale Politik*, 3, 2002, pp. 5, 8.) The Bush administration's new National Security Strategy, published in September 2002, and calling for unchallenged US military superiority and the right to use pre-emptive force against terrorist threats, sparked consternation in Europe. See 'New US doctrine worries Europeans', *Washington Post*, 30 September 2002, pp. A1, A15.

15 Stephen F. Szabo, 'Power and hubris', commentary published by the American Institute for Contemporary German Studies (Washington DC, 2002); Craig Kennedy and Marshall M. Bouton, 'The real transatlantic gap', *Foreign Policy*, November–December 2002, pp. 68–9. For complete results of the survey see www.worldviews.org. For 2003 follow-up poll, see www.transatlantictrends.org.

16 'Germany speaks', *New York Times*, 24 September 2002, p. A30; also 'New US doctrine worries Europeans'.

17 Joseph S. Nye, Jr, *The Paradox of American Power: Why the World's only Superpower can't Go it Alone* (New York: Oxford University Press, 2002), pp. xii–xvi, 40. See also his related articles: 'The American national interest and global public goods', *International Affairs*, 78, 2 (2002), pp. 233–44, and 'The dependent colossus', *Foreign Policy*, March–April 2002, pp. 74–6.

18 EU quote and position toward the ICC provided by EC delegation in Washington. Dodd quote in 'US renounces its support of new tribunal for war crimes', *Washington Post*, 7 May 2002; *Washington Post* editorial quotes in 'Red meat for unilateralists', 11 April 2002. 'Sign on, opt out', *The Economist*, 6 January 2001, p. 38. 'Role in

international court rejected', 8 December 2001, and 'US presses allies on War Crimes Court', 27 August 2002, both in *The Washington Post*. European compromise in 'Europeans to exempt US from War Court', 1 October 2002, and 'US presses for total exemption from War Crimes Court', 9 October 2002, both in *The New York Times*. The sensitivity Americans have toward constraints over the exercise of US sovereignty was expressed by Secretary of State Powell, who said of the broad coalition the President had forged to deal with the challenge of terrorism, 'There are no arrangements within this coalition which in any way shape, fashion or constrain the President in the exercise of his constitutional responsibilities to defend the United States of America'. ('Bush seeks European support'.)

19 'A transatlantic rift', *The Economist*, 19 January 2002, pp. 42–3. 'The prisoner question', *Washington Post*, 3 February 2002, pp. B1, B4. 'Geneva rules apply to captive Taliban', *International Herald Tribune*, 8 February 2002, pp. 1, 10.

20 Brad Roberts, 'Managing proliferation: a view from the United States', in Frances G. Burwell and Ivo H. Daalder (eds), *The United States and Europe in the Global Arena* (New York: St Martin's Press, 1999), pp. 130–3, 149–52. Harald Müller shares the view that transatlantic co-operation has been successful in the non-proliferation area, despite different viewpoints on a variety of questions. See Müller, 'Managing proliferation: a European perspective', in Burwell and Daalder, *The United States and Europe*, pp. 154–75.

21 'UN orders Iraq to disarm', 9 November 2002, and 'For Powell, a long path to a victory', 10 November 2002, both in *The Washington Post*.

22 'NATO approves new direction', 22 November 2002, 'Aid from NATO allies asked for Iraqi war', 6 December 2002, 'EU rejects Turkey's bid for early talks', 13 December 2002, and 'Six nations agree to a role in policing postwar Iraq, 3 May 2003, all in *The Washington Post*. Fontaine quote in third article. 'NATO: Poland will lead Iraq peacekeepers', *New York Times*, 21 May 2003.

23 'US National Missile Defence and the need to maintain strategic stability', *EU–US News*, May 2001, pp. 8, 10.

24 'Bush to tell Russia US will withdraw from '72 ABM pact', pp. A3, A14, and 'Two nuclear experts briefed Bin Laden, Pakistanis say', pp. A1, A23, both in *The Washington Post*, 12 December 2001.

25 Richard Lugar, 'Eye on a worldwide weapons cache', p. A39, and 'Nuclear warhead arsenal trimmed', p. A36, both in *The Washington Post*, 6 December 2001. Renée de Nevers, 'Russia in Europe's new equation', in Burwell and Daalder, *The United States and Europe*, p. 101. 'Bush pledges more aid for Russian arms cuts', *Washington Post*, 28 December 2001, pp. A1, A18. For fears concerning Russian WMD stocks see Jessica Stern, *The Ultimate Terrorists* (Cambridge MA: Harvard University Press, 1999), pp. 87–106.

26 Roberts, 'Managing proliferation', pp. 129–30. Harald Müller concluded that transatlantic co-operation in the non-proliferation field is most successful when exercised in a division-of-labour mode. ('Managing proliferation', p. 173.) Frances G. Burwell, 'Co-operation in US–European relations', in Burwell and Daalder, *The United States and Europe*, p. 284. Nevers, 'Russia', pp. 99–102. Philippart and Winand conclude that the US–EU record on non-proliferation has been 'meagre', despite a high level of commitment and activity. ('Deeds not words?' in Philippart and Winand, *Ever Closer Partnership*, p. 453.

27 'Weapons for sale?' *Maclean's*, 16 December 2002, pp. 35–8.

28 Author interview with Ted Whiteside in NATO Headquarters, Brussels, 11 June 2001.

29 The Nuclear Posture Review reportedly contained the justification for both a reduction of strategic warheads to as few as 1,700 and a resumption of testing. ('US to seek options on new nuclear tests', *Washington Post*, 8 January 2002, p. A4.)

30 'US fears Bin Laden gain in nuclear effort', 4 December 2001, pp. A1, A18; 'Bin Laden tells interviewer he has nuclear weapons', 11 November 2001, p. A32, both in *The Washington Post*.

31 'US boycotts nuclear test ban meeting', *Washington Post*, 12 November 2001, p. A6. 'Dancing round a ban', 17 November 2001, p. 26, and 'In America's interests', 26 May 2001, pp. 13–14, both in *The Economist*.

32 'Nations reach pact on trade of small arms', 22 July 2001, p. A17; 'US fights small arms draft', 10 July 2001, p. A1; 'Free fire at the United Nations', 10 July 2001, all in *The Washington Post*.

33 'US ends meeting on germ warfare', *Washington Post*, 8 December 2001, pp. A1, A5; 'A viral bust-up', *The Economist*, 8 December 2001, p. 46.

34 Morningstar speech at College of Europe, Bruges, 17 April 2001.

35 'Bad air over Kyoto', *Time*, European edition, 9 April 2001, pp. 16–18. Prodi quote in May 2001 publication by EC delegation in Washington. Polling results in 'Europeans object to Bush approach on foreign policy', *Washington Post*, 16 August 2001. Joffe, 'America über Alles?' *International Herald Tribune*, 16 April 2001. Polling results in Kennedy and Bouton, 'The real transatlantic gap', pp. 68, 70–71.

36 'Bush urged to negotiate global warming treaty', 2 August 2001, p. A14; 'McCain, Lieberman urge greenhouse gas curbs', 4 August 2001, pp. A1, A10; Pronk quote in 'Warming Pact a win for European leaders', 11 November 2001, p. A2, all in *The Washington Post*. 'Bush plan "positive" but EU prefers Kyoto', *International Herald Tribune*, 15 February 2002. Interview with Todd Huizinga, Office of European Union Affairs, US Department of State, 17 December 2001. The European Union plans to set up the world's largest emissions trading market by 2005. ('Europe set to create emissions trading market', *Wall Street Journal*, 11 December 2002, p. A15.)

37 'On global warming, states act locally', *Washington Post*, 11 November 2002, p. A3.

38 Philippart and Winand, 'Deeds, not words?' pp. 451–2. Statistics in May 2001 publication by EC delegation in Washington. Author interview with Huizinga, who admitted that it is difficult to 'get together' with the European Union and to get the right people within its complex organisation on board for a co-operative project. The United States sometimes follows the EU lead in Africa, as was the case when responding to Zimbabwean President Robert Mugabe's condoning of attacks on white-owned farms. ('European Union widens curbs on Zimbabwe', *Washington Post*, 23 July 2002.) With regard to US humanitarian assistance, private aid is estimated to be four times the official sum. The United States is often quicker in providing help, and it is frequently the single largest provider to a given country. "Facing responsibility", *The Economist*, 23 November 2002, p. 22. The administration of George W. Bush increased development assistance by 50 per cent in 2002, and on 27 May 2003 he signed a Bill allotting $15 billion to fight AIDS in Africa and the Caribbean over a five-year period.

39 Author interview with Whiteside. Solana quote in 'Seeing a void, EU weighs Mideast peace plan', *Washington Post*, 25 February 2002, p. A19.

40 Author interview with Mulrean. Frellesen, 'Processes', pp. 338–9. Philippart and

Winand registered good results of US–EU co-operation in the Middle East, although it remained below the level of intensity reached in co-operation in Europe. ('Deeds, not words?' p. 451.) Wallace, 'Europe', p. 23; Patten, 'Weltpolitik'. See Robert D. Blackwill and Michael Stürmer (eds), *Allies Divided: Transatlantic Policies for the Greater Middle East* (Cambridge MA: MIT Press, 1997), pp. 4–5, 299–307. Polling results in Kennedy and Bouton, 'The real transatlantic gap', p. 72. Schröder quote in 'Germany to give arms to Israel', *Washington Post*, 27 November 2002, p. A14.

41 'Despair' in 'Wake up, Europe!', *The Economist*, 15 September 2001, p. 45.

42 Author interviews with Morford and Mulrean. 'Finanzhilfen', *Das Parlament*, 20 July 2001. 'Europeans propose observer force for Middle East', *Washington Post*, 19 July 2001. 'Javier Solana', *The Economist*, 17 November 2001, p. 52. Solana quote from 'Seeing a void'. Cary quote in 'US, Europe divided over Middle East strategy', *Washington Post*, 10 November 2002, p. A18. See also 'US still trying to unfold Mideast road map', *New York Times*, 15 November 2002, p. A13. Meeting in Copenhagen in December 2002, EU Foreign Ministers, frustrated over US refusal to exert more pressure on the Israeli government, issued an unusually strong statement demanding a freeze on Israeli settlements in Gaza and the West Bank. ('Bigger EU seen as counterbalance, not threat', *Washington Post*, 16 December 2002.) For US–European co-operation in the Middle East see Volker Perthes, 'The advantages of complementarity: the Middle East peace process', in Hall Gardner and Radoslava Stefanova, *The New Transatlantic Agenda: Facing the Challenges of Global Governance* (Aldershot: Ashgate, 2001), and Roy H. Ginsberg, *The European Union in International Politics: Baptism by Fire* (Lanham MD: Rowman and Littlefield, 2001), chapter 5. Chapter 6 in Ginsberg's book deals with the European Union's political impact on the United States.

43 Patten, 'Weltpolitik'.

44 'Europeans reject role in Taiwan arms deal', *International Herald Tribune*, 27 April 2001. Daalder, 'Divorce', p. 566.

45 Müller, 'Managing proliferation', pp. 168–9. Frellesen, 'Processes', pp. 340–1, and Philippart and Winand, 'Deeds, not words?' p. 455. During the Bush administration funding for KEDO increased, and along with its European allies the United States remained a generous provider of humanitarian assistance, especially food, to North Korea. ('Eyeballing Kim Jong II', *The Economist*, 23 February 2002, p. 14.) Despite harsh rhetoric between the Bush administration and Pyongyang, the international consortium continues construction of the twin nuclear power reactors in North Korea. See 'N. Korea reactor project on course', *Washington Post*, 30 March 2002, p. A8.

46 Thomas L. Friedman, 'What game is Bush playing with Pyongyang?', *International Herald Tribune*, 10 March 2001, p. 8.

47 Interviews with Morford and Mulrean. Patten, 'Weltpolitik'. 'Europe discovers North Korea', *The Economist*, 5 May 2001, p. 36. 'EU to pursue links with North Korea', 31 March 2001; 'EU mission to Koreas is seen as rebuke to Bush', 28 March 2001, pp. 1, 8; 'On North Korea, the new administration has seen the light', 11 June 2001, all in *International Herald Tribune*. 'Powell urges resumption of N. Korea talks', 28 July 2001, p. A13; 'North Korean leader, in Moscow, says missile plan is no threat', 5 August 2001, p. A18, both in *The Washington Post*. 'Eyeballing'. Condoleeza Rice called North Korea 'the world's number one merchant for ballistic missiles, open for business with anyone, no matter how malign the buyer's inten-

tions'. ('US repeats warnings on terrorism', *Washington Post*, 1 February 2002, pp. A1, A4.)

48 'North Korea says it has a program on nuclear arms', *New York Times*, 17 October 2002, pp. A1, A8. ' North Korea says it will renew work at reactors', *Washington Post*, 13 December 2002, pp. A1, A51. Bush quote in 'Bush pledges diplomatic approach to North Korea', *Washington Post*, 22 October 2002.

Part III

Emerging security challenges

Wyn Rees

7

Combating terrorism in transatlantic relations

This chapter investigates transatlantic co-operation against the phenomenon of terrorism since the end of the Cold War. It focuses on those issues in the field of terrorism that have been pertinent to US–European collaboration, where counter-terrorist initiatives have been undertaken to prevent, deter and combat terrorism.[1] The logic of US–European co-operation against terrorism is readily apparent. All Western countries share a common abhorrence of terrorism and all are potentially vulnerable as targets. In order to combat terrorism, the most effective strategy is to maximise the amount of intelligence on the sources of the threat, and the only way to achieve this is through multilateral co-operation between governments, police forces and intelligence agencies. Yet, despite the clear rationale in favour of co-operation, the two sides of the Atlantic have found it difficult to co-operate against the menace of terrorism. The issue of terrorism has been predominantly a source of tension rather than cohesion in the transatlantic relationship.

The main obstacles to building a common transatlantic counter-terrorist strategy have included different historical experiences of the terrorist phenomenon, varying approaches to dealing with the threat and opposing attitudes to those states that are suspected of sponsoring terrorism. In addition, the Europeans have not possessed a multilateral institution of the requisite maturity to be able to react to American calls for co-operation on an equal footing. Ironically, one of the results of the terrorist attacks on the United States in September 2001 has been to inject new political will into the transatlantic relationship to co-operate in a US-led 'war against terrorism'. This has proved to be a watershed in the shared aim of countering terrorism; henceforth it will be necessary to differentiate between the period before and after the devastating attacks on New York and Washington.

A shared threat?

For the purposes of this chapter, terrorism is understood to define a type of action, namely the use of violence by a non-state actor, against civilians with the aim of creating fear. Above all, terrorism involves a psychological relationship in that the targets are usually random and the aim of the perpetrators is to generate a feeling of insecurity among a target audience. The term 'terrorism' has generated a multitude of interpretations, and authors such as Hoffman and Tucker have reviewed the many attempts to find a universal definition.[2] Among EU governments there was for a long time an inability to agree upon a common definition of terrorism or an agreed list of terrorist offences. This deadlock was resolved only after the terrorist attacks on the World Trade Center and Pentagon. There are even different definitions of terrorism within the American government, thereby exemplifying the many ambiguities in the subject.[3]

Vital to an understanding of transatlantic counter-terrorist co-operation is an appreciation of the constantly evolving nature of the problem. The ending of the Cold War marked the beginning of a period in which some terrorist movements emerged whilst others disappeared. Several trends have accompanied this reordering of international terrorism. First, there has been a trend towards groups seeking new sources of patronage and funding. As the backing of former sponsors collapsed, several movements have been forced to look elsewhere for support. This has contributed to links emerging between terrorist groups and organised crime and, in the case of Afghanistan and South America, with drug traffickers. Second, new groups have arisen with looser affiliations and a broader range of motivations. A notable trend has been towards the emergence of organisations espousing a religious cause.[4] This has been evident in the Muslim world but also in the northern hemisphere in the case of sects, such as the Aum Shinrikyo movement in Japan which conducted the Sarin gas attack on the Tokyo subway. Third, new forms of terrorism have emerged. Not only have new weapons been in evidence, such as the use of hijacked passenger aircraft, but new forms of conflict, such as cyber-terrorist disruption of advanced Western computer systems.

The number of international terrorist incidents has been decreasing since a high point in 1987. Although the number of events has been in decline, the lethality and number of casualties from attacks have been increasing. This underlines the fact that terrorist groups have become more capable and many are seeking to kill or maim ever larger numbers of people.[5] Indeed, for some terrorist groups the desire for publicity has become less important than the aim of causing death and destruction to an adversary. This may reflect the decline in terrorist groups with political motivations who are concerned not to harm their cause by large numbers of civilian casualties, and the rise of religiously inspired terrorism where it may be the object of the perpetrators to destroy as many of their enemies as possible. In the words of Bruce Hoffman, 'violence for some terrorist groups is perhaps becoming less of a means to an end than as an end in itself that does not require any wider explanation or justification beyond the group's members themselves'.[6] This has major implications if terrorist groups are successful in gaining access to weapons of mass destruction, such as chemical, biological and even nuclear weapons.

Different historical experiences have helped to forge contrasting American and European attitudes towards terrorism. Many governments in post-war Europe were forced to contend with prolonged domestic terrorist problems. Some of these resulted from colonial legacies, such as the issue of Algerian terrorism in France. Others arose from the demands of secessionist movements, such as the Basque movement in Spain and republicanism in Northern Ireland, whilst some developed from revolutionary movements that despised the modern capitalist state, such as the Baader-Meinhof group in West Germany. Terrorism has been a very diverse problem in Europe, with groups varying in terms of their origins, motivation and scale. In the words of den Boer, 'The levels of threat [among the EU members] differ greatly, and the origin of the terrorist threat is still bound up with the idiosyncrasies of the relevant member state.'[7]

This diversity has made terrorism a subject on which even West European states found it difficult to co-operate. For example, some countries have interpreted actions in their neighbours' territories as constituting 'political crimes' and have refused extradition requests on the grounds that an accused person might not receive a fair trial or because membership of an organisation is not proscribed in their state. In cases where European co-operation has taken place, it has usually been the result of bilateral agreements. This has tended to emerge from shared perceptions of danger between neighbours. Examples have included the extradition of suspected Basque terrorists from France to Spain in the latter part of the 1980s and the cross-border agreements between the United Kingdom and the Irish Republic, which resulted from the 1985 Anglo-Irish Agreement. This can be counterbalanced by cases where inter-European co-operation has been notably absent, leading to mutual recrimination. This was illustrated in the case of Belgium's refusal to extradite Father Patrick Ryan, who was suspected of involvement with the Irish Republican Army (IRA), to the United Kingdom in 1988.[8]

It was not until June 1976 that an intergovernmental organisation was established to facilitate the sharing of information between European Community (EC) members over issues relating to terrorism. The TREVI forum (Terrorisme, Radicalisme, Extremisme et Violence Internationale) became the meeting place for Interior Ministers of EC states to exchange information and discuss issues of concern as well as to serve as an interface with third-party countries. It comprised two working groups, one of which focused on terrorism and the other on broader public order matters. The working group on terrorism involved senior officials from Interior Ministries, police officers and intelligence specialists. TREVI was enhanced in 1985 and its remit was extended to drug trafficking and various aspects of international crime.[9] It became subsequently the focal point for much of the European Community's co-operation on criminal matters prior to the establishment of the 1992 Maastricht Treaty (or Treaty on European Union, TEU). In the Maastricht Treaty a substantial step forward was achieved through the creation of a dedicated intergovernmental pillar, 'Justice and Home Affairs' (JHA), which brought internal security provisions within the framework of the newly created European Union.

In contrast to Europe, the post-war American experience of terrorism was limited. The United States did not have to face a powerful indigenous terrorist movement and did not suffer a large-scale domestic terrorist outrage until the bombing of the Oklahoma Federal Building in April 1995.[10] Furthermore, the physical distance of the United States from Europe rendered it difficult for either its government or its people to appreciate the threats with which the European allies were faced. These differing experiences contributed to disagreements in transatlantic relations, as the Europeans felt that the United States did not take their domestic terrorist problems sufficiently seriously. For example, the British government expressed occasional complaints to Washington about the indulgent attitude that was shown towards Irish Republican fund raising in the United States by NORAID. Prime Minister John Major, in particular, was deeply disappointed by the willingness of the Clinton administration to receive members of Sinn Fein at the White House as part of the US government's attempts to push forward the peace process in Northern Ireland.

Whilst the US experience of domestic terrorism has been limited, the United States has found itself the principal target of terrorist attacks on its personnel and assets overseas. The severity of attacks on US overseas interests escalated in the 1980s, illustrated by the devastating attack on the US Marine base in Lebanon in 1982. Other high-profile events, such as the bombing of the Khobar Towers in Saudi Arabia in 1996 (which killed nineteen US personnel) and the attacks in 1998 on the US embassies in Kenya and Tanzania (which killed 257 people, twelve of whom were US citizens), ensured American attention was paid to terrorism. In the year 2000, for example, there were 200 terrorist attacks that were categorised as against US interests or personnel.[11] This has occurred for a number of reasons. In the first place, the United States has a global presence – in military, diplomatic, economic and cultural terms – which makes it highly vulnerable to attack. For example, the worldwide deployment of the American military was illustrated by the attack on the USS *Cole* in the port of Yemen. Secondly, American identification with countries such as Israel and Saudi Arabia has excited the hatred of Arab nationalists and Muslim fundamentalist movements. The al-Qaida network originally declared its 'holy war' against the United States because of the stationing of American forces on Saudi territory. Lastly, antipathy has been directed at the United States partly as a result of its huge wealth, which has elicited envy, and its cultural influence, through films, food and clothing.

These different experiences have influenced the responses of the United States and the Europeans towards dealing with terrorism. The European experience has taught countries to live with a low level of terrorist threat to their societies. This point was acknowledged by the European Union's High Representative, Javier Solana, who noted that the European attitude to terrorism has been conditioned by many decades of protracted struggle.[12] The Europeans have come to emphasise the importance of denying terrorists legitimacy and treating them as criminals who must be tried and punished within the judicial system. Where international action is contemplated, European governments have exhibited a predisposition to multilateral co-operation and the involvement of international organisations. Adherence to multilateral frameworks has enabled the Europeans to extol the use of legal instruments in fighting terrorism and helped them to draw upon international support.

For its part, the United States has developed five main sorts of instruments to fight terrorism: law enforcement, diplomacy, economic sanctions, covert activity and military force.[13] Whilst the United States has been quick to use its law enforcement powers against terrorist groups, it has not relied on them to the exclusion of other instruments. Terrorism has been treated by policy makers in Washington as a multi-faceted national security issue that justifies the mobilisation of all the resources of the state. This willingness to use a broader range of foreign-policy tools has distinguished the US approach from that of the European allies. It has led to open disagreement between the transatlantic allies as the Europeans have criticised the Americans for adopting a heavy-handed approach. In turn, critics in the United States have rebuked the Europeans for following policies that are geared deliberately to maintaining a low profile and minimising the risk of terrorist retribution.

The US experience of the phenomenon of terrorism – whether against a movement or against a state sponsor – has frequently led it to respond unilaterally with the use of economic sanctions and even military force. This has partly reflected America's economic strength in the world and its capacity, as the preeminent military power, to inflict retribution on an aggressor regardless of location. The United States has faced the choice of whether to pursue bilateral and multilateral forms of co-operation with its allies or to rely upon its own overwhelming strength through unilateral policies. The advantages of co-operating with European allies has been that action appears more legitimate: but the drawbacks have been the necessity for consultation and the risk of paralysis if consensus is elusive. Although the United States has generally favoured operating bilaterally or multilaterally, it has not shrunk from unilateral action when it has believed this to be in its interest or when it has been unable to obtain support from allies.

The national security approach evident in American policy on counterterrorism is reflected in the multiplicity of US agencies involved. While the State Department has primary responsibility for the co-ordination of counter terrorism activities overseas, and the FBI has principal domestic jurisdiction, there are a host of other agencies with competences in this sphere, including the Departments of Justice, the Treasury and Defense, as well as a plethora of intelligence agencies.[14] This results in the need for co-ordination mechanisms. At the top of the tree is an Interagency Coordinating Committee, chaired by the Special Assistant to the President on the National Security Council. This meets at Assistant Secretary level and helps to set long-term strategic objectives in combating terrorism. Beneath this is an Interagency Working Group on Terrorism which is chaired by the State Department Coordinator for Counterterrorism.[15] The Interagency Working Group has responsibility for developing policy goals for each of the US government agencies with an interest in counter-terrorism.

In addition to the major departments of state, another influential actor in the field of anti-terrorism has been the US Congress. As the subject of terrorism has risen higher up the foreign-policy agenda the Congress has become increasingly vocal. There has periodically been tension over policy between the administration and the Congress as the latter has pressed for a tougher stance to be adopted. In particular, the Congress has been a source of criticism of what it has perceived to be the weakness of America's allies in combating terrorism. The Clinton administration, for example, found itself squeezed, on several occasions, between European allies that were counselling caution on American policies towards suspected state sponsors of terrorist groups and a Congress that was determined to assert a muscular US approach.

Barriers to transatlantic co-operation against terrorism

Transatlantic co-operation against terrorism has been limited. In the light of the different historical experiences and the political sensitivity of the issues, perhaps this fact should not be surprising. The United States has concentrated its efforts on building bilateral links with European states: the US–UK relationship is one example. This is known to be particularly strong, partly as a result of the broader 'special relationship' between London and Washington, and partly due to the fact that Washington shares its intelligence information with London. British policy towards terrorism has consequently been closely aligned with that of the United States. Lesser describes UK policy as 'broadly supportive of US-led diplomatic, economic and military initiatives in the counter-terrorism arena'.[16] This relationship also has important wider ramifications for the United States. It provides the American government with a valuable vehicle for launching its initiatives among the Europeans and guarantees it a sympathetic voice in Brussels.[17]

Yet when one turns to examine transatlantic multilateral co-operation against terrorism, the results so far have proved to be disappointing. This is not to deny that the two sides of the Atlantic share common goals in relation to fighting terrorism: rather, it is that the political will to pursue these goals together has been insufficient. There have been three categories of obstacles to co-operation. First, some countries in Europe have not been well disposed politically towards working closely with the United States in counter-terrorist activity. France, for instance, has always been wary of allowing the United States to become disproportionately influential on the continent and has sought to circumscribe the range of activities that are carried out. The Greek government has also been an obstacle, as it has been sensitive to US criticism about its alleged lack of energy in combating its domestic terrorist problems.[18]

Second, co-operation has been rendered more difficult by European opposition to some US policy positions. For instance, the availability of the death penalty in many US states has proved to be a major obstacle. The availability of the death penalty for terrorist offences was a major feature of the Antiterrorism and Effective Death Penalty Act of 1996. The European Convention on Human Rights has rendered it problematical for a European country to extradite terrorist suspects to the United States who, if convicted, could be subject to capital punishment. The result has been opposition in Europe to any significant increase in judicial co-operation in terrorist matters with the United States.

Third, there has been an absence of suitable organisations in which to develop transatlantic counter-terrorist co-operation. NATO has been the dominant forum for promoting transatlantic military co-operation since its founding in 1949, yet it has shown little appetite to become focused on a broader, 'soft' security agenda of issues. NATO Secretary General Lord Robertson acknowledged in 2001 that the war against terrorism would be principally a legal, political and economic task,[19] and that the Alliance is 'not a police force ... and because of its nature, it is not terribly well suited to dealing with law enforcement'.[20] Although NATO's remit extends to terrorism, it has concentrated its attention on the military security issues that have traditionally been its area of expertise. This has reflected, on the one hand, a concern to avoid watering down the Alliance but, on the other, a propensity to deal with terrorism in a national context that avoids the possibility of divergences between member states. Since the Prague summit the Alliance has taken overt steps to address the issue of terrorism more actively but it is clear that the nature of the terrorist threat renders NATO only a partially suitable framework (see Chapters 2 and 6).

The inappropriateness of the NATO forum has led to the European Union becoming the main partner for counter-terrorist co-operation with the United States. This has presented problems, however, owing to the limited progress among the Fifteen to work together over terrorist issues and because of the fact that the Union's structures have been at a formative stage of development. Whilst the United States has been pressing for more substantive collaboration in the 1990s, the European Union's response has been, in effect, to ask for patience whilst it builds the appropriate machinery. An example has been American attempts to secure a working relationship with the European Police Office (Europol), based in the Hague. Despite the fact that Europol is only an information-gathering and processing centre for the EU member state police forces, and not an operational body, the United States was eager to share information. Yet American law enforcement officials were frustrated in their quest by the slow process of ratifying the Europol convention among the members and the fact that it possessed no authority to deal with terrorist issues until July 1999.[21] In the words of Chalk, 'Such a centralised body is crucial for dealing with . . . terrorism, where single pieces of information are often meaningless until they are pieced together in a larger picture'.[22] It was not until the end of 2001 that a US–EU breakthrough on the topic of Europol was achieved.

Tensions within the US–EU relationship have been compounded by the institutional complexity of the Union. The various agencies of the US government involved in fighting terrorism have been unclear about who their counterparts are in Brussels. The issue of combating terrorism crosses the three pillars of the European Union: the Community pillar, the Common Foreign and Security Policy and the Justice and Home Affairs pillar. This cross-pillarisation has rendered it difficult for states outside the Union to know with whom they must deal. For example, the American government came to find that the Commission official responsible for justice and internal security matters, resident in Washington, had no power to negotiate over issues relating to terrorism because that came under the competences of the European Union's CFSP.[23]

One attempt to break through this institutional impasse and invest co-operation with a new political dynamic was the signing of the New Transatlantic Agenda (NTA) in 1995 (see Chapter 6). The NTA deliberately specified the need for enhanced transatlantic co-operation against terrorism as one of the categories within 'New Global Challenges'.[24] Officials in the Senior Level Group of the NTA were mandated to make reports at their six-monthly meetings on the progress that had been achieved in fighting terrorism. However, in spite of the importance that was invested in raising the profile of countering terrorism through the NTA, in practice it has delivered disappointing results. The political will inside the European Union has been insufficient to satisfy US expectations and the member states have preferred to concentrate on developing their own internal ideas before engaging with outsiders.

This has led to the Group of Seven/Group of Eight leading industrial countries being used as an alternative forum for discussions and initiatives on counter-terrorism. Whilst not exclusively a transatlantic forum, it has the benefit of being an established yet flexible multilateral institution. Furthermore, unlike the situation in the European Union, the Group of Eight does not require the positions of the major European states to be negotiated before the United States can be involved. The Group of Eight has benefited from an agenda of issues that can be adapted at relatively short notice and from the ability to include other influential countries in counter-terrorist discussions, such as Russia and Japan.

The Group of Eight has been used in transatlantic relations in two ways. First, to advance US and European views on combating terrorism and to attempt to obtain a consensus among the other G-8 members. For example, at the Ottawa meeting in December 1995 the Europeans and the United States focused on practical measures that could be used to inhibit the ease of operation by terrorist groups. The European Union co-ordinated its own positions and acted as a partner to the United States; both sides promoting the objectives of information sharing and the targeting of terrorist funds. The second use to which the US–European relationship has put the Group of Eight has been the creation of a counter-terrorist consensus that can then be advanced at a global level. Agreement within the Group of Eight has often been used as a precursor for taking an issue to the United Nations in order to try and achieve universal support. Evidence of this can be seen from the Lyon summit of June 1996. At Lyon a list of forty recommendations were drawn up for states to implement in order to present a common front against terrorism. A special meeting on terrorism was convened the following month in Paris, at the suggestion of President Chirac, which emphasised the problem of terrorist fund raising and involved the work of the G-8 Financial Action Task Force. Having developed a consensus within the Group of Eight on measures against terrorist fund raising, the issue was taken to the United Nations to garner further support. The result was a UN convention which, although remaining voluntary, helped to establish a global regime against this complex problem. At the subsequent Denver summit the Group of Eight proceeded to exhort the international community to adopt all the existing UN conventions against terrorism, including the important UN International Convention on the Suppression of Terrorist Bombings.

Transatlantic differences over 'states of concern'

Countering terrorism internationally has been a major foreign-policy objective of the United States since the 1970s. Europe has been quietly supportive of many US policies around the world, including its Anti-terror Assistance Programme. This programme was initiated in 1983 and has provided states all around the world with equipment, training and technical assistance for their own counter-terrorist activities. Where the Europeans have been critical of the United States, however, has been on the occasions when America has chosen to pursue counter-terrorist policies that have not been agreed with their allies in advance.

European capitals have been especially uneasy when America has decided to undertake foreign-policy action under its own unique laws without reference to wider international law.[25] Abandoning accepted international norms of behaviour risks, in European eyes, generating the impression that the United States will defy the will of the international community if it cannot get its way. The United States demonstrated this tendency in relation to its Omnibus Terrorism Act of 1986, which enables the United States to put a suspect before an American court even when that person has been brought into the area of US jurisdiction against their will. This legislation was invoked in 1987 when a Lebanese man, Fawaz Yunis, was abducted by US personnel from a yacht in international waters in the Mediterranean and against his will was transported to America to face trial. Many European states expressed concern that by such an act the United States was likely to reduce the likelihood of receiving assistance in future cases of terrorist suspects. The United States dismissed these concerns and pointed to the fact that Yunis was duly convicted of participation in the hi-jacking of a Jordanian aircraft.[26]

A particular source of transatlantic tension has been the different attitudes of the two sides to so-called 'rogue' states or 'states of concern'. An annual certification of states considered to be sponsors of terrorism is conducted by the US Department of State.[27] Six states have preoccupied American attention during the 1990s: Cuba, Iran, Iraq, Libya, North Korea and Syria. Sudan was added to the list in 1993. Not all these are viewed as active state sponsors of terrorism – some are feared primarily as countries seeking to acquire weapons of mass destruction – but terrorism is one of the principal factors for designating states in this category. Some states are accused of actively promoting terrorism, such as Syria's support for the Hezbollah movement in Lebanon, whilst others are seen as providing safe havens for terrorist training groups or for the perpetrators of terrorist outrages. Pakistan, for example, although an ally of the United States, has been criticised by the Americans for its alleged support for armed groups fighting the Indian army in Kashmir.

American worries about the role of states of concern have been driven by two principal factors. The first has been the fact that either the United States, or its allies, are frequently the targets of attacks by groups that are receiving state support. For example, Iran is known to be a major supporter of the Hamas and Islamic Jihad groups that conduct terrorist activities in the Israeli-occupied territories. The second is the fear in the minds of American policy makers that state sponsorship could increase the chances of a terrorist group gaining access to weapons of mass destruction. This might be in the form of deliberately passing weapon technologies to a militant group or alternatively providing a secure environment in which such groups can develop materials of their own.

The US Export Administration Act of 1979[28] is the formal mechanism under which states are designated as terrorist sponsors. Under the Act such countries cannot be traded with nor can they receive US economic or military assistance. This applies in particular to the provision of dual-use technology, items that could be used for sophisticated weapons programmes. The US Congress has been active in attempting to harden the containment policies of successive administrations towards states of concern. In June 2000 the National Commission on Terrorism, a bipartisan body endorsed by Congress, issued a report calling for a more muscular range of sanctions to be instituted against suspected state sponsors.[29]

European countries, both bilaterally and in multilateral forums, have expressed their concerns at what they perceive to be a confrontational American approach. The Europeans have viewed the vilification of suspected state sponsors of terrorism as counterproductive, turning states into potential outcasts and pariahs. Instead they have advocated a 'critical dialogue' – engaging diplomatically with the state whilst expressing a comprehensive range of concerns – with the aim of modifying the target's behaviour. European attitudes have been influenced by three considerations. First, they have wanted to be convinced by evidence when the United States accuses a state of complicity with a terrorist attack, rather than relying on accusations. Second, the Europeans have been willing to acknowledge that poverty, economic deprivation and political paralysis can serve as a fertile breeding ground for the sort of extremism that gives rise to terrorism. Whilst rejecting the legitimacy of terrorism as a course of action, European states have recognised that the frustration associated with the plight of people such as the Palestinian nation has helped to foster the conditions for terrorism. Third has been the consideration, even more privately expressed, that European countries fear being identified with the sort of robust American counter-terrorist policies that could lead to retaliation.

The United States acknowledges that its priorities differ from those of its European partners: a report prepared for the June 1996 US–EU summit stated that 'We share basic objectives' (in relation to states suspected of sponsoring terrorism) but 'we take different approaches on how to address these challenges'.[30] For its part the US government, and particularly Republicans in the Congress, have been critical of the European approach and argue that the allies make an inadequate contribution towards a united Western front against terrorism. The European allies have been accused of showing weakness in the face of a common threat. The United States has suspected that they place their own selfish interests above principles in their dealings with states of concern. For example, purchases of petroleum from Libya in the early 1990s were a major factor in determining the sorts of sanctions in which the Europeans were prepared to participate.[31] America has charged its allies with seeking to maximise their own commercial trading advantage at the expense of the United States. A dim view is taken of such an approach, especially at a time in which the two sides of the Atlantic are engaged in increasing levels of commercial competition and economic rivalry.[32]

Iran has been subjected to the full ire of Washington because it has been viewed as the most active sponsor of terrorist organisations.[33] America attempted to galvanise its European allies into isolating Iran and enforcing a tightly controlled sanctions regime after 1995. The unwillingness of the Europeans to follow this lead, beyond the area of dual-use technologies, resulted in the United States introducing special legislation for the purpose, the Iran/Libya Sanctions Acts (ILSA). This initiative proved to be at the heart of a deep divide between the United States and Europe because it penalised any Western company that traded with either of the regimes.[34] European governments such as France, but also staunchly pro-American countries such as the United Kingdom, argued that the United States had no right to impose extraterritorial legislation on European firms and that it was unacceptable.[35] The European governments were influenced both by a desire to improve relations with the more moderate elements of the political leadership in Tehran, led by President Khatami, and by the interest of their oil companies in Iranian petroleum exploration.

173

When the French company Total decided to invest in the Iranian petrochemical industry, the US Congress mandated the administration to enforce the ILSA legislation. The Clinton administration complied under the terms of the Act by threatening to act against Total and its overseas interests. All West European countries expressed their opposition to the US policy and were united in the view that America's stance had to be reversed. The European Union threatened to take the United States before the World Trade Organisation in order to force it to reverse its position. In May 1998 there was an end to the stalemate when the United States agreed to waive the imposition of sanctions under the terms of ILSA.[36] Nevertheless, a sharp difference of approach in the transatlantic relationship had been exposed.[37]

An even sharper area of disagreement than over extraterritorial legislation has arisen in the past when the United States has been willing to resort to force either against terrorist organisations or against their host states. Washington's hard-line approach in its attempts to punish the activities of particular countries has caused consternation in European capitals. Even when the United States has used force in retaliation, European leaders have questioned the utility of using military power. The Europeans have tended to take the view that force is a blunt instrument to use against elusive and disparate terrorist targets and have openly expressed fears that such action could incite more terrorist action. European governments have warned of the risk of creating martyrs and encouraging others to adopt terrorist tactics in the future – thereby serving to undermine international co-operation and polarise opinion.

European states point to the experience of the US air raids against Libya in April 1986, code-named Operation El Dorado Canyon, to support their argument. The Reagan administration undertook the action in the belief that Colonel Qaddafi's regime had been responsible for terrorist attacks against US military personnel in a discotheque in Berlin. The attack against Libya was opposed by most European countries and only the United Kingdom was willing to allow American air bases on its soil to be used in the raids. The French government even went so far as to deny US planes the right to fly over its territory. The Europeans subsequently argued that the attacks were counterproductive, as Libya was suspected of involvement in terrorist attacks. These included the notorious bombing of Pan Am flight 103 over Lockerbie in December 1988 and the destruction of a French airliner over Niger in September 1989. Conversely, America took the view that the raids on Libya caused the Qaddafi government to reduce its sponsorship of terrorist activities and become far more cautious.

America's response to European condemnation of its military actions has been to contend that, even when such actions fail to arrest the use of terrorism, they play an important role in signalling US resolve to counter terrorism by all means available.[38] The United States has continued to use military power unilaterally in the 1990s when it has believed that it can strike against the perpetrators of terror. In August 1998, for example, following the terrorist attacks on the US embassies in Kenya and Tanzania, President Clinton authorised the use of military retaliation. Tomahawk cruise missile strikes were conducted against alleged terrorist bases in Afghanistan and against the al-Shaifa chemical plant in Khartoum, Sudan.

The United States argues that its willingness to use force is never a spasm response and that it has shown itself to be capable of employing a range of carefully calibrated instruments against terrorists, provided that they advance American objectives. Indeed, a novel US legal approach was evident in its subsequent attitude to Libyan complicity in the Lockerbie bombing. The Libyan government's refusal to hand over two of its nationals indicted for the outrage led the United States and the United Kingdom to pressure the United Nations into introducing sanctions in 1992.[39] Washington later agreed to the unprecedented step of allowing a prosecution to take place in relation to the death of its citizens in which the United States exercised no jurisdiction. Rather than undertake a court case with the suspects in the continental United States, it was finally agreed that the trial would take place in Holland, under Scottish law. The trial was duly conducted and secured the conviction of one of the suspects and the acquittal of the other.

11 September and the 'war against terror'

It has become commonplace to say that the world has changed since the terrorist attacks on New York and Washington in September 2001. Nevertheless, in relation to US–European co-operation against terrorism, and the impact that the attacks have caused on many Western countries, this is undoubtedly true. The scale and severity of the attacks, the *modus operandi* of the terrorists and the fact that the events were watched by countless people around the world caused shock and a deep-seated sense of outrage. Unlike most terrorist acts in the past, where violence has been employed to generate fear among a target audience, the attacks were designed to cause huge loss of life and were acts of mass murder. The perceived invulnerability of the US homeland was erased and a unique sense of fear was engendered with the subsequent cases of anthrax poisoning.

The American response to the attacks was to embark upon a 'war against terrorism', wherever it manifested itself in the world. As far as the suspected perpetrators of the attacks were concerned, the al-Qaida network headed by Osama bin Laden, the United States demanded its immediate dissolution and the hand-over of its leader to American judicial authorities. As early as 1999 the United States had imposed sanctions on the Taliban government in Afghanistan over its alleged complicity in terrorist acts.[40] After the 11 September attacks, the United States demanded that Afghanistan cease harbouring bin Laden. The failure of the Taliban to comply led this government to be designated as the first target in America's war against terrorism. The United States undertook to destroy the control of the Taliban regime over its country and to support the rebel Northern Alliance. After an intense bombing campaign the Taliban collapsed and American forces entered the country in an attempt to apprehend the principal leaders of the al-Qaida organisation.

European leaders were swift to offer support for the US war against terror. Whilst sharing in the horror at the attacks upon the United States, European countries were also concerned to be able to influence America's response. It was judged that this could best be achieved by offering to help in the US military campaign against al-Qaida. The Europeans would not have liked an outcome to the crisis that would have seen America emerge with the sense that it had succeeded alone or, worse, that it had been left to fail alone. With the offer of military forces the Europeans were showing that they favoured an engaged and multilateralist American response. European elites hoped they could encourage a new sense of American multilateralism by joining in President Bush's coalition building.[41]

Nevertheless, there were clear limits to European support for the United States. In late November 2001 President Bush doubled the number of American ground troops in Kuwait and stated that the United States would punish countries that harboured or assisted terrorists in any way, including those who 'develop weapons of mass destruction that will be used to terrorize nations'. It was clear that these remarks were aimed at Iraq and they elicited a sharp response from European capitals. Germany's Foreign Minister, Joschka Fischer, bluntly stated, 'all European nations would view a broadening [of the anti-terrorist campaign] to include Iraq highly sceptically, and that is putting it diplomatically'.[42] Europeans were reluctant to support possible US strikes against Iraq despite allegations that Baghdad had contacts with some of the terrorists involved in the 11 September attacks and confirmation by Germany's Federal Intelligence Service (BND) of reports in German newspapers that Iraq might be nuclear-capable by the year 2004 and have missiles able to reach Europe as soon as one year later.[43]

European offers of forces to the US-led conflict in Afghanistan varied. Prime Minister Tony Blair chose to seize the initiative and flew to America immediately after the disaster, visiting 'ground zero' where the World Trade Center once stood. He stated that in relation to terrorists 'There is no compromise possible with such people, no meeting of minds, no point of understanding . . . Just a choice: defeat it or be defeated by it. And defeat it we must . . .' He also travelled to the Middle East and South Asia to shore up diplomatic support for the war effort. Within two months Britain had sent 4,200 troops to the war zone and had put an additional 5,000 on alert. In the opening salvoes against the Taliban regime, British submarines fired cruise missiles at key targets, and put special forces and 100 Royal Marines on the ground to help in the Northern Alliance's rout of Taliban forces. Finally, Britain promised to 'assemble a humanitarian coalition alongside the military coalition' and allotted £25 million to humanitarian relief.[44]

France shed its usual hesitation toward collaboration with the United States.

President Chirac was the first foreign leader to visit Washington after the attacks and said that France stood 'in total solidarity' with the United States. French public opinion backed this policy. As military action against Afghanistan began, it had a refuelling ship and a frigate patrolling the waters close to the war zone. It quickly put intelligence agents on the ground to work with the Afghan opposition and readied special forces for possible use. It deployed 2,000 troops on its naval vessels, as well as combat and reconnaissance aircraft to be used if requested.

Germany's willingness to support a military effort on the other side of the globe was a major initiative. Only a decade earlier, former Social Democratic Party (SPD) leader Oskar Lafontaine had said, in reference to the Persian Gulf War, that requesting Germans to take part in any military action was 'like offering brandy chocolates to a reformed alcoholic'. But Volkmar Schultz, a member of the Bundestag's foreign relations committee, said that this attitude of mind was over: 'We have reached the end of the post-war period in German history. We cannot automatically run away from military action. Since 11 September most of the political class in Germany accept this as an unavoidable fact.' After cliffhanging negotiations and threats within his governing SPD–Green coalition, and supported by 59 per cent of the German population, Chancellor Schröder committed 3,900 troops to the war effort. Germany sent transport planes to Turkey to support operations in Afghanistan, as well as two frigates and escort vessels. Berlin offered up to 800 soldiers and 100 special forces. In addition to these military assets, Germany granted generous humanitarian aid, including US$28 million for the American victims of the terrorist attacks donated by individuals and corporations in Germany. Finally, Germany hosted a UN-sponsored political summit during November–December 2001 in the famous Petersberg Hotel overlooking Bonn, which brought together representatives of the many Afghan factions to discuss the formation of a post-Taliban regime and government.

Other European allies also provided assistance. Italy offered the aircraft carrier *Garibaldi*, other ships and up to 2,700 troops, whilst the Netherlands offered 1,200. Spain granted the United States the use of all its military installations. Even new NATO members such as Poland and the Czech Republic made pledges. Non-aligned European countries such as Sweden, Finland, Austria and Ireland signed a declaration recognising the United States' right to retaliate and offered humanitarian assistance to the Afghan people.

It was a paradox that after pressing its allies for years to take a larger part in 'out of area' operations, and after they had acted without American prompting to offer military assets for the war, Washington declined to utilise this proffered support. The Pentagon preferred to wage war in Afghanistan alone, with the subordinate back-up of Britain. This approach was frustrating for the Europeans, who were forced to stand down mobilised troops and wait for a request from Washington. Not until the White House, prodded by Colin Powell and Tony Blair, decided that it was politically prudent to involve the allies militarily, was the request sent for their help. By that time most of the hostilities had ceased. Central Command chief General Tommy Franks even objected to the subsequent deployment of thousands of international peacekeepers, led by Britain and consisting of troops from France, Germany, Italy, Canada, Turkey, Australia, Malaysia, Bangladesh and Jordan. This was on the grounds that such a force would complicate an already difficult situation. When the United Nations authorised the International Security Assistance Force (ISAF), whose mandate was to promote the stability of the post-Taliban government in Kabul, on 19 December, the US Central Command retained formal authority over the peacekeeping units in order to ensure that they would not interfere with American military objectives in Afghanistan. Thus the war in Afghanistan raised important questions about the future of American–European military co-operation against terror.

The aftermath of 11 September and the implications for transatlantic relations

The attacks of 11 September have helped to transform attitudes to transatlantic co-operation against terrorism. European countries, which had hitherto been sceptical about America's concentration on Osama bin Laden and his associates, were genuinely horrified at the events and were aware that such acts might equally have been conducted against them. German Chancellor Schröder called the attacks 'a declaration of war on the free world'.

Whilst there was an absence of a US–European counter-terrorist strategy in the past, the new international situation since the autumn of 2001 has created a different environment. The United States sought to develop counter-terrorist ties with the European Union and a meeting was swiftly organised on 21 September between the US Secretary of State Colin Powell and the EU Troika comprising of Louis Michel, Javier Solana and Chris Patten.[45] Their discussions were based upon a joint letter, written by Chris Patten and JHA Commissioner Vitorino, suggesting a range of co-operative measures. Although many of the issues had been under discussion for some time, it was only now that the political will existed to bring them into being.

Four main areas were targeted for transatlantic collaboration.[46] First, tighter airline security and closer police and judicial co-operation. A priority for judicial co-operation was the extradition of suspected terrorists, which had previously been held up over the issue of the death penalty in the United States. A compromise was mooted in which the US judicial authorities might guarantee that they would not seek the death sentence for an extradited individual. Second was the matter of terrorist financing. It was agreed that targeting both the sources of terrorist funding, as well as the ease with which groups moved and stored their money around the world, would be a major hindrance to their activities. Transatlantic co-operation would include the ratification of existing conventions on terrorist financing and the expectation that aspirant members of the European Union would sign up to the same agreements. Third was the issue of border controls, in order to make it increasingly difficult for known terrorist suspects to move into Western countries. Finally, agreement was reached in principle to improve the exchange of intelligence and information between the United States and Europe so that it could be disseminated to the greatest extent possible. Of particular importance is the sharing of information between US law enforcement agencies and Europol. Such a co-operative arrangement had hitherto been deadlocked over the issue of data protection rules in the United States.

Whilst US–EU co-operation in policing and judicial co-operation has been invigorated, it is less apparent that the United States foresees close co-operation with either the European Union or NATO in its military campaign against terrorism. The feeling has grown among European states that US consultation with them has been limited and that Washington has chosen to focus its energies on bilateral contacts with countries such as Britain and France. The approach of the Bush administration has been reinforced by the responses of the three leading European countries. The British government under Tony Blair sought to maximise its relationship with the United States by playing a role in the military campaign against Afghanistan. Even the French and German governments, hitherto the backbone of the European Union, decried the value of the 'Community method' in relation to this crisis.[47] All three governments chose at the European mini-summit in Ghent to meet outside the forum of the European Union to discuss the war in Afghanistan. Prime Minister Tony Blair subsequently organised a dinner at Downing Street on 4 November 2001 to which he invited German Chancellor Schröder and French President Chirac. Hearing of the gathering, other European leaders felt excluded and Italian Prime Minister Silvio Berlusconi, Spanish Prime Minister Jose Maria Aznar and Dutch Prime Minister Wim Kok all insisted on attending. Invitations were later extended to the Belgian Prime Minister, whose country occupied the EC presidency, and Javier Solana, the European Union's High Representative. The governments of the eight EU states that were not included were reportedly disappointed. The whole event was illustrative of the sense of competition, rather than solidarity, among the EU governments.

Meanwhile, within the confines of the European Union's own Justice and Home Affairs activities, there has been a determination to react in a muscular way to the internal security threats that were raised by the terrorist attacks on the United States. The European Union made rapid progress towards agreement on a continent-wide arrest warrant, which replaced the existing set of arrangements concerning extradition. This represented a major step forward in European co-operation, as it enables an arrest warrant issued in a country such as Greece to be enforceable within the domestic jurisdiction of the United Kingdom. In addition to the arrest warrant, there was a clear momentum to bring the 'Eurojust' concept to fruition. Eurojust is a body of European prosecutors able to co-ordinate those criminal cases that involve the judicial systems of several European states. It was agreed that these prosecutors would be accorded the right to become involved in terrorist cases. Two final measures completed this package. One was the drawing up of a common list of terrorist organisations. The other was the decision to accord Europol a dedicated anti-terrorist group within its structure.

The United States has taken its own steps to enhance its domestic security. As long ago as January 1999 the Clinton administration had undertaken efforts to improve US anti-terrorist measures both at home and abroad. Around $10 billion in funding had been appropriated to harden US infrastructure assets and to develop strategies to counter the threats from biological and cyber-terrorism. After the September 2001 attacks, Congress appropriated an additional $40 billion to pay for the 'war against terrorism'. Anti-terrorist legislation was passed in October 2001 enabling law enforcement authorities to conduct secret searches of the houses of terrorist suspects, tap phones, hold foreigners for up to seven days without charge and take steps to deport undesirables.[48] In addition, a major new Department of Homeland Security was created and Governor Tom Ridge was appointed by President Bush as the individual who would co-ordinate the work of this new government agency.[49]

Transatlantic co-operation since September 2001 has also been in evidence in other international forums. US and European efforts within the Group of Eight have led to agreement to seek ways to restrict the availability of terrorist funding. At a meeting in late September 2001, the G-8 Finance Ministers agreed to freeze the funds of terrorist groups and to use this initiative as the basis for encouraging other countries to follow suit.[50] An emergency meeting of the Financial Action Task Force was arranged in Washington at the end of October 2001 and the extension of the FATF's mandate to include terrorism was discussed. Furthermore, the two sides of the Atlantic have agreed to push for the signing of an all-embracing UN Convention on Terrorism that will draw together all the subsidiary sectors, such as the Convention on the Suppression of Terrorist Bombings and the Anti-Terrorism Financing Convention.

Conclusion

The absence of a common US–European strategy against terrorism in the 1990s has been remarkable considering that both sides shared a common abhorrence of the phenomenon. It was the different historical experiences and manifestations of the threat of terrorism that had caused America and Europe to adopt contending approaches to countering the problem. As a result, it became difficult to reconcile these different strategies and insufficient political will was evident to overcome the obstacles. This undermined what was potentially a nascent international regime. Had the transatlantic allies been more united over this issue, they might have been able to build a co-operative framework that could have been proffered to the wider world. Such a regime, had it enjoyed the backing of the leading Western countries, might have been a very powerful instrument in the global fight against terrorism.

Nevertheless, although transatlantic co-operation was limited in the past, the events of 11 September 2001 altered the situation dramatically. At the macro level, a long-term shift has occurred in the relationship between America and Europe. Issues relating to fighting terrorism are now accorded a priority that was never possible in the past. It was remarkable the way in which transatlantic debates about such issues as a common European defence capacity and the US plan to deploy an anti-missile shield were swept away by the new focus in US foreign policy. This is not to say that defence issues will not return to a more prominent place, or that counter-terrorism will always be the overriding issue in US–European relations. Rather it is to acknowledge that this issue has been accorded a new level of priority owing to the perception of the threat. As a result it will occupy a larger share of the transatlantic dialogue than ever before.

Within this shift of transatlantic emphasis, a tilting of the balance towards the US approach to counter-terrorism is under way. The newly designated 'war on terrorism' accords with America's national security approach and away from European priorities. This shift in the American response, characterised by willingness to treat the struggle as 'war', is in the ascendancy. The United States has been able to use the events of 11 September to mobilise political support for a view that sees terrorism to be an international menace that threatens global security. Added credence has been given to the US argument that the terrorist threat has mutated. The emergence of groups whose avowed aim is to destroy Western countries, that actively seek to acquire weapons of mass destruction and are likely to be prepared to use them has galvanised support for American policies.

In contrast, the European approach emphasising law enforcement and the need to engage diplomatically with states that are suspected of harbouring terrorists, to use non-forceful means such as economic sanctions, seems to have been downgraded. In prosecuting its strategy against terrorism, one of the priorities of US policy has been to build an international coalition of countries that will support action around the world. The United States has been able to exert diplomatic pressure on its European allies to support their strategy and for the time being the Europeans are reluctant to demur.

Yet it is likely that transatlantic rifts will continue in relation to counter-terrorist policy. One area of difficulty is the extension of the US 'war against terrorism' to other state sponsors around the world as well as the broadening of the remit to include states seeking access to weapons of mass destruction. Washington made it clear that the conflict in Afghanistan was only the first stage in a difficult and protracted struggle. Its decision to switch the focus from its 'war on terrorism' to a confrontation with Iraq has caused major tensions with its European allies. Traditional transatlantic differences are likely to emerge over how to deal with states of concern and whether the United States has the right to act unilaterally. US–European differences about dealing with the problem of terrorism show every sign of continuing in the future.

Notes

1 This chapter does not attempt to contribute to the academic debate about the nature of terrorism, the motivation of various terrorist movements or the trends apparent in this area.

2 B. Hoffman, *Inside Terrorism* (Guernsey: Indigo, 1998), chapter 1. D. Tucker, *Skirmishes at the Edge of Empire: The United States and International Terrorism* (Westport CT: Praeger, 1997), chapter 2.

3 For example, the FBI definition is 'the unlawful use of force or violence against persons or property to intimidate or coerce a government, the civilian population, or any segment thereof, in furtherance of political or social objectives'. This differs from other US agencies.

4 S. Simon and D. Benjamin, 'America and the new terrorism', *Survival*, 42: 1 (2000), pp. 59–76.

5 US Department of State, *Patterns of Global Terrorism* (Washington DC, 2001).

6 B. Hoffman, 'Terrorism: trends and prospects', in I. Lesser *et al.*, *Countering the New Terrorism*, (Santa Monica CA: RAND Corporation, 1999), p. 28.

7 M. den Boer, 'The fight against terrorism in the second and third pillars of the Maastricht Treaty: complement or overlap?' in F. Reinares (ed.), *European Democracies against Terrorism: Governmental Policies and Intergovernmental Co-operation* (Aldershot: Ashgate, 2000), p. 216.

8 M. Anderson, 'Counter-terrorism as an objective of European police co-operation', in Reinares, *European Democracies*, p. 234.

9 For a more detailed analysis of Trevi see J. Benyon, 'The politics of police co-operation in the European Union', *International Journal of the Sociology of Law*, 24 (1996), pp. 353–79, at pp. 361–3.

10 P. Heymann, *Terrorism and America: A Commonsense Strategy for a Democratic Society* (Cambridge MA: MIT Press, 1998).

11 US Department of State, *Patterns of Global Terrorism*, appendix C.

12 'Charlemagne: Javier Solana', *The Economist*, 17 November 2001, p. 48.

13 Testimony of J. O'Neill, Counter-terrorism Section, FBI, to Permanent Select Committee on Intelligence, US House of Representatives, July 1996, 104th Congress (Washington DC: US Government Printing Office, 1996), p. 10.

14 H. Binnendijk and P. Clawson (eds), 'International terrorism', *Strategic Assessment 1997* (Washington DC: National Defense University, 1998), p. 196.

15 E. Bazan, L. Eig, S. Cavanagh and R. Perl, *Terrorism: Background Issues for Congress*, Congressional Research Service Brief, Washington DC, 9 August 1995.

16 I. Lesser, 'Countering the new terrorism: implications for strategy', in Lesser *et al.*, *Countering the New Terrorism*, p. 116.

17 Interviews conducted by the author at the British embassy in Washington, May 2001.

18 The National Commission on Terrorism went so far as to suggest that the United States might consider imposing sanctions on Greece owing to its 'disturbingly passive response to terrorist activities'. (*Countering the Changing Threat of International Terrorism*, report of the National Commission on Terrorism, Washington DC, 5 June 2000.)

19 Transcript of press conference given by NATO Secretary General Lord Robertson following the meeting of the North Atlantic Council at the level of Foreign Ministers, NATO Integrated Data Service, Brussels, 6 December 2001.

20 NATO Secretary General Lord Robertson, 'International Security and Law Enforcement: A Look Ahead', Law Enforcement and National Security Global Forum, Edinburgh International Conference Centre, 19 June 2001.

21 Europol Annual Report 1999 (The Hague, 2000), Annex 1.

22 P. Chalk, 'The third pillar on Judicial and Home Affairs co-operation, anti-terrorist collaboration and liberal democratic acceptability', in Reinares, *European Democracies*, p. 185.

23 Interview conducted by the author with European Commission official in Washington, November 1998.

24 A. Gardner, *A New Era in US–EU Relations? The Clinton Administration and the New Transatlantic Agenda* (Aldershot: Avebury, 1997).

25 V. Stanzel, 'Dealing with the backwoods', *Washington Quarterly*, spring 1999.

26 Lesser 'Countering the new terrorism, p. 113.

27 US Department of State, *Patterns of Global Terrorism.*

28 Section 6 (j) of the Act specifies which countries are accused of being state sponsors of terrorism and the list is drawn up in consultations between the Secretary of Commerce and the Secretary of State.

29 *Countering the Changing Threat of International Terrorism*, report of the National Commission on Terrorism.

30 Senior Level Group Report to the US–EU Summit, 12 June 1996, p. 1.

31 G. Rose 'The United States and Libya', in Richard Haass (ed.), *Transatlantic Tensions: The US, Europe and Problem Countries* (Washington DC: Brookings Institution, 1999), p. 149.

32 W. Weidenfeld, 'America and Europe: is the break inevitable?' *Washington Quarterly*, 20: 3 (1997), pp. 37–53.

33 G. Kemp, 'Iran: can the US do a deal?' *Washington Quarterly*, winter 2001. See also US Department of State, *Patterns of Global Terrorism*, p. 32.

34 G. Kemp 'The challenge of Iran for US and European policy', in Haass, *Transatlantic Tensions*, p. 55.

35 A similar European position was adopted in relation to the 1996 Cuban Liberty and Democratic Solidarity Act, or 'Helms–Burton' extraterritorial legislation, passed by the United States in relation to the Castro regime.

36 Interview conducted by the author with European Commission official, Brussels, November 2000.

37 See F. Burwell and I. Daalder (eds), *The US and Europe in the Global Arena* (Basingstoke: Macmillan, 1999).

38 D. Tucker, 'Responding to terrorism', *Washington Quarterly*, winter 1998, p. 111.

39 Tucker, *Skirmishes at the Edge of Empire.*

40 P. Pillar, *Terrorism and US Foreign Policy* (Washington DC: Brookings Institution, 2001), p. 158.

41 'Bush seeks European support', *Washington Post*, 7 November 2001, p. A18, and J. Hoagland, 'All aboard in Afghanistan', *Washington Post*, 20 November 2001, p. A23.

42 'Is Saddam next?' *Maclean's*, 3 December 2001, pp. 26–8.

43 'Sleeper cells', *Washington Post*, 3 December 2001, p. A12. 'Putin warns US against expanding war to Iraq', *Washington Post*, 18 December 2001.

44 'Blair denies split with Bush over war', *Washington Post*, 22 November 2001, p. A36.

45 *Agence Europe*, No. 8052, 21 September 2001, p. 5.

46 Justice and Home Affairs Council, 'Conclusions adopted by the Council', SN 3926, Brussels, 20 September 2001.

47 'A beneficial crisis' (editorial), *The Times*, 1 November 2001, p. 21.

48 R. Dannheisser, 'Senate joins House in approving anti-terrorism Bill, 25 October 2001, *Washington File*, www.usembassy. org.uk/terror247.htm.

49 *The Economist*, 'America the unready', 22 December 2001, pp. 49–50.

50 'Seven most industrialised countries decide to join forces to combat financing of terrorism', *Agence Europe*, No. 8077, 27 September 2001, p. 15.

8

Transatlantic co-operation against organised crime and drug trafficking

During the 1990s there was a perception that international organised crime and the trafficking of proscribed drugs were growing problems. No one would claim that transnational organised crime[1] is a new phenomenon; rather that its scale and consequent level of danger have much increased. In part this has reflected a changing sense of the security agenda as the threat of major inter-state war has receded for developed states in the western hemisphere. In place of the traditional preoccupation with military security issues has arisen a more differentiated agenda in which non-military concerns have been accorded greater priority. It has also reflected a more favourable global situation in which various forms of transnational crime can flourish. The ease of international communications, the dismantling of barriers between East and West, the emergence of new market economies and newly independent states – in short, the 'globalisation' of inter-state interactions – have all contributed to a more permissive environment for crime.

Crime has long been recognised to have an international as well as a local dimension but in recent times it is the growing scale of the problem that has caused alarm. The United Nations International Drug Control Programme estimated in 1997 that drug trafficking amounted to a US$300 billion industry.[2] Many of the major criminal organisations now operate on a worldwide basis and are known to conduct a range of illegal activities. Chinese Triads and the Japanese Yakuza, for example, are involved in illegal immigration activities and drug trafficking in various parts of the world. Crime, like other forms of business, has sought global market opportunities. This can be seen most clearly in relation to illegal drugs: they are cultivated and processed in various parts of the world and then delivered to consumers on a global basis.

As a country with far-flung interests, the United States has been concerned to counter the dangers posed by international criminals and drug traffickers. Following the exposure of US personnel serving in Vietnam to the availability of cheap illegal drugs, the American government took a hard-line approach to countering these problems.[3] In the case of Europe, these concerns have not received the same level of priority but they have been accorded a higher priority since the ending of the Cold War. The emergence of a Russian-organised crime problem has helped the two sides of the Atlantic to identify shared interests in combating this menace. The Russian Mafia has been able to penetrate state structures and conduct a wide range of illegal activities, ranging from drug smuggling to people trafficking and prostitution. Its threat is insidious because its organisations link up with ethnic communities based in the United States and Europe, using them either as a source of recruits or as a kinship group upon which to prey. The former CIA Director John Deutch, for example, warned that up to 200 large Russian criminal organisations were conducting their activities on a transnational basis.[4] Former Director of the FBI Louis Freeh made a speech in Moscow in July 1994 in which he said that '[Russian] organised crime groups also pose a significant and direct threat to the United States . . . America is an increasingly desirable target of opportunity for Russian organised crime groups.'[5]

The two sides of the Atlantic agree that international co-operation is necessary to overcome the problems of international crime and drug trafficking. Co-operation between national police forces, judicial collaboration, the sharing of information and the extradition of suspects are all necessary elements in a successful counter-crime strategy. The fact that a problem is experienced only on one side of the Atlantic does not mean that it cannot spread to the other side over time. There is also the risk of the displacement of these problems when they are energetically countered by law enforcement agencies: organised crime groups may react by moving their activities to other territories.

Co-operation against organised crime and drug trafficking have presented a very real challenge in transatlantic relations. Actually realising the goal of co-operation has been much more difficult than policy makers expected. Three principal reasons account for these difficulties. First, Europe and the United States have been required to move beyond established patterns of bilateral co-operation and create new ways of dealing with each other. This has demanded the establishment of new structures and new forms of interaction, all of which need to prove their effectiveness before they are trusted. Second, this new sphere of working together has been undertaken in relation to a dynamic and ill defined problem: namely organised criminal activity. By its nature this problem is secretive and a difficult subject on which to obtain reliable information. Third, this sphere of transatlantic co-operation has been developing during a time of on-going political integration in Western Europe which has meant that the Europeans have been experiencing a constant process of change.

Differing transatlantic conceptions of the problem of organised crime

The US approach to dealing with problems of organised crime and drug trafficking has been conditioned by its historical experience. In relation to organised crime, the US concept of the problem has been based upon a 'Mafia' model of ethnically homogeneous and interlinked criminal groups. These groups have been seen as alien to American society and structured in a hierarchical fashion. This view of organised crime derived from US investigations of its domestic Italian-American crime phenomenon, conducted in the 1950s and 1960s. Such public hearings into the nature of organised crime as the Kefauver Commission of 1950 exercised a disproportionate influence on American thinking for subsequent decades.[6] The 'Mafia conspiracy' model was evident in the assumptions of subsequent investigations, such as the presidential commission in 1967, and led to published works adopting this approach.[7] The model has represented the dominant paradigm for much of American discussion about the problem of organised crime ever since.[8]

The US model of ethnically based and hierarchical crime groups has been less appropriate to the European experience. Whilst some crime groups operating in Europe, such as Turkish organisations, have indeed been shown to be ethnically homogeneous, and there have been examples of rival ethnic groups fighting for territorial control, other research has demonstrated evidence of heterogeneous criminal operations. Van Duyne has argued that groups are attracted by criminal opportunities and will often co-operate with others in new localities in order to gain the local knowledge that will enable them to maximise their economic advantage.[9] For example, Mafia groups in Italy have been found providing services to foreign drug traffickers, such as Albanians, in the form of forged documentation, transport services and jobs in the black economy. Less evidence has also been forthcoming of hierarchically based groups. Den Boer refers to a 1996 parliamentary report from the Netherlands which found that organised crime was being conducted by networks and coalitions of criminal entrepreneurs rather than by hierarchical organisations.[10]

The American tendency to accentuate the externally driven nature of the crime threat has also been questioned by European experience. It is undeniable that there has been an influx of Russian, Chechen and Albanian crime groups into Europe since the end of the Cold War as the political rigidities in those areas have splintered. Yet, after some of the alarmism about waves of organised crime groups entering Western Europe that characterised the first half of the 1990s subsided, it has come to be acknowledged that much of the organised crime problem is home-grown. Where foreign crime groups continue to be blamed for the problem it is possible that governments in both Eastern and Western Europe have found it convenient to blame foreign sources for rising numbers of domestic offences. Reports from the European Police Office (Europol), drawing upon statistics provided by member states, have noted that the external organised crime phenomenon should not be exaggerated and that pre-existing indigenous crime organisations help to account for much of the increase in activity.[11]

In the sphere of drug trafficking, the United States has drawn on its own experience of trying to combat hierarchical crime organisations both on its home soil and overseas. US efforts to fight the major drug trafficking structures in South America, such as the Medellin and Cali cartels in Colombia, have helped to structure their thinking.[12] The experience in Europe has been different. Because drugs have usually been imported from much larger distances, there has rarely been a single crime organisation controlling the process, from harvesting the raw material through to distribution of the refined product on the streets of European cities. Different groups tend to control the trafficking and the street-level distribution of the drugs. There has even been evidence of collaboration between organisations; for example, within Italy, Albanian drug trafficking groups have established themselves in some of the northern cities with the complicity of the resident Mafia families.[13]

The scale of the organised crime problem has been an additional subject of disagreement between the United States and Europe. A growing body of opinion in American law enforcement and academic circles has identified evidence of linkages between transnational organised crime groups across the world. Analysts such as Shelley[14] have regarded this development as reflecting an attempt to exploit greater market opportunities, whilst others, such as Sterling,[15] have viewed it in terms of a global criminal conspiracy. The best known example of linkages between different crime groups is that between different parts of the Italian Mafia and the American Cosa Nostra. The Cosa Nostra built its position principally on drug trafficking but later diversified into gambling and contracts from public works projects. The United States points to regions of the world where crime and drug trafficking threaten national economies and nascent democratic structures: Russia presents a particular cause for concern.[16]

Many analysts in Europe have viewed this American assessment as alarmist and have suspected it could be driven by domestic politics. Whilst there has been undeniable evidence of a growing Russian organised crime problem and some evidence of collusive arrangements being forged between criminal organisations, the extent of the activity is subject to dispute. Organised crime may represent a far bigger threat internally to the political and economic stability of Russia rather than to neighbouring states.[17] As for evidence of a global criminal conspiracy, there can be a variety of linkages between groups which fall significantly short of a unified conspiracy. A spectrum of co-operation may develop, ranging from the demarcation of territorial limits to avoid inter-group conflict, through to single ventures or tactical alliances in order to exploit market opportunities.

Transatlantic approaches to illegal drugs

There is far more that unites than divides the Europeans and the United States on the subject of illegal drugs. Both sides of the Atlantic work to combat the production and the trafficking of narcotics and carry out programmes to this end in various parts of the world. Both the United States and its European allies are key supporters of efforts within the United Nations to decrease the supply and demand for drugs. Nevertheless, differing experiences over drugs and differing policy strategies have made some forms of co-operation problematical.

The United States has adopted a more hard-line approach to the drug problem than its European counterparts.[18] This is demonstrated by the fact that both illegal narcotics (through Presidential Decision Directive 42 in October 1995) and transnational organised crime have been defined by the American government as national security issues, thereby mobilising the agencies and resources of the whole US government. This approach began as early as 1969 when President Richard Nixon declared a 'total war' on illegal drugs.[19] Subsequent presidents, notably Ronald Reagan and George H. Bush, authorised a range of measures, including the use of military capabilities, to interdict the flow of drugs into North America. Under the Clinton administration the various strands of policy against organised criminals and drug traffickers were drawn together in an International Crime Control Strategy and were accompanied in 1998 by the passing of the International Crime Control Act.[20] The International Crime Control Strategy focused on a range of policies, including reinforcing US borders, imposing tougher penalties for smuggling, combating money laundering and restricting the movements of known traffickers.

The punitive US approach to the problem of illegal drugs has been driven by perceptions of the damage that it causes to the economy and the welfare of people. US citizens consume approximately 50 per cent of the world's supply of illegal narcotics and the annual cost to the US economy has been estimated at about $68 billion.[21] This estimate includes money spent on law enforcement activities and the cost to the health care system. It also includes the number of drug-related prisoners within the penal service; a figure noted by Singh to comprise 75 per cent of those entering federal prisons and 35 per cent of those entering state institutions.[22] The scale of the problem has led to an American drug control approach that has prioritised supply reduction and the imposition of robust penalties within the criminal justice system. A strong and influential lobby exists in the United States that is opposed to any relaxation in the laws governing the use of narcotics.

Washington has focused part of its attention on states producing drugs for the US market. This has resulted in pressure being exerted on South American countries to cease the cultivation of coca, the basis of cocaine, which has long been the principal illegal narcotic smuggled into the United States. America has targeted the Andean states of Colombia, Bolivia and Peru, as they are the main exporters of cocaine, as well as states such as Mexico, which have acted as transit routes. Since 1986 the US President has conducted an annual certification process of those countries that are believed to be linked with the cultivation and transit of drugs. Those states that are judged not to have co-operated with American efforts are at risk of suffering decertification, leading to the imposition of sanctions and the blackballing of that country from international aid programmes involving US money.[23]

The United States has also identified the danger of drug money financing political movements in the region with destabilising consequences. Guerrilla movements such as the Revolutionary Armed Forces of Colombia (FARC) are known to draw strength from coca cultivation in the areas where they exercise control.[24] Panama, under its erstwhile leader General Manuel Noriega, provided an example of a state accused of acting as a regional facilitator of the drugs trade. The United States intervened militarily in Panama in 1989, overthrew the government and put Noriega on trial.

The European experience of the drug problem has been different from that of the United States. Europe's main problem has been from the smoking and injecting of heroin, rather than cocaine. The source of heroin production has been the 'Golden Triangle' states of Thailand, Laos and Myanmar and the 'Golden Crescent' countries of Afghanistan, Pakistan and Iran. Between them the Golden Triangle and Golden Crescent regions traditionally account for approximately 90 per cent of the world's supply of opium.[25] The US-led war to oust the Taliban, from the autumn of 2001, has thrown the issue of opium production in Afghanistan into confusion. The conflict has undoubtedly disrupted the growing of the opium crop and the capacity of traffickers to disseminate the manufactured drug. But the Taliban had built up a major stockpile of opium in the years before the conflict and it is therefore possible that large quantities could still emanate from this source.[26]

The extent of the cocaine problem in Europe is still relatively small and consumption is only about a third of the US figure.[27] Nevertheless, the trend has been moving upward, particularly in highly addictive derivations such as 'crack cocaine'. Officials in the US drug enforcement community warn that as the American cocaine market shows signs of becoming saturated, so the problem in Europe could escalate rapidly. Some drugs flow the other way, from Europe across to the United States. In the 1970s and 1980s the Sicilian Mafia were estimated to be importing approximately 80 per cent of the heroin into the United States, but strenuous law enforcement activity and shifting supply patterns appear to have undermined this trade.[28] Nowadays, what flows from Europe to the United States is mainly the softer end of the drug spectrum. For example, approximately 80 per cent of the ecstasy currently trafficked and consumed in the United States comes from the Netherlands or, to a lesser degree, from Belgium.[29]

The Europeans' attitude towards drugs has led them to concentrate attention on 'harm reduction' and public health.[30] For instance, heroin and its substitute, methadone, can be obtained on prescription in some European countries, while clean syringes and safe injecting facilities are also available. The European rationale has been to try and minimise the social damage associated with criminalising drugs and reducing the risks of infection such as HIV/AIDS. There has also been a process under way in Europe of relaxing the laws in relation to the recreational use of cannabis. For example, so-called 'coffee shops' in the Netherlands are allowed to sell up to 5 g of cannabis to customers.[31] In the United Kingdom the criminal status of cannabis is being downgraded and, since 2001, police officers in various regional constabularies have been told only to caution a person found in possession of the drug in small quantities. In short, European approaches to drugs are more diverse and there has been a stronger debate about their legalisation; based on the arguments that they would be easier to control, they could be licensed and that the profits for organised criminals would be removed.

The United States is often critical of what it regards as a more lax European approach to drug trafficking. The argument in the US law enforcement community is that European attempts at harm reduction, such as the controlled access to narcotics, undermine law enforcement efforts to curb the availability of those drugs. The United States has been vociferously opposed to ideas about decriminalisation and expresses a sense of frustration that the Europeans do not view the problems more seriously. A frequently expressed view in US official circles is that the European experience of the drug problem is around two decades behind that of the United States and that thinking in Europe will change as the issue becomes more difficult.[32] The Europeans' response is that their data on the threat from drugs do not accord with those of the United States and therefore they remain to be convinced.

Whilst the United States and Europeans have placed a different emphasis on the domestic management of their drug problems, they have also differed on some of the foreign-policy dimensions of combating drug trafficking. European states have been uncomfortable with the way in which the drug issue is employed as a weapon in the US foreign-policy armoury, through the process of the annual certification of countries by the State Department. As a result, when Washington has encouraged European governments to join its efforts in arresting cocaine production among the Andean states, through crop eradication and substitution programmes, it has largely been disappointed with the response.[33] In the case of Colombia the United States went a step further and provided large quantities of money and equipment to help the government defeat the FARC. 'Plan Colombia', approved in June 2000, provided US$1.3 billion in US military aid for the project.[34] This was followed by the Andean Regional Initiative (ARI) which was spread among the countries in the region and provided a balanced assistance programme targeted at alternative development as well as law enforcement.[35] Whilst the Europeans have argued that such approaches amount to bullying, and impact on many of the poorest farmers in drug-producing countries, the US response has been that the majority of the poor in the Andean states are not dependent on drugs and that the principal measures are aimed at the illegal traffickers.

Transatlantic bilateral co-operation

Co-operation between national police forces takes place all over the world when shared interests are at stake. However, it tends to occur only in relation to specific cases and depends upon the respect and expectations of reciprocity that have been built up over a period of time between professional police officers.[36] When attempts are made to try to regularise patterns of co-operation between countries, then the situation invariably becomes more complex. The involvement of Foreign Ministries takes the matter out of the hands of police officers and invests it with a raised political salience. It often results in the process proceeding at a slow pace and leads to wider foreign policy considerations being drawn into play.

Transatlantic co-operation in combating crime has been built upon a foundation of extensive bilateral linkages. Direct contacts between national European police forces and their American counterparts have been transformed into systematic patterns of collaboration. Where this has reflected a shared security threat, the collaboration has become particularly close and durable. For example, in seeking to counter the problem of Italian-American organised crime, the co-operation between the American Federal Bureau of Investigation (FBI) and the Italian Carabineri has been remarkable. It led to the creation of a joint US–Italian Working Group on organised crime that shared intelligence information and discussed detection techniques. The co-operation between the two sides took a further step forward in July 1997 when the FBI and the Italian police agreed upon a common strategy to combat the spread of Russian organised crime.[37]

There have been many examples where co-operation between US and Italian law enforcement agencies has led to major successes. The famous 'Pizza connection' case in 1985 exposed the way in which Italian restaurants on the east coast of the United States were being used to distribute heroin that had been shipped there from Sicily, with the profits being repatriated to the Sicilian Mafia. In 1992–93 collaboration between the two legal authorities resulted in Operation Green Ice, which targeted the transatlantic supply of cocaine from the United States to Italy as well as the corresponding money laundering activities. The operation resulted in the arrest of over 200 suspects of Colombian, Spanish and Canadian nationality.[38] Operation Dinero in 1994 involved the US Drug Enforcement Administration tracing money laundering connected with the sale of cocaine from Colombia to the United States, Italy and Spain and resulted in eighty-four arrests.[39]

The United States has enshrined co-operation with partner countries in Western Europe in a series of bilateral legal agreements, known as Mutual Legal Assistance Treaties (MLATs). By the spring of 2002 these existed between the United States and nine EU member states, with two more signed but awaiting ratification. The MLATs concern information that can be shared for criminal investigations and prosecutions. This exchange of information has proved to be of enormous value in helping to build criminal cases on occasions when evidence is drawn from more than one national jurisdiction, as well as in fostering expectations of rapid assistance in gathering data. The issue of the extradition of criminal suspects is separate from the MLATs and is covered by the extradition treaties that the United States has signed with all the EU countries.

Alongside the success of MLATs, the United States also stations law enforcement personnel overseas. For example, the FBI and the Drug Enforcement Administration (DEA) have representatives in more than thirty embassies, with a particular concentration in Western Europe. The FBI's legal attachés, or 'Legats', act as liaison officials overseas – as they have no operational powers outside of the United States – but they can greatly assist the speed and depth of co-operation when complex transnational criminal cases arise. Personal contacts built up with national police forces can smooth the process of information sharing and ensure that a high degree of confidence exists on both sides of the Atlantic when sensitive sources of information are involved. Similarly, DEA officials interact with their counterparts in counter-drugs organisations in the host countries. The DEA are known to have built very close working relationships with the Central Narcotics Office in France, the Central Anti-drugs Service in Italy and the National Criminal Intelligence Service in the Netherlands.[40] The United States also seconds some of its attorneys from the Department of Justice to serve in important embassies.[41] These individuals can ensure that the correct legal documentation is provided in such matters as extradition arrangements and can prevent some of the notorious experiences in the past where high-profile criminal suspects have been released because of failures in the extradition procedures between countries.

One example of successful bilateral co-operation is in the German Federal Criminal Police Office (Bundeskriminalamt, BKA) headquarters in Wiesbaden. A computer terminal has been made operational there which is linked directly to the US National Criminal Information Center. This was established under a US–German agreement in September 1997 and enables officers of the BKA to access US police files on criminal suspects. It represents a major step forward, as it circumvents the need for the German police to make a formal application to the US authorities for information and then wait for the request to be processed and the information provided. A degree of trust is also demonstrated in the way in which the recipients of the information will employ the data.[42]

Yet problems have impeded even bilateral attempts to improve transatlantic co-operation. One particular stumbling block has been the variety of legal instruments that states have considered necessary to combat organised crime and drug trafficking. The United States, drawing on past experience of its domestic problem of organised crime, has tended to be more robust in the powers that it invests in its law enforcement officials. For instance, since 1970, the United States has possessed legislation to counter racketeering, namely the Racketeer Influenced and Corrupt Organizations Act (RICO), which is a part of the Organized Crime Control Act. This law enables membership of particular organisations to be proscribed. In addition, the legislation makes possible the confiscation of criminally derived property, the freezing of financial assets and access to the bank accounts of suspects.[43] The American government has also been willing to grant clandestine powers to law enforcement agencies, such as the use of *agents provocateurs* and the employment of multiple wire taps of a target for the purpose of electronic surveillance. A federal judge can authorise surveillance – the material being admissible in a court of law – and in special cases of organised crime the Attorney General can give the necessary authority for a period of up to forty-eight hours.

European countries have traditionally been more conservative in the legislation that they have been prepared to draft against organised crime, and this has rendered co-operation with the United States problematical. Some of the evidence gathered against a criminal by US authorities would not be admissible in a European court. Consequently a European prosecution could risk being undermined by the involvement of US authorities. This has caused the United States to express disquiet that, in their view, some of their European allies are not taking the problem of transnational crime sufficiently seriously. The US ambassador to the European Union admitted in December 2001 that 'Differing legal systems and approaches to the protection of civil liberties, both among EU member states and between the United States and Europe, have hampered full collaboration.'[44]

Only some European countries have enacted the sort of legislation against organised crime that the United States has long advocated. Italy, for example, is one of the few European countries that can boast a dedicated Anti-Mafia Investigative Directorate in its police force. It has also drafted a range of anti-money laundering legislation and has enacted a witness protection programme. In the early 1990s, in response to a wave of Mafia violence, the Italian government passed measures to improve its crime-fighting powers, such as stiffening the prison penalties for senior Mafia figures and increasing the range of under-cover methods available to the police. Germany, in 1992, introduced legislation that authorised the use of under-cover agents and electronic surveillance. Anderson has noted that several European countries, including Britain, the Netherlands and Belgium, have all increased the powers available to the police to counter the activities of organised crime gangs.[45]

Yet it has been difficult to obtain agreement among all European states to achieve common standards in measures to combat sophisticated criminal activity. For example, the European Commission has been pressing the member states to amend the 1991 Money Laundering Directive in order to bring all countries up to a higher standard on the identification, seizure and confiscation of the profits from criminal activities.[46] It is worth remembering that the instigation of such measures can involve costs as well as benefits, and depends on the perception of the scale of the organised crime problem that each country confronts. A heavy financial burden can be placed upon the state: in Italy, for example, the so-called *pentiti* witness protection programme now extends to over 2,000 people.[47]

US–EU co-operation

Whilst bilateral co-operation between the United States and various European countries has been built up over a long period of time, attempts to multilateralise co-operation have been more problematical. Established patterns of co-operation have existed within the framework of Interpol[48], but when the United States has tried to develop linkages with the European Union, the results have been disappointing. This has led the American government to express frustration at the slow pace of progress in its relations with the European Union and to suspect certain countries in Europe of deliberately trying to stifle anything other than bilateral co-operation. It has caused the United States to question the utility of seeking such enhanced co-operation. The European Union does not have a central authority for mutual legal assistance, nor does it possess powers over extradition arrangements. As a result, the United States relies upon its bilateral agreements with member states for mutual legal assistance and extradition.[49] The United States debated for some time whether to try to negotiate a criminal judicial agreement with the European Union which would cover these areas, fearing that what it might achieve would be less than what it currently enjoys from the existing MLATs. Nevertheless, the impact of 11 September created a climate in which US policy makers considered it was worth risking such an effort.

One of the difficulties in fashioning co-operation has been that the United States and the European Union represent quite different sorts of actors. The United States is self-evidently a nation state with its own government, law enforcement agencies and legal system. There is acknowledged to be some diversity within the American system, between the federal and state level, and there are a plethora of policing agencies, with overlapping interests and competences. This diversity and plurality of policing bodies can complicate co-operation with other external actors, and European states have expressed disappointment when their requests have been transmitted to the United States but have failed to elicit a satisfactory response. The European Union is thus aware from its member states that the United States has its own limitations in the area of transatlantic legal co-operation.[50]

Nevertheless, the problems presented by the American system are small relative to the difficulties faced by the United States in trying to secure co-operation with the European Union. The Union is not a state but a complex, multi-level polity, comprised of fifteen countries that will, as a result of the Copenhagen agreement, expand to twenty-five states by 2004. All the existing, as well as future, members have varied histories and separate priorities. The European Union has to reach a consensus among all its member states before it can move forward and it only requires the objection of a single country to bring its decision-making process grinding to a halt. Because of its complexity many officials in the United States have struggled to understand its nature and have been disappointed when the Union has not reacted swiftly to their initiatives. In turn, European officials have perceived US pressure for co-operation as illustrative of Americans' expectation that their power and status in international relations guarantee them the right to special treatment.

The difficulties for the United States in the 1990s of obtaining co-operation from the European Union were exacerbated by the fact that the Union was in the process of institution building, resulting from the Treaty on European Union (TEU). The structures of the intergovernmental Third Pillar on Justice and Home Affairs (JHA) were not ratified until November 1993 and consequently the European Union was incapable of responding positively to US overtures. The TEU created expectations of a developing internal security agenda for the member states with the attendant issue of border controls being managed through the Schengen system. Yet little progress was realised in this new and innovative area of EU competence in the period following the ratification of the TEU until the next treaty-making summit at Amsterdam in 1997. It was in the Treaty of Amsterdam that substantial steps forward were achieved, through 'communitarising' some of the Third Pillar activities, moving them into the First Pillar.[51] The subsequent special European Council meeting at Tampere in 1999 further developed these policies. Responsibility for the JHA portfolio is now divided between the First and Third Pillars, with roles for both the Council and the Commission.

EU Justice and Home Affairs continue to touch on two areas of particular sensitivity for member states. One is the issue of internal law enforcement and police and judicial co-operation. These matters have traditionally been at the heart of national sovereignty and, despite recognising the growing need to work together to overcome new threats, agreeing areas of practical co-operation has been slow. The other issue is external relations. It is evident that internal security has an external dimension in the need to work with third countries against the source of threats or over the extradition of suspects. This results in the need for the European Union to agree upon foreign policy issues – a further area of traditionally sovereign concern. In all of these ways, JHA represents an issue of profound complexity for the European Union which has made co-operating with Washington particularly difficult.

An illustration of the problems attendant upon EU institution building is the case of Europol. This organisation, based in the Hague, was built on the foundations of the European Drugs Unit and was designed to be a centre for the sharing of criminal intelligence information among the EU member states. Throughout the 1990s the United States sought to develop an information-sharing relationship with Europol but it faced the problem that the organisation was incapable of co-operation because it was at too early a stage of development. Europol was left in suspension while the member states ratified its convention; a process not achieved until 1998. Since that time the organisation has been building up its competences and expertise, and it has seen its mandate extended to cover a wider variety of crimes.

Even since 1998 the American government has been frustrated in its attempts to improve co-operation with Europol, for two reasons. First, the process of enlarging the European Union to countries in Central and Eastern Europe (CEECs) has presented an obstacle because those states could obtain access to information that the United States has shared with Europol. Officials in Washington have expressed misgivings that sensitive information on US citizens suspected of criminal offences might leak from the future members of the European Union and could place American prosecutions at risk.[52] The second issue has been data protection, following the adoption of a Europol Data Protection Policy in September 1999. Information in the US judicial process has to be available in the court system, which is incompatible with the guidelines laid down for Europol. This led to an impasse as Europol was unable to conclude an agreement with the United States concerning the sharing of data. Not until the 11 September terrorist attacks on New York and Washington was the political will forthcoming to resolve this stand-off. In December 2001 an agreement was concluded between the United States and Europol that allowed for the exchange of strategic and technical information,[53] with the expectation that this will be extended to personal data in the future.

Contributing to the complexity of the European Union has been the fact that European countries have evolved with different types of police forces – some 120 on one estimate[54] – and different legal systems. For example; France, Italy, and Spain have developed *gendarmerie* policing traditions, with an armed force organised along military lines. This force is accorded responsibility for the policing of the entire national territory. In contrast, countries such as Germany have developed a federal policing model, which is similar in nature to that of the United States. A third model, exemplified by Great Britain, is decentralised in nature, with regional police forces granted substantial autonomy.[55]

Europe lacks a unified judicial system. There is no European criminal law system and there are a variety of different legal structures, with differing roles for Interior Ministers, magistrates, judges and prosecutors. French Roman-based law, with its system of investigating magistrates, exists at one end of the spectrum, whilst at the other end stands the British common-law tradition, relying upon the creation of legal precedents. States in Europe do not have the same definition of illegal acts, and this presents a major obstacle in cases necessitating the extradition of suspects. The United Kingdom, for instance, does not have legislation which formally recognises 'organised crime' but refers to the problem instead as 'serious crime'. This has made it difficult for the United Kingdom to extradite an individual to a country such as Italy on the grounds of membership of an illegal organised crime group. Yet the growth of crime and the increasing sophistication of criminal groups have provided a powerful incentive to cooperation. At the Tampere European Council the decision was taken to pursue a policy of mutual recognition of member states' legal decisions.[56] It was decided that mutual recognition was likely to offer a more fruitful way forward than attempting to harmonise the criminal codes of all fifteen countries.

US–EU initiatives

The New Transatlantic Agenda (NTA) of 1995 identified organised crime and drug trafficking as two of the global challenges that the United States and

Europe had to address. The NTA was conceived as a mechanism for not only identifying common interests, but also putting the necessary political pressure behind them to ensure they were prioritised. In relation to law enforcement co-operation the emphasis has been upon practical and achievable targets. For instance, the NTA has sought to improve information sharing, assist in the creation of a transatlantic judicial network and enhance the mechanisms for the extradition of criminal suspects. The European Union's Multi-disciplinary Group (MDG) on Organised Crime, consisting of national experts, was made partly responsible for implementing some of the NTA's goals in this area of security.

What has tended to emerge from the NTA has been a series of initiatives between the European Union and the United States. These initiatives have reflected the priorities of particular EU presidencies and have lacked a long-term perspective. In the eyes of critics, they have represented the desire of particular countries to achieve a politically high-profile form of co-operation with the United States, involving only a limited cost.

Examples of such initiatives were the measures taken to combat the growing incidence of the trafficking of women. Women are being smuggled to the West primarily from CEE countries, usually to be sold against their will into prostitution or other parts of the sex industry. Such activities are recognised to have become a major business for transnational criminals worth billions of dollars per year and subject to relatively modest penalties. There was transatlantic agreement about the nature of the problem, and at the EU–US summit in the Hague, in May 1997, it was decided to undertake a joint initiative. Two public information campaigns were orchestrated to try and contain the problem and to warn the potential victims about the dangers. The first campaign was conducted in Ukraine and Poland from April to June 1998 and the second in Bulgaria and Hungary from January to June 2000.[57] These were at best limited initiatives and reflected a desire to achieve rapidly realisable results.

Three more substantial EU–US initiatives have been in other areas of activity: two in counter-drug trafficking and one in countering computer crime. Their relative success has reflected the importance that the United States has invested in combating these problems. Counter-drug trafficking has focused on the Caribbean, where both sides of the Atlantic share a sense of danger. The US experiences drug flows of cocaine and heroin from South America, through the Caribbean and into Florida, whilst European countries have witnessed an increasing proportion of cocaine shipments transiting through the many islands of the region *en route* to European destinations. For example, a US report estimated that up to 30 per cent of the drugs entering the United Kingdom were being trafficked through the Caribbean.[58] The initiative was built upon existing patterns of bilateral co-operation between the United States and interested European countries: namely Britain, France, the Netherlands and Spain. It aimed at improving co-ordination and establishing some new forms of co-operation, rather than creating a truly joint policy.[59]

The EU–US Caribbean Drug Initiative, as it has come to be called, has resulted in some practical improvements. A summit was held in Bridgetown, Barbados, in May 1997 and resulted in the negotiation of an Action Plan. This provided a joint funding programme for a range of activities, including coast-guard services and support equipment for the interdiction of drug traffickers; money for the training of local personnel and the creation of a specialist judicial network capable of prosecuting drug cases. The United States sponsored a second Action Plan, which broadened the emphasis from drugs to related issues such as the fight against corruption and the strengthening of the rule of law. America also stimulated the sharing of intelligence between countries with an interest in the area. However, co-operation has served to highlight the different approaches between the European Union and the United States and has led to the latter expressing frustration with the time it takes for the European Union to divide and enact responsibilities among its members.[60]

The second substantive US–EU initiative has been in the field of chemical precursors. These are the essential foundation chemicals used in the manufacture of illegal narcotics. This is an unusual subject for the European Union because it falls under the Commission's trade portfolio, rather than JHA, but nevertheless the transatlantic allies designed an agreement to prevent the diversion of chemicals from legitimate to illegal uses.[61] The Chemical Precursors Agreement was signed in May 1997 and has provided an effective instrument in tracking the movement of relevant substances. Chemicals used in the production of cocaine, such as potassium permanganate, were the first to be targeted but the success of the agreement has led it to be extended to include chemicals used for the manufacture of heroin. The United States and the European Union have been able to share data on producer countries and exercise their considerable joint political influence to control the flow of these substances. They have proceeded to establish a Follow-up Working Group to determine where best their efforts can be directed in the future.[62]

The third initiative has been in the area of combating computer or 'cyber' crime. This has been a particular cause for concern in the United States with its advanced and interlinked computer networks. American officials have become alarmed at the vulnerability of computer systems, ranging from those belonging to government agencies through to commercial banking networks. All such systems are potentially vulnerable to hacking from criminals, the insertion of destructive viruses or penetration by groups with a malicious objective against the state.[63] Cyber-crime can originate from any source in the world and successful prosecutions often necessitate crossing multiple legal jurisdictions. As a result of these factors the United States has pressed for agreements to combat cyber-crime in conjunction with its technologically advanced European allies. In relation to the Internet, the Austrian government pioneered an agreement with the United States, during its EU presidency, to combat the spread of pornographic images.

Both sides of the Atlantic have recognised the need to assist Central and Eastern European countries experiencing the transition from communist to democratic political systems. These countries have faced a plethora of problems. On the one hand, their development of market economies has helped to stimulate an increase in organised crime activity – both indigenous and from neighbouring countries such as Russia, Ukraine and Belarus. This has been compounded by the fact that these countries have been used for the transiting of drugs into Western Europe and for the shipment of stolen goods, such as prestige cars, from Europe to the Balkans and the Middle East. On the other hand, the law enforcement and judicial systems of many of the CEECs have been in a poor condition since the end of the Cold War. Their systems been under-funded, owing to the difficult economic conditions pertaining during the transition process, and they have lacked legitimacy as a result of being identified with the control mechanisms of former communist regimes.[64]

Unfortunately, US and EU approaches to the Central and East European region have tended to be competitive rather than co-operative, which has weakened the influence that they could have jointly brought to bear. West European states have regarded the CEE area as their own back yard and have resented American attempts to cultivate influence within the region. France in particular has been obstructive of co-operative ventures between Europe and the United States because it has suspected America of trying to export its law enforcement approaches and philosophies into the CEECs. Where collaborative programmes between the United States and the European Union have been undertaken, such as the South East Europe Co-operation Initiative – designed to channel funds and improve the governance of states in that corner of the continent – progress has been episodic and limited.[65]

Transatlantic rivalries were evident when the United States attempted to obtain EU participation in a police academy it founded in Budapest. The International Law Enforcement Academy (ILEA) was part of an on-going US programme to train police forces in the CEECs in the latest American policing techniques. In 1994 the FBI opened a legal attaché's office in Moscow and signed an agreement with the Hungarian national police to open the ILEA in 1995.[66] The United States was eager for the European Union to participate in the project and offered it a vice-presidential position. A team of law enforcement officers from the EU troika visited the academy to pursue the proposal,[67] but France refused to support EU participation and thereby vetoed the discussions. As a result, individual EU countries have decided to appoint training officers to work at the academy on a bilateral basis.

A final area of transatlantic co-operation has been in countering money laundering. Until relatively recently the laundering of the profits of organised crime through the international financial system has been accorded insufficient attention. This was because the activity was highly secretive and its scale was difficult to measure. Two other, more sensitive, reasons help to account for its neglect. First, it was not apparent where responsibility lay for the policing of the international financial system, nor was it evident under what legal basis it could be carried out. Financial crimes throw into sharp relief the difficult issue of legal jurisdiction, as a crime could be committed across a number of territories and it is difficult to determine the framework and the location for a prosecution. Second, there were countries in the West that were profiting from money laundering that took place within their territories and they were reluctant to stop this abuse of the system.

The United States has been critical of the attitudes of its EU allies towards banking secrecy and what it has regarded as weak forms of financial accountability. Washington protested against the policies of states, such as Luxembourg, that have used their reputations for banking anonymity to attract large inflows of money from abroad without thoroughly investigating the source of the funds. The United States has also denounced the European toleration of offshore tax havens and cases where allied governments have appeared reluctant to conduct investigations when accusations of impropriety have been made. For example, there has been friction between the United States and the United Kingdom over the Cayman Islands and the Virgin Islands due to the American belief that organised crime groups have laundered their profits in such territories. There has been some justification for American concern: the Cayman Islands have become the world's fifth largest financial centre in terms of monetary flows.[68]

Owing to this American pressure, transatlantic co-operation in combating money laundering has flourished. They have discussed the most appropriate legislation to prohibit money laundering activities; instituting the obligation on finance professionals to report suspicious transactions; asset forfeiture in the event of criminal activity; tight regulations on firms offering financial services and sanctions against states that permit their territories to be used as havens for illegal profits. The European Union traditionally restricted money laundering agreements to the sphere of drug trafficking but in October 2001, after urging from Washington, there was agreement between the Council and the European Parliament to a directive that broadened the ban to include all types of organised crime.[69]

Encouraging global co-operation

US–European co-operation in countering organised crime and drug trafficking has led to efforts to build broader international frameworks. Transatlantic efforts have been viewed as one step, albeit an important one, in a process of creating international regimes, through 'transform[ing] the "soft laws" of international conventions into the "hard laws" that are enacted by nation states'.[70] The intention has been to make it more difficult for criminal groups and drug trafficking organisations to find sanctuaries around the world where they can perpetrate their activities undisturbed.

The transatlantic allies have advanced their co-operative efforts in the context of the United Nations because it is the most comprehensive and high-profile intergovernmental forum. The utility of the United Nations was demonstrated in

1988 when the Convention against Illicit Traffic in Narcotic Drugs and Psychotropic Substances was drawn up. This UN convention provided an international framework in which signatories were expected to draw up legislation relevant to combating the drugs trade and focused on the cultivation of plants for making drugs, the production of narcotics, their transportation to markets and the financing of such operations. The United States and the European Union have proceeded to apply this experience in countering drug trafficking to the sphere of organised crime and have attempted to secure a concomitant convention.

One of the first major successes on the path to global agreements against organised crime was the holding of a UN World Ministerial Conference on Organised Transnational Crime in Naples in November 1994.[71] The conference resulted in the 'Naples Political Declaration and Global Action Plan', which made a series of recommendations for countering the organised crime phenomenon.[72] The United States and the European Union were active in supporting the conference and ensured that the momentum was maintained. Both sides of the Atlantic went on to lobby for a UN 'Convention against Transnational Organised Crime', which was eventually presented for signing at Palermo in December 2000. The convention aims at improving co-operation on extradition, on mutual legal assistance and on facilitating joint investigations and has been considered to be a major breakthrough in creating a global norm against international crime.[73]

The United States and key European states have also been active in other forums. The Group of Eight leading industrial states has been noteworthy, both because of its innate flexibility and the fact that it includes countries with indigenous and globally active crime organisations, namely Japan and Russia. As early as 1987 the Group of Seven (without Russia) sponsored the creation of the Financial Action Task Force (FATF), which has been a particularly effective instrument in countering the problem of money laundering. With Russia's membership the Group of Eight has been a powerful voice calling for agreement on the UN convention against transnational crime.

Conclusion

It is evident that efforts to combat organised crime and drug trafficking have not received the same level of priority on both sides of the Atlantic. This has partly reflected different experiences and attitudes towards these problems – in particular, a history of domestic organised crime and the debilitating effect of cocaine imported from South America have led the United States to accord these problems a far higher priority than European states. The United States has been the principal motivator behind attempts to secure greater transatlantic co-operation and it has expressed frustration with the response that it has received. Throughout the 1990s, efforts to combat transnational crime have been accorded a relatively low political profile and progress in building co-operation has been slow. In one sense this has been beneficial, because co-operation in this matter has been insulated from the vagaries of the broader transatlantic political relationship, enabling work to proceed unhindered between law enforcement officials on both sides. But, in another sense, its low profile has been a handicap because it has not received the sort of political backing that would have expedited progress.

For their part, the Europeans have struggled to respond to an American-led agenda of issues. Whilst some European countries have long-established patterns of bilateral co-operation with the United States, efforts to translate these into multilateral forums have been only partially successful. Diversity among the European states in relation to their policing structures and judicial systems has been part of the problem. But it has been compounded by the fact that the European Union has been in an early stage of building its own JHA structures and it has treated American overtures for collaboration as premature. The result has been that co-operation between the transatlantic allies has been disappointing. Where joint initiatives have taken place they have tended to be modest in nature and their successes have been limited.

Enhancing US–European co-operation will require efforts in a number of overlapping directions. First is the need for European states to improve their own arrangements to combat international organised crime. This can be most readily achieved by the European Union realising the ambitious targets set within the Tampere agenda. Second, the EU member states should ratify all the various conventions that they have signed on the subject of countering crime, including those undertaken in other forums such as the Council of Europe and the United Nations. This would overcome the problem of differential commitments among the European countries. Finally, the United States and the European Union need to redouble their efforts in those areas where only marginal progress has been achieved. In particular, they need to find ways to share intelligence information on known criminal groups and build more confidence in the integrity of each side's judicial processes. Only after such foundations have been put in place will it be possible to take substantial steps forward.

Two factors give grounds for optimism about the future of transatlantic co-operation. One is the shared perception in Europe and the United States that the problems of transnational organised crime and drug trafficking are growing. The world community is facing a challenge from organised criminals who are able to benefit from globalised communications, easier travel and increasing international trade. There is a recognition on both sides of the Atlantic that only by greater law enforcement co-operation can the threat be mitigated. This is particularly the case for the European Union as it prepares to welcome new members from Central and Eastern Europe. Such a step is likely to exacerbate the problem of transnational crime and will therefore stimulate demand for collaboration with like-minded Western states.

The other factor is the impact of the 11 September 2001 terrorist attacks upon the United States. This event raised the salience of transatlantic security co-operation against non-military threats. Although co-operation against these challenges was neglected in the past, renewed political will should ensure that they will be accorded priority in the future. Co-operation against transnational organised crime is similar in nature to co-operation against terrorism and will benefit from the linkages. Already since September 2001 it is possible to identify a range of measures that have been taken to counter terrorism that will also be relevant against crime. For example, US–EU action against money laundering, the increased sharing of intelligence information and the discussion of new extradition arrangements. The United States and the European Union have also resolved their impasse over data protection that was obstructing the sharing of information between the United States and Europol. Such evidence of new patterns of co-operation will ensure that this facet of the transatlantic relationship will repay careful watching in the future.

Notes

1 The term 'transnational' is used in this context to denote activity across state boundaries that is carried out by non-governmental actors.
2 P. Stares, *The Global Habit: The Drug Problem in a Borderless World* (Washington DC: Brookings Institution, 1996), p. 2.
3 J. de Gazia, *DEA: The War against Drugs* (London: BBC, 1991).
4 H. Binnendijk and P. Clawson (eds), *International Crime, Strategic Assessment 1997* (Washington DC: National Defense University, 1998), p. 199.
5 Quoted in C. Ulrich, *The Price of Freedom: The Criminal Threat in Russia, Eastern Europe and the Baltic Region*, Conflict Studies (London: Research Institute for the Study of Conflict and Terrorism, 1994).
6 M. Woodiwiss, 'Crime's global reach', in F. Pearce and M. Woodiwiss (eds), *Crime's Global Reach* (Basingstoke: Macmillan, 1993).
7 See, for example, D. Cressey, *Theft of a Nation* (New York: Harper and Row, 1969).
8 M. Beare and R. Taylor, *Major Issues relating to Organised Crime, Within the Context of Economic Relationships* (Ottawa: Law Commission of Canada, 1999).
9 P. van Duyne, 'The phantom threat of organised crime', *Crime, Law and Social Change*, 24 (1996).
10 Quoted in M. den Boer, 'The European Union and organised crime: fighting a new enemy with many tentacles', in E. Viano (ed.), *Global Organised Crime and International Security* (Aldershot: Ashgate, 1999), p. 16.
11 See EU Organised Crime Situation Report, Report for the Year 2000 (The Hague: Europol), http://www.europol.eu.int/content.htm.
12 See the Staff Report to the US Senate Committee of Foreign Relations, 'Corruption and Drugs in Colombia: Democracy at Risk' (Washington DC: Government Printing Office, 1996).
13 M. Massari, 'Transnational Organised Crime: Between Myth and Reality', paper presented to the Workshop on Organised Crime, European Consortium for Political Research conference, Grenoble, March 2001.
14 L. Shelley, 'Transnational organised crime: an imminent threat to the nation state?' *Journal of International Affairs*, 2 (1995), pp. 463–89, at p. 466.
15 C. Sterling, *Thieves' World: The Threat of the new Global Network of Organized Crime* (New York: Simon and Schuster, 1994). See also L. Raine and F. Cillufo (eds), *Global*

Organized Crime: The New Empire of Evil (Washington DC: CSIS, 1994), and Senator J. Kerry, *The New War: The Web of Crime that Threatens America's Security* (New York: Simon and Schuster, 1997).

16 Binnendijk and Clawson, 'International crime', p. 197. See also CSIS Task Force report, *Russian Organized Crime* (Global Organized Crime Project, Washington DC: CSIS, 1996).

17 A. Surikov, *Crime in Russia: The International Implications* (Centre for Defence Studies pamphlet 25, London: Brassey's, 1995).

18 E. Nadelmann, *Cops across Borders: The Internationalization of US Criminal Law Enforcement* (University Park PA: Pennsylvania State University Press, 1993).

19 Stares, *The Global Habit*, p. 26.

20 'International Crime Control Strategy', White House, May 1998.

21 Binnendijk and Clawson, 'International crime', p. 202.

22 R. Singh, 'Law and order' in G. Peele, C. Bailey, B. Cain and G. Peters (eds), *Developments in American Politics* (4th edn, Basingstoke: Palgrave, 2002), p. 196.

23 M. Levitsky, 'US foreign policy and international narcotics control: challenges and opportunities in the 1990s and beyond', in R. Perl (ed.), *Drugs and Foreign Policy: A Critical Review* (Boulder CO: Westview Press, 1994), pp. 41–59. See also R. Perl, *Drug Control: International Policy and Options*, Congressional Research Service Brief, 20 April 2001, Washington DC.

24 A. Rabasa and P. Chalk, *Colombian Labyrinth: The Synergy of Drugs and Insurgency and its Implications for Regional Stability* (Santa Monica CA: RAND Corporation, 2001). See also A. Schmid, 'The links between transnational organised crime and terrorist crimes', *Transnational Organised Crime*, 2: 4 (1996), pp. 40–82.

25 V. Ruggiero and N. South, *Eurodrugs: Drug Use, Markets and Trafficking in Europe* (London: UCL Press, 1995).

26 *The Economist*, 'Special report: another powder trail', 20 October 2001, p. 21.

27 Office of National Drug Control Policy, *National Drug Control Strategy 1999* (Washington DC: ONDCP, 1999).

28 N. Dorn, J. Epsen and E. Savona, *European Drug Policies and Enforcement* (Basingstoke: Macmillan, 1996).

29 Interview conducted by the author with official at the US Mission to the European Union, Brussels, 29 September 2000.

30 Dorn *et al.*, *European Drug Policies*.

31 A. Travis, 'Dutch point to benefit of "coffee shop" experiment', *Guardian*, 10 October 2000.

32 Interviews conducted by the author with officials in various US government departments, Washington DC, November 2000.

33 *The Economist*, 'The Andean coca wars: a crop that refuses to die', 4 March 2000, pp. 25–7.

34 Testimony of Michael Shifter before the House Committee on International Relations, US Congress, 21 September 2000, www.house.gov/international_relations/wh/colombia/shifter.htm.

35 R. Beers, 'On-the-record Briefing on the Andean Regional Initiative', US Department of State, 16 May 2001.

36 E. Savona, *The Organisational Framework of European Crime in the Globalisation Process* (Transcrime Working Paper 20, Trento: Transcrime, 1998).

37 Testimony of Giovanni de Gennaro, Italian National Police, to hearing before the

Committee on International Relations, US House of Representatives, October 1997, 105th Congress (Washington DC: US Government Printing Office, 1997), p. 13.
38 Ruggiero and South, *Eurodrugs*.
39 A. Jamieson, 'The transnational dimension of Italian organised crime', *Transnational Organised Crime*, 1: 2 (1995), pp. 156–7.
40 Nadelmann, *Cops across Borders*.
41 Interview conducted by the author with an attorney from the US Department of Justice, US embassy to the United Kingdom, London, 1 November 2000.
42 Testimony of Louis Freeh, Director of the FBI, to hearing before the Committee on International Relations, US House of Representatives, October 1997, 105th Congress (Washington DC: US Government Printing Office, 1997), p. 6.
43 R. Naylor, 'From Cold War to crime war: the search for a new "national security" threat', *Transnational Organized Crime*, 1: 4 (1995), pp. 37–56, at p. 39.
44 US ambassador to the European Union Rockwell Schnabel, 'US Ambassador to the EU on Terrorism, Transatlantic Co-operation', Washington file, 13 December 2001, www.usembassy.org.uk/euro167.html.
45 M. Anderson, 'The merging of internal and external security', in M. Anderson, M. den Boer, P. Cullen, W. Gilmore, C. Raab and N. Walker, *Policing the European Union* (Oxford: Clarendon Press, 1995), p. 172.
46 Speech by A. Vittorino, Commissioner of Justice and Home Affairs, conference 'Strategies of the EU and the US in combating Transnational Organised Crime', Ghent, 24 January 2001.
47 Interview conducted by the author at Europol headquarters, The Hague, 28 September 2000.
48 Interpol has a membership of 177 states and has its headquarters in Lyon, France. A telecommunications network links each country's 'National Central Bureau' and provides access to a database on international criminal activities.
49 Interview conducted by the author at the Bureau for International Narcotics and Law Enforcement Affairs, Washington DC, 17 May 2001.
50 Interview conducted by the author at the European Commission offices in Washington DC, 14 May 2001.
51 J. Monar, 'An "area of freedom, justice and security"?' Progress and deficits in justice and home affairs', in P. Lynch, N. Neuwahl and W. Rees (eds), *Reforming the European Union: From Maastricht to Amsterdam* (Harlow: Longman, 2000).
52 Interview conducted by the author at the Bureau for International Narcotics and Law Enforcement Affairs, Washington DC, 17 May 2001.
53 Council of the European Union, 'Draft Agreement between Europol and USA', Document 13359/01, Brussels, 31 October 2001.
54 *The Economist*, 'Europe's borders: a single market in crime', 16 October 1999, p. 28.
55 Anderson *et al.*, *Policing the European Union*, p. 168.
56 Special European Council held at Tampere, Finland, 15–16 October 1999.
57 B. Steffenson, 'The Institutionalisation of EU–US Relations: Decision Making, Institution Building and the New Transatlantic Agenda' (Ph.D. thesis, University of Glasgow, 2001).
58 Bureau for International Narcotics and Law Enforcement Affairs, 'International Narcotics Control Strategy Report' (Washington DC: US Department of State, 1996).
59 Interview conducted by the author at the Foreign and Commonwealth Office, London, 1 November 2000.

60 Interview conducted by the author in the Caribbean Programs section of the US State Department, Washington DC, 15 May 2001.

61 Senior Level Group Report to the US–EU Summit, 12 June 1996, p. 2.

62 Interview conducted by the author at the US Department of Justice, Washington DC, 16 May 2001.

63 Senior Level Group Report to the US–EU Summit, 16 December 1996, p. 4.

64 J. Monar, *Enlargement-related Diversity in EU Justice and Home Affairs: Challenges, Dimensions and Management Instruments* (Working Document W112, The Hague: Scientific Council for Government Policy, 2000), pp. 41–2.

65 Interview conducted by the author at the Bureau for International Narcotics and Law Enforcement Affairs, Washington DC, 17 May 2001.

66 Written evidence of the FBI to the hearing before the Committee on International Relations, US House of Representatives, October 1997, 105th Congress (Washington DC: US Government Printing Office, 1997), p. 64. See also A. Wright, 'Organised crime in Hungary: the transition from state to civil society', *Transnational Organised Crime*, 3: 1 (1997), p. 69.

67 Senior Level Group Report to the US–EU Summit, 12 June 1996, p. 5.

68 W. Lucas, 'Global financial systems under assault', in Raine and Cillufo, *Global Organized Crime*.

69 *Agence Europe*, 'EU money laundering', *Agence Europe*, 8068, 12 October 2001.

70 Savona, *The Organisational Framework*.

71 P. Williams and E. Savona (eds), *The United Nations and Transnational Organised Crime* (London: Frank Cass, 1996).

72 United Nations, Naples Political Declaration and Global Action Plan, www.un.org/documents/ga/res/49/a49r159.htm.

73 United Nations, Convention against Transnational Organised Crime, Palermo, Italy, 12–15 December 2000, www.odccp. org/palermo/convmain.html.

Conclusion:
the challenge of change

Wyn Rees

The United States and Europe are potential partners in shaping the post-Cold War world. Their ability to co-operate will have a major impact on whether the emerging era of international relations turns out to be one that is more or less violent, prosperous and democratic.[1]

Any attempt to survey the transatlantic security relationship must start by celebrating its strengths and achievements. Post-Cold War doomsayers predicted that the relationship would degenerate into competition and mutual recrimination once the Soviet threat had been removed. They foresaw that transatlantic organisations such as NATO would lose their cohesion as competitive national interests reasserted themselves. Those gloomy prognostications of a transatlantic divorce proved to be wrong. The complex web of linkages and shared interests that have bound the United States and Europe together in the post-1945 period have exhibited great durability and have been stronger than the issues that divide them.

In the post-Cold War era the United States has continued to possess vital interests on the continent. Despite initial hesitations over the precise role it wanted to play in European security, at the 1994 NATO Brussels summit it became clear that America was recommitting itself to taking a leadership function. Through the vehicle of an adapted NATO, the United States galvanised its allies into responding to a variety of security challenges. NATO enlarged its functions by undertaking peace enforcement and peacekeeping tasks on Europe's perimeter, most notably in the Bosnia and Kosovo conflicts. It accepted a role in preventive diplomacy in operations such as in Macedonia. In addition, the United States has been in the vanguard of enlarging the membership of the Alliance. At the 1997 Madrid summit, Poland, Hungary and the Czech Republic were invited to join NATO, whilst at the 2002 Prague Summit a further seven states were invited to begin the process of accession.

NATO has provided a versatile and tested forum for the United States. Since the 1997 NATO–Russia Founding Act it has offered an additional means of conducting a dialogue with Moscow, whilst the main channel remains the bilateral relationship between Russia and the United States. The relationship has grown closer following Russia's support for America's War on Terrorism. The Alliance is also host to a special NATO–Ukraine Commission (NUC) as well as to the wider European Atlantic Partnership Council, comprising forty-six countries. The European Atlantic Partnership Council enables the Americans and the Europeans to engage in regular consultations with a diverse range of states across a breadth of security issues and to structure the process by which aspirant states could be considered for NATO membership.

The American–European relationship embodied in NATO is at the core of a Western-led international order. The broad agreement over values between the two sides of the Atlantic serves not only as a valuable model of co-operative and peaceful relations, but also as a foundation to reach out to the wider world. The sense of solidarity within the Alliance acts as a platform for the transatlantic allies to shape global norms of behaviour. This was evidenced in the Kosovo campaign, where agreement amongst the nineteen NATO members to a humanitarian intervention provided the legitimacy for an operation that was not forthcoming from the United Nations, because of the opposition of China and Russia. The transatlantic relationship has furthermore been the corner-stone for international regime building in subjects as varied as nuclear non-proliferation and countering new transnational security challenges such as international crime.

This is not to say that the success of the Alliance is immutable for all time. As contended in Chapter 4, it is paradoxically at the height of its success that doubts are raised about the future of the Alliance. For all its achievements, NATO's role as a transatlantic security forum must continue to adapt to new realities. The conflicts in the Balkans exposed the disparities of capability within the Alliance and contributed to the sense in Washington that the European allies expect the United States to bear almost the exclusive burden in peace enforcement tasks. This reflected the inability of the Europeans to develop a consensus around a course of action as well as their inability to do more in military terms. The Europeans have been unsuccessful in convincing the United States that they have made significant contributions in other ways. Europe has shouldered the major part of the burden of post-conflict reconstruction and state building in Bosnia and Kosovo and has demonstrated that military conflict is only one stage in the long process of addressing the problems of these countries. Yet the United States has offered little recognition to the Europeans for this form of effort and has continued to berate them for offering only a limited contribution to the prosecution of coercive diplomacy.

Another pressure upon NATO, predominantly from the United States, is to reassess the focus of the Alliance's activities. The argument is that the growing security threats lie outside of the continent and take such forms as nuclear proliferation and international terrorism. This would mean reorientating NATO from its traditional concentration on the security of the European continent to more of a global role, addressing security threats wherever they arise in the world. Those commending this approach regard it as a way of addressing new concerns by building on established patterns of transatlantic co-operation. In the eyes of its advocates it would represent a natural extension of the Alliance's role and it would guarantee the United States both a leadership position as well as a group of allies upon which it could rely.

This approach has received strong endorsement in the United States from leading figures, such as Senator Richard Lugar. They believe that for the Alliance to confine itself to military tasks in Europe would risk it being sidelined and might lead the United States to neglect NATO. Lugar argued that 'NATO has to decide whether it wants to participate in this war (on terrorism and against states developing WMD). It has to decide whether it wants to be relevant in addressing the major security challenge of our day'.[2] Evidence of this pressure was apparent at the NATO summit in Prague in November 2002. Agreement was reached over the establishment of a NATO Response Force whose primary mission will be to address security challenges a long way from the territories of member states. This was a very explicit attempt to address US demands for a more globally relevant Alliance.

Critics of such a change of focus argue that NATO is too important an organisation to put at risk by demanding it take on tasks for which it was never designed. The danger would be that the existing continental security functions performed by the Alliance might be jeopardised. This would have the effect of undermining its credibility. Furthermore, NATO has no experience in fulfilling roles outside Europe. For example, although NATO headquarters now possesses a centre responsible for monitoring weapons of mass destruction, most of the efforts to counter this problem have hitherto been taken by the United States. The 'Nunn–Lugar Co-operative Threat Reduction Programme', undertaken between the United States and Russia, was an initiative pursued independently of the Alliance (see Chapter 6). Similarly, NATO has little expertise in dealing with terrorism and there was little that it could offer substantively to the US operation in Afghanistan. It may be that NATO will be steered to develop its expertise, assets and operational philosophy to engage more actively with 'low security' threats, such as terrorism, but there are many who fear that this will detract from the existing strengths of the organisation.

An additional argument against 'globalising' NATO is that such an approach misunderstands both the nature of emerging threats and the likely Western responses. Unlike the Cold War, the Alliance no longer faces an easily identifiable and consistent enemy. As a result, there is no common agreement about the nature of threats to be contended with, or a firm commitment for all to act together. States in the post-Cold War environment can now decide whether an international crisis justifies their active participation or whether to remain unengaged. Such an approach would allow the United States to assemble *ad hoc* groups of countries to participate in particular military expeditions – something Haass refers to as the concept of 'foreign policy by posse'.[3] The limitation imposed by the requirement for unanimity in NATO makes such 'coalitions of the willing' an attractive option: offering the benefits of flexibility and removing the need to build a consensus. The Alliance's function, in the event of such future scenarios, would be to provide a fund of experience of conducting exercises together, rendering it possible to assemble a coalition of countries, with knowledge of how to operate jointly, at relatively short notice.

Whether or not NATO is selected as the vehicle for addressing extra-European threats, it is clear that new security issues will present thorny problems for the transatlantic relationship. Some of these security issues, such as nuclear proliferation, have been matters on which the United States has traditionally taken the lead, whilst on others, such as transnational organised crime and drug trafficking, there is no fund of co-operative experience upon which to draw. Consequently, they pose problems for two reasons. First, because they impact to varying extents and create different perceptions among European countries and America. Transatlantic attitudes towards weapons of mass destruction and illegal drugs serve as potent examples of these differences. Although both sides of the Atlantic agree that these are security concerns, they differ over the principal sources of these threats as well as the severity of the danger. America, for instance, regards the potential acquisition of nuclear weapons by a state such as Iraq as a direct threat to US security, and to that of its allies in the Middle East, in a way that is not shared by any European country. Many of these new security issues possess the capacity to exacerbate tensions within the transatlantic relationship, rather than promote unity.

Second, the transatlantic allies differ over the appropriate solutions to these problems. Europeans are more inclined to believe that threats are better dealt with through dialogue and engagement than through containment. The United States has exhibited a tendency to be far more hard-line than the Europeans in its approach across a range of instruments, including diplomatic isolation, economic sanctions and military force. In the 1990s the United States conducted punitive sanctions against Iraq, attempted to enforce extra-territorial sanctions against Iran, Libya and Cuba and conducted cruise missile strikes against Afghanistan, Iraq and Sudan. These were occasions on which various European countries expressed misgivings about American policies. They were also unconvinced by the arguments put forward in the United States to develop a missile defence system that, whilst potentially offering invulnerability to the American homeland from ballistic missile attack, would threaten the framework of international arms control. Since 11 September 2001 the US attitude towards external threats has hardened and the United States appears to be determined to confront each of them in turn. In its National Security Strategy it has made clear its willingness to use force pre-emptively,[4] which is likely to place ever greater strains on the transatlantic relationship. The build-up to war with Iraq in 2003 demonstrated how allies as traditionally close as Germany and the United States can disagree fundamentally about security issues outside the continent.

One of the most unpredictable factors in the future of US–European relations is likely to be the interaction between the long-established security agenda, focused around the European continent, and the global agenda of nuclear non-proliferation and countering terrorism and organised crime. It will be impossible to isolate the two agendas, not least because the United States is likely to emphasise the issue of burden sharing if it perceives its allies to be reluctant to contribute to extra-European security roles. The global agenda will require new patterns of co-operation to negotiated and established. Such new patterns of co-operation can quickly be put at risk if transatlantic tensions develop – witness the friction that arose between the Europeans and the United States as the latter switched its priority from the War on Terrorism to targeting Iraq as a proliferator of WMD. If the Europeans remain preoccupied, in US eyes, with the security concerns of their own continent, then the US response may be to demand a clearer division of labour. Washington may expect its allies to do more for themselves in Europe and will offer to contribute progressively less. With the two halves of the Atlantic preoccupied with different issues, the potential for sclerosis in the relationship increases.

The fact that NATO has no experience in addressing extra-European security issues increases the possibility of enhanced US–EU security co-operation in the future. The benefit of focusing activity within the US–EU nexus is that it enables a breadth of security problems to be considered. Unconstrained by NATO's legacy of continental military security expertise, the European Union has found itself free to concentrate on combating threats from international organised crime and drug trafficking as well as counter-terrorism. Such threats impact on both internal and external security and call for responses that range from trade policies and financial controls through to economic sanctions. The Union, with its capacity for multi-level governance and its extensive competences, is uniquely well placed to meet these demands.

The New Transatlantic Agenda (NTA), and its accompanying Joint Action Plan (JAP), were a recognition by the United States and the European Union of the need to co-operate on issues as diverse as nuclear non-proliferation and international crime. The aim was to find a forum in which to discuss these evolving challenges and agree upon common strategies for addressing them. It is apparent that, so far, the NTA has not lived up to expectations. The range of issues on which it has tried to focus has been over-ambitious and relatively little has been accomplished (see Chapter 5). Whilst the NTA and the JAP have contributed to improved consultation and co-ordination across the Atlantic, they have intentionally eschewed areas of persistent disagreements, such as over states of concern. Thus they have not solved many of the thorniest problems in the relationship.

The challenges of this evolving global security agenda have led analysts such as Blackwill to call for the United States and the European Union to go beyond initiatives such as the NTA to create a 'global strategic partnership to shape the international system in the new era'.[5] This theme was echoed at the policy elite level when the United States' former ambassador to the European Union, Richard Morningstar, said that

> the US genuinely wants the European Union to be a strategic global partner, one we can work closely with to address political, security and economic issues of common concern around the world. But being a global player means the European Union will have to take on global responsibilities – this requires financial resources and political will. We hope they can deliver on both.[6]

The risks for the United States in such a strategic partnership with the European Union would be that it would have minimal input into the policy positions agreed beforehand amongst the EU member states. Thus tensions could arise as European policy would be formulated without the United States and policy positions might clash. This has already occurred, to some degree, in relation to US–EU policies towards the Middle East. The United States, for example, has been forced to share its pre-eminence on the Middle East peace process with an increasingly confident and critical Europe that has sought to chart an independent course. However, the risk of the European Union asserting itself at the expense of the United States should not be exaggerated. In the view of Kupchan, the more significant danger is that Europe will be unable to convince the United States that it is a worthy partner in global issues. He warns that 'The main threat to the Atlantic link stems from too little Europe, not too much.'[7]

The European Union has confronted three principal problems in attempting to act alongside the United States on the global stage. First, there remains a diversity of perspectives on parts of the world among EU members. This has frequently reduced the attempt to develop a single policy into the search for the lowest common denominator to which all can subscribe. Many of the smaller EU countries have been content to follow policies agreed within the Union but some of the larger states have been reluctant to abandon their national foreign policies. Countries such as the United Kingdom and France, for instance, have always regarded themselves as powers with global interests and have sought to pursue independent policies towards the United States. The United Kingdom has sought to exert influence in Washington by demonstrating its willingness to act alongside America in military operations, such as in the policing of the Iraqi 'No-fly Zone'. It has also tried to act as a bridge between European policy positions and those of the United States, particularly when transatlantic relations have been in the process of diverging. France, on the other hand, has tended to follow an independent path in which it has been critical of US policy, arguing that it is the duty of an ally to highlight errors in the policies of its friends.

Second, there is a question mark over whether the European Union can develop the necessary institutional structures to enable it to take timely foreign policy decisions. In the 1990s the Common Foreign and Security Policy provided a new and important organisational coherence to the European Union's external actions[8] and this was subsequently strengthened by the appointment of Javier Solana as the EU High Representative and the creation of a Policy Planning and Early Warning Unit. But there have remained obstacles to efficient decision making such as the overlapping competences between the European Commissioner for External Affairs and the EU presidencies, as well as the problem of majority voting in CFSP. Proposals presented to the European Commission have included the appointment of a single person to represent the European Union in foreign affairs and the extension of majority voting. The prospects of a major improvement in the machinery of decision making appear to be bleak in the short term, especially in the light of the influx of ten new member states in 2004.

The third problem is whether the European Union can mobilise the political will to underpin its foreign-policy objectives with the credible threat of the use of force. The European Security and Defence Policy has achieved modest operational goals but it is unclear where this capability might be deployed in the world, what interests it will underpin and the extent to which it will be kept compatible with NATO. Whether the Europeans can remedy their military weaknesses, such as in power projection, satellite intelligence and precision guided munitions, is similarly uncertain but vital if they wish to be taken seriously by the United States.[9] The two key European instigators of the ESDP initiative, France and the United Kingdom, maintain different visions about its role. France has been eager to promote the European Union's autonomy of action from NATO, whilst the United Kingdom has been determined to ensure that the Alliance would always be offered the choice of leading in a crisis.

The inability of the European Union to rectify its weaknesses and redress its disparity in power with the United States has enabled America to avoid the question of treating its European allies as equals. As Wallace notes, 'The United States now acknowledges the European Union as an economic partner, but the idea of sharing leadership in political and military matters has yet to gain acceptance in Washington.'[10] America calls for greater burden sharing by its European allies yet appears unwilling to treat them as more than subordinates in US-led policies. The 11 September terrorist attacks appear to have reinforced this attitude because they have given the United States a renewed sense of mission in the world that had faded after the demise of communism. Having suffered an attack upon its own territory the United States has once more picked up the baton of leadership and appears reluctant to defer to its allies in deciding upon its list of foreign-policy priorities.

The United States is itself ambivalent about the extent to and the manner in which it wants to work alongside allies on this global agenda. On the one hand, allies help to accord legitimacy to international action and contribute to the sharing of risk. US engagement in military conflict over the last decade has demonstrated its proclivity to risk aversion. On the other hand, allies bring with them constraints in terms of diluting decision making, necessitating consultation and building consensus. A tension between multilateralism and unilateralism has been characteristic of successive periods in American foreign policy and unilateralism is a potent strand of thinking within the US Congress. The 2001 Bush administration has been forced to confront the dilemma posed succinctly by Tucker: 'In employing American power, should efforts bend as far as possible toward action collectively, even to the extent of making cooperative action a prerequisite for acting at all?'[11] In the case of the conflict in Afghanistan, America's overwhelming military strength and technological preponderance made it unnecessary to seek contributions from elsewhere. Only the offer of bilateral assistance from the United Kingdom was accepted by the United States in that conflict.

The answer in practice to this conundrum may lie in the limits of American power. The United States cannot do everything alone, even its resource base is not infinite, and when it confronts the broad range of security challenges America must seek to work with its closest allies, the Europeans. This is compounded both by the American public's reluctance to be the solitary 'world policeman' and international pressure to be seen to be acting legitimately. The transatlantic relationship will have to find ways to adapt to a constantly evolving security agenda. The challenge of managing this process of adaptation should not be underestimated but the rewards justify the effort. In the words of President George W. Bush, speaking at the University of Warsaw on 15 June 2001, 'All in Europe and America understand the central lesson of the century past: When Europe and America are divided, history tends to tragedy; when Europe and America are partners, no trouble or tyranny can stand against us.'

Notes

1 R. Haass (ed.), 'Introduction', in *Transatlantic Tensions: The US, Europe and Problem Countries* (Washington DC: Brookings Institution, 1999), p. 3.

2 'Senator R. Lugar calls war on terrorism "most critical issue" facing NATO', *Washington File*, 18 January 2002, www.usembassy.org.uk/natol42.html.

3 R. Haass, *The Reluctant Sheriff: The United States after the Cold War* (Washington DC: Council on Foreign Relations, 1996), pp. 93–7.

4 'The National Security Strategy of the United States', The Whitehouse, November 2002, www.whitehouse.gov/nsc/nss.html.

5 R. Blackwill, 'The future of transatlantic relations', *Report of Independent Task Force sponsored by the Council on Foreign Relations* (Washington DC: CFR, 1999), p. 3.

6 US ambassador to the European Union, Richard Morningstar, 'Speech to the EU Committee of the American Chamber of Commerce', 23 January 2001.

7 C. Kupchan, 'The US–European relationship: opportunities and challenges', testimony before the House of Representatives International Relations Committee, 25 April 2001, www.house.gov/intemational-relations/kupc0425.htm.

8 D. Dinan, *Ever Closer Union: An Introduction to European Integration* (2nd edn, Boulder CO: Lynne Rienner, 1999), p. 533, and C. Piening, *Global Europe: The European Union in World Affairs* (Boulder CO: Lynne Rienner, 1997), p. 101.

9 J. Ruggie, 'Consolidating the European pillar: the key to NATO's future', *Washington Quarterly*, winter 1997, pp. 109–24, at p. 122.

10 W. Wallace, 'Europe, the necessary partner', *Foreign Affairs*, 80: 3 (2001), pp. 16–34, at p. 16.

11 R. Tucker. 'Alone or with others? The temptations of post-Cold War power', *Foreign Affairs*, 78: 6 (1999), pp. 15–21.

Bibliography

Books and articles

Adomeit, H. (1999), 'Russische Aussen- und Sicherheitspolitik. Zwischen Anspruch und Wirklichkeit', *AP 3091*, Berlin: Stiftung Wissenschaft und Politik.

Afanasyev, Y. (1994), 'A new Russian imperialism', *Perspective*, 4: 3, www.bu.edu/iscip/vol4/Afanasyev.

Alp, Y. (2000), 'Turkey's Place in the Newly Emerging European Security Architecture', M.A. thesis, Bruges: College of Europe.

Andersen, M. (2000), 'Russia and the former Yugoslavia', in M. Webber (ed.), *Russia and Europe: Conflict or Co-operation?* New York: St Martin's Press.

Anderson, M. (1995), 'The merging of internal and external security', in M. Anderson, M. den Boer, P. Cullen, W. Gilmore, C. Raab and N. Walker, *Policing the European Union*, Oxford: Clarendon Press.

Anderson, M. (2000), 'Counter-terrorism as an objective of European police co-operation', in F. Reinares (ed.), *European Democracies against Terrorism: Governmental Policies and Intergovernmental Co-operation*, Aldershot: Ashgate.

Anderson, M., den Boer, M., Cullen, P., Gilmore, W., Raab, C., and Walker, N. (1995), *Policing the European Union*, Oxford: Clarendon Press.

Andréani, G., Bertram, C. and Grant, C. (2001), *Europe's Military Revolution*, London: Centre for European Reform.

Andreasen, S. (2001), 'The Bush strategic plan', *Survival*, 43: 3.

Andren, N. (1998), 'Is NATO an option for ex-neutrals and ex-Soviets on the Baltic?' in P. Dutkiewicz and R. Jackson (eds), *NATO Looks East*, Westport CT: Praeger.

Bacevich, A. J. (2002), *American Empire: The Realities and Consequences of US Diplomacy*, Cambridge MA: Harvard University Press.

Bazan, E., Eig, L., Cavanagh, S., and Perl, R. (1995), *Terrorism: Background Issues for Congress*, Congressional Research Service brief, Washington DC, 9 August.

Beare, M., and Taylor, R. (1999), *Major Issues relating to Organised Crime, within the Context of Economic Relationships*, Ottawa: Law Commission of Canada.

Beevor, A. (2002), *The Fall of Berlin, 1945*, New York: Viking Press.

Benyon, J. (1996), 'The politics of police co-operation in the European Union', *International Journal of the Sociology of Law*, 24.

Bernier, J. and Keohane, D. (2001), 'Europe's aversion to NMD', *Strategic Review*, winter.

Biden, J. R., Jr (2000), 'Unholy symbiosis: isolationism and anti-Americanism', *Washington Quarterly*, 23: 4.

Binnendijk, H., and Clawson, P., eds (1998), *Strategic Assessment 1997*, Washington DC: National Defense University.

Black, J. L. (2000), *Russia Faces NATO Expansion: Bearing Gifts or Bearing Arms?* Lanham MD: Rowman and Littlefield.

Blackwill, R. (1999), 'The future of transatlantic relations', *Report of Independent Task Force sponsored by the Council on Foreign Relations*, Washington DC: CFR.

Blackwill, R., and Sturmer, M., eds (1997), *Allies Divided: Transatlantic Policies for the Greater Middle East*, Cambridge MA: MIT Press.

Blinken, A. J. (2001), 'The false crisis over the Atlantic', *Foreign Affairs*, 80: 3.

Boer, M. den (1999), 'The European Union and organized crime: fighting a new enemy with many tentacles', in E. Viano (ed.), *Global Organized Crime and International Security*, Aldershot: Ashgate.

Boer, M. den (2000), 'The fight against terrorism in the second and third pillars of the Maastricht Treaty: complement or overlap?' in F. Reinares (ed.), *European Democracies against Terrorism: Governmental Policies and Intergovernmental Co-operation*, Aldershot: Ashgate.

Bordachev, T. V. (2001), 'The Russian challenge for the European Union: direct neighbourhood and security issues', in Iris Kempe (ed.), *Beyond EU Enlargement: The Agenda of Direct Neighbourhood for Eastern Europe*, Gütersloh: Bertelsmann Foundation.

Brenner, M. (2002), *Europe's New Security Vocation*, Washington DC: National Defense University.

Brusewitz, G. (2001), 'Towards a European Defence Capacity: The Franco-British Discrepancy and its Implications for the European Security and Defence Policy (ESDP)', M.A. thesis, Bruges: College of Europe.

Burwell, F. (1999), 'Co-operation in US–European relations', in F. Burwell and I. Daalder (eds), *The United States and Europe in the Global Arena*, New York: St Martin's Press.

Burwell, F. and Daalder, I., eds (1999), *The United States and Europe in the Global Arena*, New York: St Martin's Press.

Calleo, D. (2001), *Rethinking Europe's Future*, Princeton NJ: Princeton University Press.

Carr, F., ed. (1998), *Europe: The Cold Divide*, New York: St Martin's Press.

Çelik, Y. (1999), *Contemporary Turkish Foreign Policy*, Westport CT: Praeger.

Center for the Study of International Security (1996), *Russian Organized Crime*, Task Force Report, Washington DC: Global Organized Crime Project.

Chalk, P. (2000), 'The third pillar on judicial and home affairs co-operation, anti-terrorist collaboration and liberal democratic acceptability', in F. Reinares (ed.), *European Democracies against Terrorism: Governmental Policies and Intergovernmental Co-operation*, Aldershot: Ashgate.

Chalmers, M. (2001), 'The Atlantic burden-sharing debate: widening or fragmenting?' *International Affairs*, 77: 3.

Clark, W. (2001), *Waging Modern War: Bosnia, Kosovo, and the Future of Combat*, New York: Public Affairs.

Clemens, W. C. (1991), *Baltic Independence and Russian Empire*, Basingstoke: Macmillan.

Clemens, W. C. (2001), *The Baltic Transformed. Complexity Theory and European Security*, Boulder CO and Oxford: Rowman and Littlefield.

Council of the European Union (2001), 'Draft Agreement between Europol and USA', Document 13359/01, Brussels, 31 October.

Cowles, M. G. (2001), 'Private firms and US–EU policy making: the transatlantic business dialogue', in E. Philippart and P. Winand (eds), *Ever Closer Partnership: Policy Making in US–EU Relations*, Brussels: Lang.

Cressey, D. (1969), *Theft of a Nation*, New York: Harper and Row.

Croft, S., Redmond, J., Rees, W., and Webber, M. (1999), *The Enlargement of Europe*, Manchester: Manchester University Press.

Daalder, I. H. (2001), 'Are the United States and Europe heading for divorce?' *International Affairs*, 77: 3.

Daalder, I. H. and Makins, C. (2001), 'A consensus on missile defence?' *Survival*, 43: 3.

D'Aniello, C. (2001), 'Interactions between Common Foreign and Security Policy related to Civil Crisis Management', paper presented to the conference 'Integrated Security in Europe: A Democratic Perspective', Bruges, 16 November, *Collegium*, 22 (News of the College of Europe), special edition.

Davis, M. J. (1995), *Security Issues in the post-Cold War World*, Brookfield: Edward Elgar.

Devuyst, Y. (2001), 'European unity in transatlantic commercial diplomacy', in E. Philippart and P. Winand (eds), *Ever Closer Partnership: Policy Making in US–EU Relations*, Brussels: Lang.

Dewitt, D., and Rattinger, H., eds (1992), *East–West Arms Control: Challenges for the 1992 Western Alliance*, London and New York: Routledge.

Dinan, D. (1999), *Ever Closer Union: An Introduction to European Integration*, 2nd edn, Boulder CO: Lynne Rienner.

Dorn, N., Epsen, J., and Savona, E. (1996), *European Drug Policies and Enforcement*, Basingstoke: Macmillan.

Duetsch, K., *et al.* (1957), *Political Community and the North Atlantic Area: International Organisation in the Light of Historical Experience*, Princeton NJ: Princeton University Press.

Duignan, P. (2000), *NATO: Its Past, Present and Future*, Stanford CA: Hoover Institution Press.

Dunn, L. (2001), 'Co-ordinated security management: towards a "new framework"', *Survival*, 43: 3.

Dutkiewicz, P. and Jackson, R. J., eds (1998), *NATO Looks East*, Westport CT: Praeger.

Duyne, P. van (1996), 'The phantom threat of organised crime', *Crime, Law and Social Change*, 24.

EU Organised Crime Situation Report (2000), *Report for the Year 2000*, The Hague: Europol, www.europol.eu.int/content.htm.

Flenle, P. (1998), 'Russia in the new Europe', in F. Carr (ed.), *Europe: The Cold Divide*, New York: St Martin's Press.

Foye, S. (1995), 'Russia and the "near abroad"', *Post-Soviet Prospects*, 3: 12, Washington DC: Center for Strategic and International Studies, www.csis.org/ruseura/psp/pspiii12.html.

Frellesen, T. (2001), 'Processes and procedures in EU–US foreign policy: from the Transatlantic Declaration to the New Transatlantic Agenda', in E. Philippart and P. Winand (eds), *Ever Closer Partnership: Policy Making in US–EU Relations*, Brussels: Lang.

Gardner, A. (1996), *A New Era in EU–EU Relations? The Clinton Administration and the New Transatlantic Agenda*, Aldershot: Avebury.

Gardner, A. (2001), 'From the Transatlantic Declaration to the New Transatlantic Agenda: the shaping of institutional mechanisms and policy objectives by national and supranational actors', in E. Philippart and P. Winand (eds), *Ever Closer Partnership: Policy Making in US–EU Relations*, Brussels: Lang.

Garnett, J. C. (1995), 'European security after the Cold War', in M. J. Davis (ed.), *Security Issues in the post-Cold War World*, Brookfield: Edward Elgar.

Gärtner, H., Hyde-Price, A., and Reiter, E., eds (2001), *Europe's New Security Challenges*, Boulder CO: Lynne Rienner.

Gazia, J. de (1991), *DEA: The War against Drugs*, London: BBC.

Gebhard, P. (1994), *The United States and European Security*, Adelphi Paper 286, London: Brassey's, for the International Institute of Strategic Studies.

Gerbert, P. (1999), *La Construction de l'Europe*, Paris: Imprimerie Nationale.

Giersch, C. (1998), *Konfliktregulierung in Jugoslawien 1991–1995. Die Rolle von OSZE, EU, UNO und NATO*, Baden-Baden: Nomos.

Ginsberg, R. H. (2001), *The European Union in International Politics: Baptism by Fire*, Lanham MD: Rowman and Littlefield.

Gompert, D. C. (2002), 'The EU on the world stage', *Transatlantic Internationale Politik*, 3.

Gower, J. (2000) 'Russia and the European Union', in M. Webber, *Russia and Europe: Conflict or Co-operation?* New York: St Martin's Press.

Gower, J. (2001), 'The Baltic states: bridge or barrier to the east?' in M. A. Smith and G. Timmins (eds), *Uncertain Europe: Building a New European Security Order*, London: Routledge.

Haass, R. (1996), *The Reluctant Sheriff: The United States after the Cold War*, Washington DC: Council on Foreign Relations.

Haass, R., ed. (1999), *Transatlantic Tensions: The US, Europe and Problem Countries*, Washington DC: Brookings Institution.

Haglund, A. (2000), 'Baltic Sea Regional Security and Multilateral Security Co-operation: Towards a Co-operative Security Regime?' M.A. thesis, Bruges: College of Europe.

Ham, P. van (2001), 'Security and culture, or, Why NATO won't last', *Security Dialogue*, 32: 4.

Heisbourg, F. (2001), 'A view from Europe', *Survival*, 43: 3.

Heisbourg, F. *et al.* (2000), *European Defence: Making it Work*, Chaillot Papers 42, Paris: WEU Institute of Security Studies.

Henrikson, A. K. (2001) 'The role of metropolitan regions in making a new Atlantic community', in E. Philippart and P. Winand, *Ever Closer Partnership: Policy Making in US–EU Relations*, Brussels: Lang.

Hewish, M. (2000), 'Raising the ballistic shield: the latest advances in ballistic missile defense are emerging', *Jane's International Defense Review*, 9.

Heymann, P. (1998), *Terrorism and America: A Commonsense Strategy for a Democratic Society*, Cambridge MA: MIT Press.

Hoffman, B. (1998), *Inside Terrorism*, Guernsey: Indigo.

Hoffman, B. (1999), 'Terrorism: trends and prospects', in I. Lesser *et al.* (eds), *Countering the New Terrorism*, Santa Monica CA: RAND Corporation.

Holmes, J. (1997), *The United States and Europe after the Cold War: A New Alliance?* Columbia SC: University of South Carolina Press.

Holsti, K. (1983), *International Politics: A Framework for Analysis*, 4th edn, Englewood Cliffs NJ: Prentice Hall.

Hopkinson, W. (2001), *Enlargement: A new NATO*, Chaillot Papers 49, Paris: WEU Institute for Security Studies.

Hopmann, P. T. (2001), 'An evaluation of the OSCE's role in conflict management', in H. Gärtner, A. Hyde-Price and E. Reiter (eds), *Europe's New Security Challenges*, Boulder CO: Lynne Rienner.

Howorth, J. (2000), *European Integration and Defence: The Ultimate Challenge?* Chaillot Papers 43, Paris: WEU Institute of Security Studies.

Jamieson, A. (1995), 'The transnational dimension of Italian organised crime', *Transnational Organised Crime*, 1: 2.

Kagan, R. (2002), 'Power and weakness', *Policy Review*, 113, www.policyreview.org/JUN02/kagan.html

Kagan, R. (2003), *Paradise and Power: America and Europe in the New World Order*, New York: Knopf.

Kamp, K-H. (2001), *Die nächste Runde der NATO-Erweiterung. Kriterien und Optionen*, Sankt Augustin: Konrad-Adenauer-Stiftung.

Kamp, K-H., and Weilemann, P. (1997), 'Germany and the Enlargement of NATO', study based on the conference 'NATO Enlargement: The Debates over Ratification', held in Washington DC on 7 October, www.nato.int/acad/conf/enlarg97/ kampweil.htm.

Kemp, G. (1999), 'The challenge of Iran for US and European policy', in R. Haass (ed.), *Transatlantic Tensions: The US, Europe and Problem Countries*, Washington DC: Brookings Institution.

Kemp, G. (2001), 'Iran: can the US do a deal?' *Washington Quarterly*, winter.

Kennedy, C. and Bouton, M. M. (2002), 'The real transatlantic gap', *Foreign Policy*, November–December.

Kerry, J. (1997), *The New War: The Web of Crime that Threatens America's Security*, New York: Simon and Schuster.

Kissinger, H. A. (1962), *Nuclear Weapons and Foreign Policy*, Boulder CO: Westview Press.

Klöcker, G. (2001), *Ten Years after the Baltic States re-entered the International Stage*, Baden-Baden: Nomos.

Kramer, H. (2000), *A Changing Turkey: The Challenge to Europe and the United States*, Washington DC: Brookings Institution.

Krepon, M. (1999), 'Missile defense: not such a bad idea', *Bulletin of the Atomic Scientists*, May–June.

Krepon, M. (2001), 'Moving away from MAD', *Survival*, 43: 2.

Kupchan, C. A. (2002), *The End of the American Era: U.S. Foreign Policy and the Geopolitics of the Twenty-first Century*, New York: Knopf.

Lesser I. (1999), 'Countering the new terrorism: implications for strategy', in I Lesser *et al.* (eds), *Countering the New Terrorism*, Santa Monica CA: RAND Corporation.

Lesser, I. *et al.*, eds (1999), *Countering the New Terrorism*, Santa Monica CA: RAND Corporation.

Levine, N. (1995), 'A transatlantic bargain', *Journal of Commerce*, 10 May.

Levitsky, M. (1994), 'US foreign policy and international narcotics control: challenges and opportunities in the 1990s and beyond', in R. Perl (ed.), *Drugs and Foreign Policy: A Critical Review*, Boulder CO: Westview Press.

Light, M., Löwenhardt, J., and White, S. (2000), 'Russian perspectives on European security', *European Foreign Affairs Review*, 5.

Lodal, J. M. (2001), 'For modest defences and low offensive numbers', *Survival*, 43: 3.

Lucarelli, S. (2000), *Europe and the Breakup of Yugoslavia: A Political Failure in Search of a Scholarly Explanation*, The Hague: Kluwer.

Lucas, W. (1994), 'Global financial systems under assault', in L. Raine and F. Cillufo (eds), *Global Organized Crime: The New Empire of Evil*, Washington DC: CSIS.

Lynch, P., Neuwahl, N., and Rees, W., eds (2000), *Reforming the European Union: From Maastricht to Amsterdam*, Harlow: Longman.

Macintosh, J. (1992), 'Confidence-building processes. CSCE and MBFR: a review and assessment', in D. Dewitt and H. Rattinger (eds), *East–West Arms Control: Challenges for the 1992 Western Alliance*, London and New York: Routledge.

Mahncke, D. (1972), *Nukleare Mitwirkung. Die Bundesrepublik Deutschland in der atlantischen Allianz 1954–1970*, Berlin and New York: de Gruyter.

Mahncke, D. (1987), *Vertrauensbildende Maßnahmen als Instrument der Sicherheitspolitik. Ursprung – Entwicklung – Perspektiven*, Melle: Ernst Knoth.

Mahncke, D. (2001), 'Regional Co-operation: Security Aspects', paper presented at the Dubrovnik Diplomatic Summer School, August–September.

Mahncke, D. (2001), 'Russia's attitude to the European Security and Defence Policy', *European Foreign Affairs Review*, 6: 4.

Mahncke, Dieter (2001) 'Questions to be asked', in D. Mahncke (ed.), *Old Frontiers – New Frontiers: The Challenge of Kosovo and the Implications for the European Union*, Berne: Lang.

Mahncke, D., ed. (2001), *Old Frontiers – New Frontiers: The Challenge of Kosovo and the Implications for the European Union*, Berne: Lang.

Massari, M. (2001), 'Transnational Organised Crime: Between Myth and Reality', paper presented to the Workshop on Organised Crime, European Consortium for Political Research conference, Grenoble, March.

Mathews, J. T. (2001), 'Estranged partners', *Foreign Policy*, 127.

Mearsheimer, J. (1990), 'Back to the future: instability in Europe after the Cold War', *International Security*, 41: 1.

Moltmann, G. (1973), *Atlantische Blockpolitik im 19. Jahrhundert. Die Vereinigten Staaten und der deutsche Liberalismus während der Revolution von 1848–49*, Düsseldorf: Droste.

Monar, J. (2000), 'An "area of freedom, justice and security"? Progress and deficits in justice and home affairs', in P. Lynch, N. Neuwahl and W. Rees, (eds), *Reforming the European Union: From Maastricht to Amsterdam*, Harlow: Longman.

Monar, J. (2000), *Enlargement-related Diversity in EU Justice and Home Affairs: Challenges, Dimensions and Management Instruments*, Working Document W112, The Hague: Scientific Council for Government Policy.

Monar, J., ed. (1998), *The New Transatlantic Agenda and the Future of EU–US Relations*, London: Kluwer.

Müller, H. (1999), 'Managing proliferation: a European perspective', in F. Burwell and I. Daalder (eds), *The United States and Europe in the Global Arena*, New York: St Martin's Press.

Nadelmann, E. (1993), *Cops across Borders: The Internationalization of US Criminal Law Enforcement*, University Park PA: Pennsylvania State University Press.

Nadoll, J. (2000), 'Die Europäische Union und die Konfliktbearbeitung in ex-Jugoslawien 1991–1998. Mühl- oder Meilenstein?' in Klaus Schubert and Gisela Müller-Brandeck-Bocquet (eds), *Die Europäische Union als Akteur der Weltpolitik*, Opladen: Leske + Budrich.

National Commission on Terrorism (2000), *Countering the Changing Threat of International Terrorism: Report of the Commission*, Washington DC: NCT.

Nau, Henry R. (2002), *At Home Abroad*, Ithaca NY and London: Cornell University Press.

Naylor, R. (1995), 'From Cold War to crime war: the search for a new "national security" threat', *Transnational Organized Crime*, 1: 4.

Nevers, R. de (1999), 'Russia in Europe's new equation', in F. Burwell and I. Daalder (eds), *The United States and Europe in the Global Arena*, New York: St Martin's Press.

Newhouse, J. (1997), *Europe Adrift*, New York: Pantheon Books.

Newhouse, J. (2001), 'The missile defense debate', *Foreign Affairs*, July–August.

Nye, J. S., Jr (2000), 'The US and Europe: continental drift?' *International Affairs*, 76: 1.

Nye, J. S., Jr (2002), 'The American national interest and global public goods', *International Affairs*, 78, 2.

Nye, J. S., Jr (2002) 'The dependent colossus', *Foreign Policy*, March–April.

Nye, J. S., Jr (2002), *The Paradox of American Power: Why the World's only Superpower can't Go it Alone*, New York: Oxford University Press.

Office of National Drug Control Policy (1999), *National Drug Control Strategy 1999*, Washington DC: ONDCP.

Osgood, R. E. (1953), *Ideals and Self-interest in American Foreign Relations*, Chicago: University of Chicago Press.

Osgood, R. E. (1962), *NATO: The Entangling Alliance*, Chicago: University of Chicago Press.

Patten, C. (2001), 'Weltpolitik, warum nicht?' *Die Zeit*, 25.

Pearce, F., and Woodiwiss, M., eds (1993), *Crime's Global Reach*, Basingstoke: Macmillan.

Pearson, R. (1991), 'Nationalities: decolonising the last empire', in D. W. Spring (ed.), *The Impact of Gorbachev: The First Phase, 1985–90*, London and New York: Pinter.

Peele, G., Bailey, C., Cain, B., and Peters, G., eds (2002), *Developments in American Politics*, 4th edn, Basingstoke: Palgrave.

Pellerin, A. (1997), *NATO Enlargement: Where we Came from and Where it Leaves us*, Aurora Paper 29, Military Analysis Network.

Perl, R. (2001), *Drug Control: International Policy and Options*, Congressional Research Service Brief, Washington DC, 20 April.

Perl, R., ed. (1994), *Drugs and Foreign Policy: A Critical Review*, Boulder CO: Westview Press.

Perthes, V. (2001), 'The advantages of complementarity: the Middle East peace process', in H. Gardner and R. Stefanova (eds), *The New Transatlantic Agenda: Facing the Challenges of Global Governance*, Aldershot: Ashgate.

Peterson, J. (2001), 'Shaping, not making: the impact of the American Congress on US–EU relations', in E. Philippart and P. Winand (eds), *Ever Closer Partnership: Policy Making in US–EU Relations*, Brussels: Lang.

Philippart, E. (2001) 'Assessing, evaluating and explaining the output of US–EU relations', in E. Philippart and P. Winand (eds), *Ever Closer Partnership: Policy Making in US–EU Relations*, Brussels: Lang.

Philippart, E. and Winand, P. (2001), 'Deeds, not words?' in E. Philippart and P. Winand, *Ever Closer Partnership*.

Philippart, E. and Winand, P., eds (2001), *Ever Closer Partnership: Policy Making in US–EU Relations*, Brussel: Lang.

Piening, C. (1997), *Global Europe: The European Union in World Affairs*, Boulder CO: Lynne Rienner.

Pierre, A. J. (2001), 'Europe and missile defense: tactical considerations, fundamental concerns', *Arms Control Today*, May.

Pillar, P. (2001), *Terrorism and US Foreign Policy*, Washington DC: Brookings Institution.

Prodi, R. (2001), in *EU–US News: A Review of Transatlantic Relations*, II, 7 May.

Rabasa, S., and Chalk, P. (2001), *Colombian Labyrinth: The Synergy of Drugs and Insurgency and its Implications for Regional Stability*, Santa Monica CA: RAND Corporation.

Raine, L., and Cillufo, F., eds (1994), *Global Organized Crime: The New Empire of Evil*, Washington DC: CSIS.

Rees, W. (1998), 'US–European security relations: surfing or sinking?' in J. Monar (ed.), *The New Transatlantic Agenda and the Future of EU–US Relations*, The Hague: Kluwer.

Reinares, F., ed. (2000), *European Democracies against Terrorism: Governmental Policies and Intergovernmental Co-operation*, Aldershot: Ashgate.

Reynolds, C. (2001), 'Future Tense? ESDP and the Challenge for Transatlantic Relations', M.A. thesis, Bruges: College of Europe.

Roberts, B. (1999), 'Managing proliferation: a view from the United States', in F. Burwell and I. Daalder (eds), *The United States and Europe in the Global Arena*, New York: St Martin's Press.

Rodman, P. W. (1999), *Drifting Apart? Trends in US–European Relations*, Washington DC: Nixon Center, www.nixoncenter.org/publications/monographs/ drifting.pdf.

Rose, G. (1999), 'The United States and Libya', in R. Haass (ed.), *Transatlantic Tensions: The US, Europe and Problem Countries*, Washington DC: Brookings Institution.

Ruggie, J. (1997), 'Consolidating the European pillar: the key to NATO's future', *Washington Quarterly*, winter.

Ruggiero, V., and South, N. (1995), *Eurodrugs: Drug Use, Markets and Trafficking in Europe*, London: UCL Press.

Savona, E. (1998), *The Organisational Framework of European Crime in the Globalisation Process*, Working Paper No. 20, Trento: Transcrime.

Schmid, A. (1996), 'The links between transnational organised crime and terrorist crimes', *Transnational Organised Crime*, 2: 4.

Schneider, H. (1998), 'Europäische Identität: historische, kulturelle und politische Dimensionen', in Rudolf Hrbek, Mathias Jopp, Barbara Lippert and Wolfgang Wessels (eds), *Die Europäische Union als Prozeß*, Bonn: Europa Union.

Schneider, H. (2000), 'Die Europäische Union als Wertegemeinschaft auf der Suche nach sich selbst', *Die Union*, 1.

Schonberg, K. K. (2001), 'Paradigm regained: the new consensus in US foreign policy', *Security Dialogue*, 32: 4.

Serfaty, S. (1997), *Stay the Course: European Unity and Atlantic Solidarity*, Washington Paper 171, Westport CT and London: Center for Strategic and International Studies.

Shake, K. (2002), *Constructive Duplication: Reducing EU Reliance on US Military Assets*, London: Centre for European Reform.

Shelley, L. (1995), 'Transnational organized crime: an imminent threat to the nation state?' *Journal of International Affairs*, 2.

Simon, S., and Benjamin, D. (2000), 'America and the new terrorism', *Survival*, 42: 1.

Singh, R. (2002), 'Law and order', in G. Peele, C. Bailey, B. Cain and G. Peters (eds), *Developments in American Politics*, 4th edn, Basingstoke: Palgrave.

Sloan, E. C. (2002), *The Revolution in Military Affairs*, Montreal: McGill–Queen's University Press.

Sloan, S. R. (2003), *NATO, the European Union, and the Atlantic Community. The Transatlantic Bargain Reconsidered*, Lanham MD: Rowman and Littlefield.

Smith, M. (2000), 'NATO enlargement and European security', in L. Aggestam and A. Hyde-Price (eds), *Security and Identity in Europe: Exploring the New Agenda*, Basingstoke: Macmillan.

Smith, M. A. and Timmins, G. (2000), *Building a Bigger Europe: EU and NATO Enlargement in Comparative Perspective*, Aldershot: Ashgate.

Smith, M., and Woolcock, S. (1993), *The United States and the European Community in a Transformed World*, Chatham House Papers, London: Pinter.

Soofer, R. M. (1988), *Missile Defenses and Western European Security: NATO Strategy, Arms Control and Deterrence*, New York and London: Greenwood Press.

Sperling, J., ed. (1999), *Two Tiers or Two Speed? The European Security Order and the Enlargement of the European Union and NATO*, Manchester: Manchester University Press.

Spring, B. (2001), 'Achieving agreement on nuclear weapons, missile defence and arms control', *Survival*, 43: 3.

Spring, D. W. (1991), *The Impact of Gorbachev: The First Phase, 1985–90*, London and New York: Pinter.

Stanzel, V. (1999), 'Dealing with the backwoods', *Washington Quarterly*, spring.

Stares, P. (1996), *The Global Habit: The Drug Problem in a Borderless World*, Washington DC: Brookings Institution.

Steffenson, B. (2001), 'The Institutionalisation of EU–US Relations: Decision Making, Institution Building and the new Transatlantic Agenda', Ph.D. thesis, University of Glasgow.

Sterling, C. (1994), *Thieves' World: The Threat of the new Global Network of Organized Crime*, New York: Simon and Schuster.

Stern, J. (1999), *The Ultimate Terrorists*, Cambridge MA: Harvard University Press.

Surikov, A. (1995), *Crime in Russia: The International Implications*, Centre for Defence Studies Pamphlet 25, London: Brassey's.

Szabo, S. F. (2002), 'Power and hubris', Washington DC: American Institute for Contemporary German Studies.

Thiel, E. (1979), *Dollar-Dominanz. Lastenteilung und amerikanische Truppen-präsenz in Europa. Zur Frage kritischer Verknüpfung währungs- und stationierungspolitischer Zielsetzungen in den deutsch-amerikanischen Beziehungen*, Baden-Baden: Nomos.

Tucker, D. (1997), *Skirmishes at the Edge of Empire: The United States and International Terrorism*, Westport CT: Praeger.

Tucker, D. (1998), 'Responding to terrorism', *Washington Quarterly*, winter.

Tucker, R. (1999), 'Alone or with others? The temptations of post-Cold War power', *Foreign Affairs*, 78: 6.

Ulrich, C. (1994), *The Price of Freedom: The Criminal Threat in Russia, Eastern Europe and the Baltic Region*, Conflict Studies, London: Research Institute for the Study of Conflict and Terrorism.

United Nations (1995), *Naples Political Declaration and Global Action Plan*, www.un.org/documents/ga/res/49/a49r159.htm.

United Nations (2000), Convention against Transnational Organised Crime, Palermo, Italy, 12–15 December, www.odccp. org/palermo/convmain.html.

United States Department of State (2001), *Patterns of Global Terrorism*, Washington DC.

Varwick, J. and Woyke, W. (2000), *Die Zukunft der NATO. Transatlantische Sicherheit im Wandel*, Opladen: Leske + Budrich.

Viano, E., ed. (1999), *Global Organized Crime and International Security*, Aldershot: Ashgate.

Vlachos-Dengler, K. (2002), *Getting there: Building Strategic Mobility into ESDP*, Occasional Paper 38, Paris: European Union Institute for Security Studies.

Wallace, W. (2001), 'Europe, the necessary partner', *Foreign Affairs*, 80: 3.

Wallander, C. A. (2000), 'Russia's new security policy and the ballistic missile defense debate', *Current History*, October.

Walt, S. (1987), *The Origins of Alliances*, Ithaca NY: Cornell University Press.

Washington Summit communiqué (1999), Press Release NAC-S(99)64, Washington DC, 24 April.

Webber, M. (1996), *The International Politics of Russia and the Successor States*, Manchester: Manchester University Press.

Webber, M., ed. (2000), *Russia and Europe: Conflict or Co-operation?* New York: St Martin's Press.

Weidenfeld, W. (1996), *America and Europe: Is the Break Inevitable?* Gütersloh: Bertelsmann Foundation.

Weidenfeld, W. (1997), 'America and Europe: is the break inevitable?' *Washington Quarterly*, 20: 3.

White House (1998), 'International Crime Control Strategy', May.

Wijk, Rob de (1997), *NATO on the Brink of the New Millennium: The Battle for Consensus*, London and Washington DC: Brassey's.

Williams, P., and Savona, E., eds (1996), *The United Nations and Transnational Organized Crime*, London: Frank Cass.

Winand, P. 'The US mission to the EU in Brussels, the European Commission delegation in Washington DC and the New Transatlantic Agenda', in E. Philippart and P. Winand (eds), *Ever Closer Partnership: Policy Making in US–EU Relations*, Brussels: Lang.

Winand, P. (1996), *Eisenhower, Kennedy and the United States of Europe*, New York: St Martin's Press.

Winand, P. and Philippart, E. (2001), 'From "equal partnership" to the "New Transatlantic Agenda": enduring features and successive forms of the US–EU relationship', in E. Philippart and P. Winand, *Ever Closer Partnership: Policy Making in US–EU Relations*, Brussels: Lang.

Woodiwiss, M. (1993), 'Crime's global reach', in F. Pearce and M. Woodiwiss (eds), *Crime's Global Reach*, Basingstoke: Macmillan.

Woolcock, S. (1999), 'The United States and the European Union in the global economy', in F. Burwell and I. Daalder (eds) *The United States and Europe in the Global Arena*, New York: St Martin's.

Wright, A. (1997), 'Organised crime in Hungary: the transition from state to civil society', *Transnational Organised Crime*, 3: 1.

Yost, D. S. (1998), *NATO Transformed: The Alliance's New Roles in International Security*, Washington DC: US Institute of Peace Press.

Newspapers

Agence Europe
The Economist
EU Institutions Press Release
European Voice
The Financial Times

Frankfurter Allgemeine Zeitung
Guardian
International Herald Tribune
Jerusalem Post
Maclean's
Newsweek
Neue Zürcher Zeitung
Nordamerikanische Wochen-Post
Das Parlament
Rossiiskaya gazeta
Time (European edition)
The Times
The Washington Post
Die Welt

Index

Page references for notes are followed by 'n'.